Why you should use this book

- **It is written entirely for the Apple Mac version of Excel 2019.** While this book covers the same material as our acclaimed *Excel 2019 for Windows* course, the book has been completely re-written for the (very different) Apple Mac version.

- **It is up-to-date.** This book is fully updated for Excel 2019. This means that the screenshots printed in the book will match what you see on your screen. This makes the lessons easy to follow. It can be very frustrating to try to learn Excel 2019 using an out-of-date book.

- **Learning success is guaranteed.** For over fifteen years, Smart Method® courses have been used by large corporations, government departments and the armed forces to train their employees. This book has been constantly refined (during hundreds of classroom courses) by observing which skills students find difficult to understand and then developing simpler ways of explaining them. We have never had a student who has failed to learn Excel after taking one of our courses.

- **It is the book of choice for teachers.** As well as catering for those wishing to learn Excel by self-study, Smart Method® books have long been the preferred choice for Excel teachers as they are designed to teach Excel and not as reference books. Books follow best-practice adult teaching methodology with clearly defined objectives for each learning session and an exercise to confirm skills transfer. With single, self-contained lessons, the books cater for any teaching or self-learning period (from minutes to hours).

- **Smart Method® books are #1 best sellers.** Every paper printed Smart Method® Excel book (and there have been ten of them starting with Excel 2007) has been an Amazon #1 best seller in its category. This provides you with the confidence that you are using a best-of-breed resource to learn Excel.

- **No previous exposure to Excel is assumed.** You will repeatedly hear the same criticism of most Excel books: "you have to already know Excel to understand the book". This book is different. If you've never seen Excel before, and your only computer skill is using a web browser, you'll have absolutely no problems working through the lessons. No previous exposure to Excel is assumed and everything is explained clearly and in a simple way that absolutely any student, of any age or ability, can easily understand.

- **It focuses upon the everyday Excel skills used in the workplace.** This *Essential Skills* book will equip you with excellent Excel 2019 skills, good enough to impress any employer, but it doesn't confuse by attempting to teach skills that are not common in the workplace. Only users who have advanced requirements need progress to the *Expert Skills* book.

- **It doesn't confuse Excel 2019 with Excel 365.** There are now two current Mac versions of Excel: **Excel 2019** (the pay-once version) and **Excel 365** (the subscription version). Where there are differences you'll always find them clearly documented within the text of this book.

Learn Excel in just a few minutes each day (or in as little as one full day)

Excel is a huge and daunting application and you'll need to invest some time in learning the skills presented in this book. This will be time well spent as you'll have a hugely marketable skill for life. With 1.2 billion users worldwide, it is hard to imagine any non-manual occupation today that doesn't require Excel skills.

This book makes it easy to learn at your own pace because of its unique presentational style. The book contains short self-contained lessons and each lesson only takes a few minutes to complete.

You can complete as many, or as few, lessons as you have the time and energy for each day. Many learners have developed Excel skills by setting aside just a few minutes each day to complete a single lesson. Others have worked through the entire book in a single day.

Every lesson is presented on two facing pages

> Pray this day, on one side of one sheet of paper, explain how the Royal Navy is prepared to meet the coming conflict.
> *Winston Churchill, Letter to the Admiralty, Sep 1, 1939*

Winston Churchill was aware of the power of brevity. The discipline of condensing thoughts into one side of a single sheet of A4 paper resulted in the efficient transfer of information.

A tenet of our teaching system is that every lesson is presented on *two* facing sheets of A4. We've had to double Churchill's rule as they didn't have to contend with screenshots in 1939! If we can't teach an essential concept in two pages of A4 we know that the subject matter needs to be broken into two smaller lessons.

How this book avoids wasting your time

Over the years I have read many hundreds of computer text books and most of my time was wasted. The big problem with most books is that I must wade through thousands of words just to learn one important technique. If I don't read everything I might miss that one essential insight.

Many presentational methods have been used in this book to help you to avoid reading about things you already know how to do, or things that are of little interest to you.

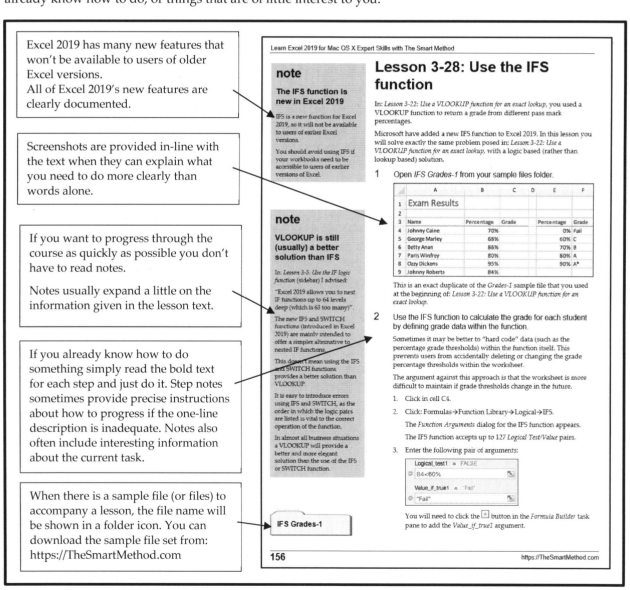

Learning by participation

> Tell me, and I will forget. Show me, and I may remember. Involve me, and I will understand.
>
> *Confucius, Chinese teacher, editor, politician and philosopher (551-479 BC)*

Confucius would probably have agreed that the best way to teach IT skills is hands-on (actively) and not hands-off (passively). This is another of the principal tenets of The Smart Method® teaching method.

Research has backed up the assertion that you will learn more material, learn more quickly, and understand more of what you learn if you learn using active, rather than passive methods.

For this reason, pure theory pages are kept to an absolute minimum with most theory woven into the hands-on lessons, either within the text or in sidebars.

This echoes the teaching method used in Smart Method classroom courses where snippets of pertinent theory are woven into the lessons themselves so that interest and attention is maintained by hands-on involvement, but all necessary theory is still covered.

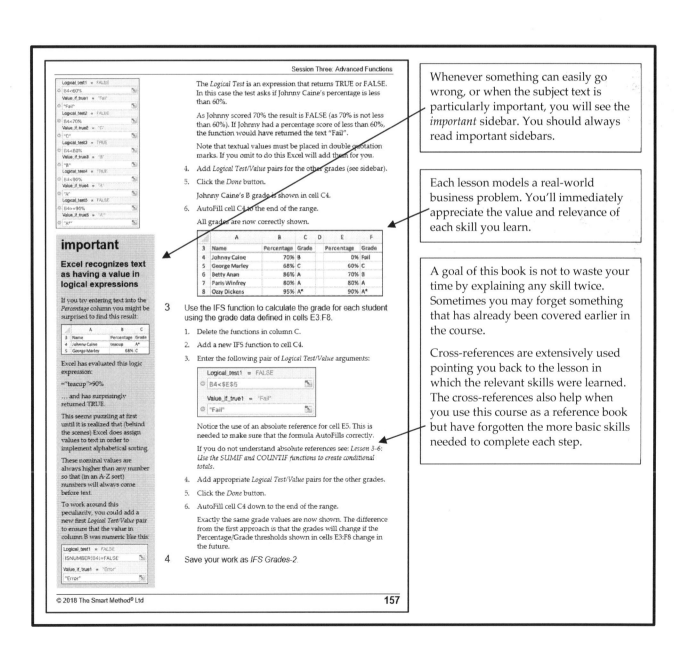

Whenever something can easily go wrong, or when the subject text is particularly important, you will see the *important* sidebar. You should always read important sidebars.

Each lesson models a real-world business problem. You'll immediately appreciate the value and relevance of each skill you learn.

A goal of this book is not to waste your time by explaining any skill twice. Sometimes you may forget something that has already been covered earlier in the course.

Cross-references are extensively used pointing you back to the lesson in which the relevant skills were learned. The cross-references also help when you use this course as a reference book but have forgotten the more basic skills needed to complete each step.

Hardly anybody understands how to use <u>every</u> Excel feature

It is important to realize that Excel is probably the largest and most complex software application ever created. Hardly anybody understands how to use *every* Excel feature and for almost all business users, large parts of Excel's functionality wouldn't even be useful.

Many learners make the fundamental error of trying to learn from an Excel reference book that attempts to document (though not teach) *everything* that Excel can do. Of course, no single book could ever actually do this. (There are some advanced Excel features that easily justify an entire book of their own).

By the end of this *Essential Skills* book you will have excellent Excel skills, good enough to impress any employer, and your Excel skills will be better than most office workers (even those with many years of experience). You'll be able to create beautifully laid-out worksheets that will really impress. You'll also have mastered many advanced features that few Excel users understand such as absolute and relative cell references, visualizations, advanced charts, conditional formatting, date serial numbers, themes and cloud computing.

We also have a follow-on book that will teach you expert-level skills

The *Expert Skills* book teaches Excel to an extremely high level of competence that is very rarely found in the workplace (even amongst top professionals). At *Expert* level your skills will be greater and broader than almost all other Excel users and you will understand (and be able to use) absolutely every Excel feature. You'll have a complete mastery of skills that are often even a mystery to Excel power users.

The full course outlines for the *Expert Skills* book can be viewed at the https://thesmartmethod.com web site.

Who Is This Book For?

If you need good Excel skills for your work or want to add Excel skills to your resume or CV, you've found the right book.

If you've never used *Excel 2019 for Mac* before, this book will give you all of the skills you need to be thoroughly competent. By the end of the book, your Excel skills will be better than most office workers with many years of experience.

This book is for *Excel 2019 for Mac* users who:

■ Need to acquire essential Excel skills quickly.

■ Have never used Excel before, or who have only basic Excel skills.

■ Want to learn Excel skills from first principles.

■ Are moving to *Excel 2019 for Mac* from an earlier version.

Use of this book as courseware

This book is also the official courseware for The Smart Method's *Excel 2019 for Mac Essential Skills* course.

Smart Method courses have been taken by a varied cross-section of the world's leading companies. We've had fantastic feedback from the vast number of professionals we've empowered with Excel skills.

This book is also suitable for use by other training organizations, teachers, schools, colleges and universities to provide structured, objective-led, and highly effective classroom courses.

This book is not suitable for learning *Excel 2019 for Windows*

You could be forgiven for thinking that *Excel 2019 for Windows* (suitable only for Windows desktop and laptop computers) was "just the same" as *Excel 2019 for Mac*. Unfortunately, this is not the case. The *Excel 2019 for Windows* version has a different feature set and a radically different user interface to the *Excel 2019 for Mac* version.

We've produced a different version of this book suitable for Windows users:

Learn Excel 2019 Essential Skills for Windows with The Smart Method
ISBN: 978-1-909253-34-6

Learn Excel 2019 for Mac Essential Skills with The Smart Method

Mike Smart

Learn Excel 2019 for Mac Essential Skills with The Smart Method®

Published by:

The Smart Method® Ltd
Burleigh Manor
Peel Road
Douglas, IOM
Great Britain
IM1 5EP

Tel: +44 (0)845 458 3282 Fax: +44 (0)845 458 3281

E-mail: Use the contact page at https://TheSmartMethod.com/contact
Web: https://TheSmartMethod.com (this book's dedicated web site)

FIRST EDITION

International Standard Book Number (ISBN13): 978-1-909253-32-2

The Smart Method® is a registered trademark of The Smart Method Ltd.

2 4 6 8 10 9 7 5 3 1

Contents

Session Three: Taking Your Skills to the Next Level   113

Session Four: Making Your Worksheets Look Professional — 159

Session Five: Charts and Graphics — 211

Introduction

Welcome to *Learn Excel 2019 for Mac Essential Skills with The Smart Method®*. This book has been designed to enable students to master Excel 2019 for Mac by self-study. The book is equally useful as courseware in order to deliver courses using The Smart Method® teaching system.

Smart Method publications are continually evolving as we discover better ways of explaining or teaching the concepts presented.

Feedback

At The Smart Method® we love feedback – both positive and negative. If you have any suggestions for improvements to future versions of this book, or if you find content or typographical errors, the author would always love to hear from you.

You can make suggestions using the online form at: https://TheSmartMethod.com/contact

If you have any difficulty understanding or completing a lesson, or if you feel that anything could have been more clearly explained, we'd also love to hear from you. We've made hundreds of detail improvements to our books based upon reader's feedback and continue to chase the impossible goal of 100% perfection.

Downloading the sample files

In order to use this book, it is necessary to download sample files from the Internet. The sample files are available from: https://thesmartmethod.com/sample-files

The process of downloading the free sample files will be explained later, in: *Lesson 1-7: Download the sample files and open/navigate a workbook.*

Problem resolution

If you encounter any problem using any aspect of the course, you can contact us using the online form at: https://TheSmartMethod.com/contact

The Excel version that was used to write this book

This book is written purely for *Excel 2019*. You'll discover exactly which version your computer is running in: *Lesson 1-3: Check that your Excel version is up to date.* You can also use this book if you are using the subscription version of Excel 2019 (also known as Excel 365), but there may be some minor differences.

If you are using Excel 2016, you should either upgrade to Excel 2019 or purchase the earlier version of this book. You'll find the relevant ISBN numbers at the end of this book.

This edition was also written using the *macOS (OS X) High Sierra (10.13)* operating system. Excel 2019 for Mac can also run under *Sierra (10.12)* and any future macOS version. If you're using a different version of macOS this book will be equally relevant, but you may notice small differences in the appearance of some of the screenshots in the book. This will only occur when describing an operating system (rather than an Excel) feature.

Users of earlier operating system versions should also consider updating their operating system to Sierra, as Apple offer a free update (or at least they did at the time of writing this book in August 2018).

Typographical Conventions Used In This Book

This guide consistently uses typographical conventions to differentiate parts of the text.

When you see this	Here's what it means
Click *Line Color* on the left-hand bar and then click *No line.*	Italics are used to refer to text that appears in a worksheet cell, an Excel dialog, on the Ribbon, or elsewhere within the Excel application. Italics may sometimes also be used for emphasis or distinction.
Click: →File→Open… 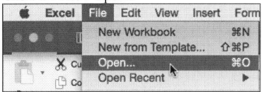	Move the cursor to the Menu Bar at the top of the screen. Click the File menu and click the Open… option from the drop-down list.
Click: Home→Underline. 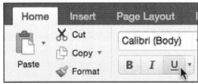	Click on the Ribbon's *Home* tab and then click the *Underline* button (that's the left-hand side of the button, not the drop-down arrow next to it). Don't worry if this doesn't make sense yet. You will cover the Ribbon in depth in session one.
Click: Home→ Underline Drop Down→Double Underline. 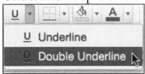	Click on the Ribbon's *Home* tab and then look for the *Font* group. Click the drop-down arrow next to the Underline button (that's the right-hand side of the button) within this group and then choose *Double Underline* from the drop-down list.
Click: →Excel→Preferences→ Formulas and Lists→Custom Lists→ Import	This is a more involved example. 1. Move the cursor to the Menu Bar at the top of the screen. 2. Click the *Excel* menu and click *Preferences* from the dropdown list. The *Excel Preferences* dialog appears. 3. Find the *Formulas and Lists* group in the dialog and click the *Custom Lists* button. Another dialog pops up. 4. Click the *Import* button.
Type: **European Sales** into the cell.	Whenever you are supposed to actually type something on the keyboard it is shown in bold faced text.

Press <Cmd> + <Z>.	You should hold down the **Cmd** (⌘) key and then press the **Z** key.
Σ AutoSum ▾	When a lesson tells you to click a button, an image of the relevant button will often be shown either in the page margin or within the text itself.

note In Excel 2019 there are a possible 16,585 columns and 1,048,476 rows. This is a great improvement on earlier versions.	If you want to read through the book as quickly as possible, you don't have to read notes. Notes usually expand a little on the information given in the lesson text.
important Do not click the *Delete* button at this point as to do so would erase the entire table.	Whenever something can easily go wrong, or when the subject text is particularly important, you will see the *important* sidebar. You should always read important sidebars.
tip **Moving between tabs using the keyboard** You can also use the <Cmd>+<PgUp> and <Cmd>+<PgDn> keyboard shortcuts to cycle through all of the tabs in your workbook.	Tips add to the lesson text by showing you shortcuts or time-saving techniques relevant to the lesson. The bold text at the top of the tip box enables you to establish whether the tip is appropriate to your needs without reading all of the text. In this example you may not be interested in keyboard shortcuts so do not need to read further.
anecdote I ran an Excel course for a small company in London a couple of years ago...	Sometimes I add an anecdote gathered over the years from my Excel classes or from other areas of life. If you simply want to learn Excel as quickly as possible you can ignore my anecdotes.
trivia The feature that Excel uses to help you out with function calls first made an appearance in Visual Basic 5 back in 1996 …	Sometimes I indulge myself by adding a little piece of trivia in the context of the skill being taught. Just like my anecdotes you can ignore these if you want to. They won't help you to learn Excel any better!
The World's Fastest Cars	When there is a sample file (or files) to accompany a lesson, the file name will be shown in a folder icon. You can download the sample file from: *https://TheSmartMethod.com*. Detailed instructions are given in: *Lesson 1-7: Download the sample files and open/navigate a workbook.*

How to use this course

This course utilizes some of the tried and tested techniques developed after teaching vast numbers of people to learn Excel during many years teaching Smart Method classroom courses.

In order to master Excel as quickly and efficiently as possible you should use the recommended learning method described below. If you do this there is absolutely no doubt that you will master the advanced Excel skills taught in this book.

Three important rules

#1 - Complete the course from beginning to end

It is always tempting to jump around the course completing lessons in a haphazard way.

We strongly suggest that you start at the beginning and complete lessons sequentially.

That's because each lesson builds upon skills learned in the previous lessons and one of our goals is not to waste your time by teaching the same skill twice. If you miss a skill by skipping a lesson you'll find the later lessons more difficult, or even impossible to follow. This, in turn, may demoralize you and make you abandon the course.

#2 If possible, complete a session in one sitting

The book is arranged into *sessions* and *lessons*.

You can complete as many, or as few, lessons as you have the time and energy for each day. Many learners have developed Excel skills by setting aside just a few minutes each day to complete a single lesson.

If it is possible, the most effective way to learn is to lock yourself away, switch off your telephone, and complete a full session, without interruption, except for a 15-minute break each hour. The memory process is associative, and we've ensured that the lessons in each session are very closely coupled (contextually) with the others. By learning the whole session in one sitting, you'll store all that information in the same part of your memory and will find it easier to recall later.

The experience of being able to remember all of the words of a song as soon as somebody has got you "started" with the first line is an example of the memory's associative system of data storage.

#3 Rest at least every hour

In our classroom courses we have often observed a phenomenon that we call "running into a wall". This happens when a student becomes overloaded with new information to the point that they can no longer follow the simplest instruction. If you find this happening to you, you've studied for too long without a rest.

You should take a 15-minute break every hour (or more often if you begin to feel overwhelmed) and spend it relaxing rather than catching up with your e-mails. Ideally you should relax by lying down and closing your eyes. This allows your brain to use all of its processing power to efficiently store and index the skills you've learned. We've found that this hugely improves retention of skills learned.

How to work through the lessons

At the end of each session, complete the session exercise

Keep attempting the exercise at the end of each session until you can complete it without having to refer to lessons in the session. Don't start the next session until you can complete the exercise from memory.

At the end of each session, review the objectives

The session objectives are stated at the beginning of each session.

Read each objective and ask yourself if you have truly mastered each skill. If you are not sure about any of the skills listed, revise the relevant lesson(s) before moving on to the next session.

You will find it very frustrating if you move to a new session before you have truly mastered the skills covered in the previous session. This may demoralize you and make you abandon the course.

How to best use the incremental sample files

Many lessons in this course use a sample file that is incrementally improved during each lesson. At the end of each lesson an interim version is always saved. For example, a sample file called Sales-1 may provide the starting point to a sequence of three lessons. After each lesson, interim versions called Sales-2, Sales-3 and Sales-4 are saved by the student.

A complete set of sample files (including all incremental versions) are provided in the sample file set. This provides three important benefits:

- If you have difficulty with a lesson it is useful to be able to study the completed workbook (at the end of the lesson) by opening the finished version of the lesson's workbook.

- When you have completed the book, you will want to use it as a reference. The sample files allow you to work through any single lesson in isolation, as the workbook's state at the beginning of each lesson is always available.

- When teaching a class one student may corrupt their workbook by a series of errors (or by their computer crashing). It is possible to quickly and easily move the class on to the next lesson by instructing the student to open the next sample file in the set (instead of progressing with their own corrupted file or copying a file from another student).

The time you spend learning Excel is hugely worthwhile

Excel is a huge and daunting application and you'll need to invest some time in learning the skills presented in this course. This will be time well spent as you'll have a hugely marketable skill for life. With 1.2 billion users worldwide, it is hard to imagine any organization of any size that does not value Excel skills.

If you persevere with this course there is no doubt that you will master Excel. A little time and effort is needed but the skills you'll acquire will be hugely valuable for the rest of your life.

Enjoy the course.

Session One: Basic Skills

A bad beginning makes a bad ending.

Euripides, Aegeus (484 BC - 406 BC).

Even if you are a seasoned Excel user, I urge you to take Euripides' advice and complete this session. You'll fly through it if you already know most of the skills covered.

In my classes I often teach professionals who have used Excel for over ten years and they *always* get some nugget of fantastically useful information from this session.

In this session I teach you the absolute basics you need before you can start to do useful work with Excel 2019.

I don't assume that you have any previous exposure to Excel (in any version) so I have to include some very basic skills.

Session Objectives

By the end of this session you will be able to:

- Configure your mouse and understand right clicking
- Start Excel and open a new blank workbook
- Check that your Excel version is up to date
- Change the Office Theme
- Minimize, re-size, move and close the Excel window
- Understand Full Screen view
- Download the sample files and open/navigate a workbook
- Save a workbook to a local file
- Understand common file formats
- Pin a workbook and understand file organization
- View, move, add, rename, delete and navigate worksheet tabs
- Use the Ribbon
- Understand Ribbon components
- Customize the Quick Access Toolbar and preview the printout
- Understand views
- Hide and show the Formula Bar and Ribbon
- Use the help search system

Lesson 1-1: Configure your mouse and understand right clicking

note

If you have a very old mouse

If you have an Apple mouse that was manufactured before 2005, it's possible that it truly has only one button and can't be configured to allow a 'right click'.

If this is the case, I'd strongly recommend purchasing a mouse that has two buttons.

This book will always use the terms 'left click' and 'right click' to indicate which of the mouse buttons you should use.

If you can't attach a two-button mouse, you can simulate a 'right click' by holding down the <Ctrl> key before clicking with the mouse.

note

If you are using a trackpad

If you're using a laptop computer you might use a trackpad instead of a mouse. In this case you will see a *Trackpad* option under System Preferences instead of the *Mouse* option.

You can use this to configure right clicking using a trackpad, which is done either by clicking with two fingers, clicking in the bottom-right corner or clicking in the bottom-left corner.

It's usually easier to use Excel with a mouse, but you should be able to complete this course using a trackpad without any problems.

If you're using your Mac with default settings and hardware, it's likely that your mouse appears to only have one button instead of two. This is great for simple programs, but makes it more difficult to use complex business applications like Excel.

It is possible to work with Excel using a single mouse button, but many features are much easier to use if you're able to 'right click' to access a contextual menu.

Even if your mouse only appears to have a single button, it's likely that it can be configured to recognize the difference between a 'left click' and 'right click'. Only very old mice truly only have one button (see sidebar if this is the case).

This lesson will show you how to enable two-button functionality on your mouse.

1   Test your mouse.

Move your mouse pointer down to any of the icons on the Dock at the bottom of the screen and click the right mouse button.

Even if your mouse only seems to have one button, click the mouse with your finger on the right side of the mouse.

If a contextual menu appears as shown above, your mouse is already configured for right clicking and you don't need to do anything else. If no menu appears and a program opens instead, read on to learn how to enable right-clicking.

2   Open the System Preferences dialog.

If it hasn't been removed, you should see the System Preferences icon on the Dock at the bottom of the screen:

If you don't see this icon, you can access System Preferences by going to the Launchpad by either clicking its icon on the Dock or pressing the <F4> key.

Click the System Preferences icon.

The *System Preferences* dialog appears:

trivia

The history of the Apple mouse

The very first Apple mouse was included with the Apple Lisa system, released in 1983. The Lisa mouse had only one button, setting a standard that Apple followed for over 22 years.

The design of Apple's mice remained very similar to the Lisa Mouse until the Apple Desktop Bus II mouse was released in 1993. This was the first of Apple's mice to use the rounded shape that is used by almost every computer mouse today.

The Apple Desktop Bus mouse was followed by the Apple USB Mouse in 1998. Nicknamed the 'hockey puck' because of its round shape, the USB Mouse was not very well received due to its short cable and tendency to rotate.

In the year 2000, the Apple Pro Mouse was released. The Apple Pro Mouse was Apple's first optical mouse, and the first to use the '0-button' design that has continued in Apple's latest generation.

The Apple Mighty Mouse was released in 2005, and was the first Apple mouse capable of both left and right-click, as well as including a trackball.

The most recent Apple mouse as of 2018 is the Apple Magic Mouse 2, first released in 2015. The Magic Mouse 2 replaces the trackball with the ability to perform gesture controls on the surface of the mouse itself.

3   Open the Mouse settings dialog.

Click the *Mouse* icon in the *System Preferences* dialog (the 4th icon from the left on the second row).

The *Mouse* dialog appears:

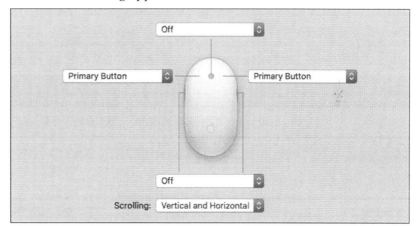

Note that this dialog may look different depending upon the type of mouse you are using.

4   Set the right mouse button to *Secondary Button*.

1.   Click the drop-down menu pointing to the right mouse button and click *Secondary Button* from the shortcut menu.

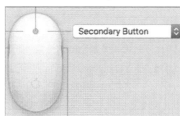

2.   Close the *Mouse* dialog by clicking the red *Close* button.

5   Test your mouse again.

Try right-clicking one of the Dock icons again. This time you should find that the contextual menu appears.

Lesson 1-2: Start Excel and open a new blank workbook

1 Move your mouse cursor to the bottom of the screen to display the Dock if it's not already visible.

2 Click the *Launchpad* icon on the Dock.

All of your installed applications are displayed, including *Microsoft Excel*.

3 Add the *Microsoft Excel* icon to your Dock.

You'll be using Excel a lot, so it makes sense to add it to the Dock. This will make it appear at the bottom of the screen in future so you'll be able to start Excel with just one click.

To add Excel to the Dock, point to the *Microsoft Excel* icon in the list, then click and drag it down onto the Dock.

4 Click the *Microsoft Excel* icon to start Excel.

You can click the *Microsoft Excel* icon either from the Dock or from the Launchpad screen.

Excel starts and is displayed on the screen:

After you've started Excel 2019

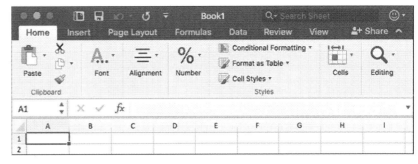

Now that Excel 2019 has started, it needs to know whether you want to create a new workbook, or whether you want to open a workbook that was created earlier.

When creating a new workbook, Excel also offers to give you a "flying start" by using a template. Templates are sample workbooks that you can adapt and modify for your own needs. The idea is very good but, in reality, templates are not usually a good choice as it can take longer to adapt them to your true needs than to design from scratch (see sidebar).

In this lesson you'll create a blank workbook.

1   Create a new blank workbook.

  1.   Click the left mouse button on the *Blank Workbook* template.

  2.   Click the *Create* button in the bottom-right corner.

  Alternatively, you can double-click on the *Blank Workbook* template.

  The Excel 2019 screen is displayed, showing a blank workbook:

2   Leave the workbook open for the next lesson.

---

note

Office 365 and feature updates

There are now two ways of purchasing Excel – either as a one-off purchase or as part of a subscription service called Office 365.

You will receive monthly security and bugfix updates regardless of how you purchased Excel, but you will only receive new features if you have an Office 365 subscription.

The screenshots in this course show the most up-to-date version of Excel 2019, so some things may appear differently if you are using Excel 365 (the subscription version).

Lesson 1-3: Check that your Excel version is up to date

Automatic Updates

Normally Microsoft Office (including Excel) will look after updates without you having to do anything if Automatic Updates are enabled.

If you don't enable Automatic Updates, there is a danger that you may have an old, buggy, out of date version of Excel installed.

This lesson will show you how to enable Automatic Updates and make sure that you are using the latest (most complete, and most reliable) version of Excel 2019.

1   Start Excel and open a new blank workbook (if you have not already done this).

You learned how to do this in: *Lesson 1-2: Start Excel and open a new blank workbook.*

2   Make sure that Automatic Updates are enabled.

1. If the Menu Bar isn't visible at the top of the screen, move the mouse cursor to the top of the screen to make it appear.

    You should see the following options:

    If you see a different set of options, it means the Excel window isn't selected. Make sure that the Excel window is selected either by clicking on it or by clicking the Microsoft Excel icon on the Dock.

2. Click: ⌘→Help→Check for Updates.

    The Microsoft AutoUpdate dialog appears.

note

The Office Insider program

You might have noticed the tempting option to *Join the Office Insider program* in the *Microsoft AutoUpdate* dialog.

Joining the Office Insider program allows Microsoft to install updates on your computer that have not yet been fully tested. This means that you get early access to new features, but it also greatly increases the chances of encountering bugs in the untested early releases.

Microsoft offer two options for Office Insider: *Office Insider Slow* and *Office Insider Fast*.

The *Slow* option gives you early access to new updates that have already had some significant testing but are not yet considered ready for release.

The *Fast* option gives you significantly earlier updates, but with significantly more risk of encountering bugs and errors.

Joining the Office Insider program is not a good idea for most users. It is better to wait for the final versions that have been fully tested than to risk the potentially disastrous consequences of downloading untested updates.

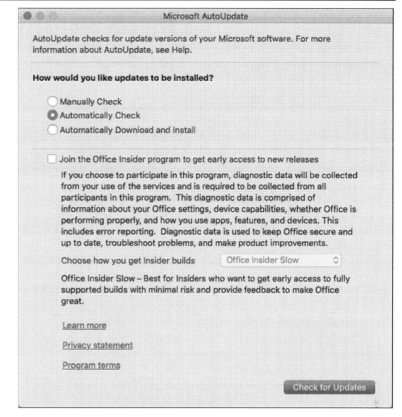

3. Make sure that *Automatically Check* is selected.

3 Check for updates and update to the latest version if necessary.

1. Click the *Check for Updates* button.

    You may be prompted to enter your password to confirm that updates should be allowed.

2. Install any updates that are available.

3. Click the red *Close* button ⬛ in the top-left corner of the *Microsoft AutoUpdate* window to close it.

4 Click the *Close* button ⬛ in the top-left corner of the Excel window to close Excel.

Lesson 1-4: Change the Office Theme

Excel 2019 allows you to change the colors of screen elements (such as the Menu Bar and Ribbon) by selecting one of two *themes*. The available themes are called *Colorful,* and *Classic*.

Colorful

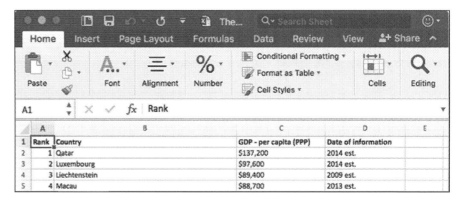

Excel 2019 uses the *Colorful* theme as the default. The Colorful theme makes it clear which of the Office applications you are using as Word, Excel, PowerPoint, Outlook and other Office applications each have their own unique color.

The previous version of Excel for the Mac (Excel 2011) didn't provide the option to change themes and was fixed to the *Classic* color scheme.

Classic

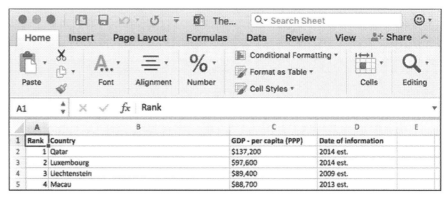

The *Classic* theme doesn't have the unique color scheme for each Office application and instead uses the gray color scheme that was used by Excel 2011 and earlier versions of Excel for the Mac.

1   Open Excel and open a new blank Excel workbook.

2   Change the *Office Theme.*

    1.   Click: →Excel→Preferences.

tip

You can also open the *Excel Preferences* dialog by using the **<Cmd>+<,>** keyboard shortcut.

The *Excel Preferences* dialog appears.

2. Click *General* from the *Authoring* group.

The dialog changes to show the *General* options.

3. In the *Personalize* group, click the *Office theme* dropdown menu and select *Classic*.

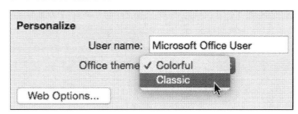

A dialog pops up to inform you that this change will affect all Office applications (see sidebar).

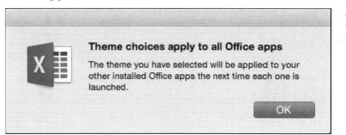

note

Themes affect every Office application

When you set a theme in Excel you are actually changing the theme for the entire Office 2019 application.

This means that you will have a consistent experience when using other Office applications such as *Word* and *PowerPoint*.

4. Click *OK* to close the dialog.

The color scheme changes immediately.

Experiment with each theme until you discover the one you prefer. All of the screenshots in this book were done using the *Colorful* theme. If you choose the *Classic* theme, the screenshots in the book may look slightly different to what you see on your computer screen.

3   Close Excel.

Lesson 1-5: Minimize, re-size, move and close the Excel window

The main Excel window has a dazzling array of buttons, switches and other artifacts. By the end of this book they will all make sense to you and you'll feel really comfortable with Excel.

For now, you'll explore the big picture by looking at how the Excel window can be sized and moved. The details will come later.

1 Open Excel.

2 Use the *Blank Workbook* template to open a new blank workbook.

   You learned how to do this in: *Lesson 1-2: Start Excel and open a new blank workbook.*

3 Understand the *Close*, *Minimize*, and *Zoom* buttons

   At the top left corner of the Excel window you can see three buttons.

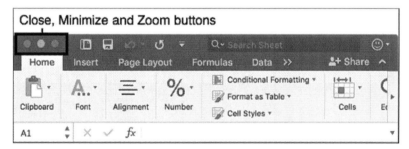

   These are the Close, Minimize and Zoom buttons:

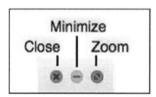

   Don't worry if they look like empty circles on your screen. The icons will appear when you move your mouse close to them.

   You'll learn more about the Zoom button and Full Screen view in the next lesson: *Lesson 1-6: Understand Full Screen view.*

4 Minimize and restore the Excel window

   Try clicking the *Minimize* button.

   Minimize reduces Excel to a button on right side of the Dock.

   Click this button again to restore the window to its previous size.

You can also restore the Excel window by clicking the Excel icon on the Dock (the same icon that you use to start Excel).

5   Re-size the Excel window.

Hover over either the side of the Excel window, or a corner of the window, with your mouse cursor. The cursor shape changes to a double-headed arrow.

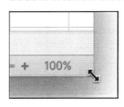 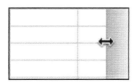

When you see either cursor shape, hold down the mouse button and move the mouse (this is called *click and drag*) to re-size the window.

Clicking and dragging a corner allows you to change both the height and width of the window.

Clicking an edge allows you to change only one dimension.

6   Move the Excel window.

Click and drag the *Title Bar* (the bar at the very top of the window) to move the Excel window around the screen.

7   Close Excel.

Click on the *Close button* at the top left of the Excel window.

This is the most common way to close an Excel window.

There are also two lesser known (and lesser used) methods of closing Excel windows (see sidebar).

Note that, on the Mac, closing all Excel windows is not the same as quitting Excel (see sidebar for more on this).

note

Other ways to close Excel

There are two other ways of closing an Excel window.

1. Click:

       →File→Close

2. Press the **<Cmd>+<W>** keys on your keyboard.

note

Closing Vs Quitting

Excel doesn't exit completely, even if you close every open Excel window. Instead, it stays running in the background so it can quickly reopen if it is needed again.

This usually isn't a problem, but large numbers of open programs can eventually cause your computer to run slowly.

To completely close Excel, click:

 →Excel→Quit Excel

You can also do this by pressing the **<Cmd>+<Q>** keys on your keyboard or right-clicking on the Excel icon on the Dock and clicking *Quit* from the shortcut menu.

Lesson 1-6: Understand Full Screen view

You saw how to use the Minimize and Close buttons in the previous lesson, but you haven't yet used the Zoom button.

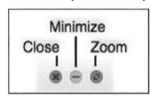

The Zoom button allows you to enter Full Screen view, which dedicates as much screen space as possible to the Excel window. You'll see how to use the Zoom button in this lesson.

1   Open Excel.

2   Use the *Blank Workbook* template to open a new blank workbook.

3   Enter Full Screen view.

Click the *Zoom* button to enter Full Screen view. 🔘

The Excel window expands to fill the entire screen.

4   Access the Dock and Menu Bar while in Full Screen view.

The first thing you may notice is that the Menu Bar has disappeared from the top of the screen and the Dock has disappeared from the bottom. They have been hidden so that as much screen space as possible can be dedicated to Excel, but they can still be accessed.

1. Move the mouse cursor to the top of the screen.

The Menu Bar appears, along with the *Close, Minimize* and *Zoom* buttons.

2. Move the mouse cursor to the bottom of the screen.

The Dock appears.

5   Exit Full Screen view.

1. Move the mouse cursor to the top of the screen to make the *Close, Minimize* and *Zoom* buttons appear.

tip

Alternative ways to enter and exit Full Screen view

As well as using the Zoom button, there are a few other ways to enter and exit Full Screen view.

One alternative is to click:
⌘→View→Enter Full Screen

...or to exit full screen view:

⌘→View→Exit Full Screen

You can also enter and exit full screen view by using the keyboard shortcut:
<Ctrl>+<Cmd>+<F>

...finally, you can also exit full screen view by simply pressing the **<Esc>** key.

note

If there is no Alt key on your keyboard

Before 2006, Apple keyboards used the *Option* key instead of the *Alt* key.

If you don't have an *Alt* key on your keyboard, use the *Option* key instead. It will work in exactly the same way.

Notice that the *Zoom* button has a different appearance while in Full Screen view.

2. Click the *Zoom* button once more to exit Full Screen view.

See sidebar for alternative ways to enter and exit Full Screen view.

6   **Maximize the Excel window without entering Full Screen view.**

Full Screen view is useful when you need as much screen space as possible, but it also makes it more difficult to access the Menu Bar and Dock, and can interfere with Excel's window management features.

Windows in Full Screen view can't be automatically rearranged by Excel, as you'll see in: *Lesson 2-2: Create a new workbook and view two workbooks at the same time.*

Fortunately, there's a solution that enables you to maximize a window without entering Full Screen view.

1. Move the mouse cursor to the Close, Minimize and Zoom buttons so that their icons appear.

2. Hold down the **<Alt>** key (see sidebar if there is no **<Alt>** key on your keyboard).

    When you hold down the **<Alt>** key, the *Zoom* icon changes into a + symbol.

3. Keeping **<Alt>** held down, click the *Zoom* button.

    The window expands to fill the screen without entering Full Screen view.

    This method of maximizing the window doesn't allow Excel to fill as much screen space as Full Screen view, because it allows the Dock and Menu Bar to remain visible.

    Unless you have a very small screen, it's usually better to avoid Full Screen view. Keeping the Dock and Menu Bar visible makes it easier to switch between programs and windows, as well as providing more convenient access to Excel's own features.

7   **Close Excel.**

Lesson 1-7: Download the sample files and open/navigate a workbook

Excel uses the analogy of a book that has many pages. In Excel terminology the term: *Workbook* is used for the entire book and *Worksheet* for each of the pages. You'll be learning more about worksheets later in this session in: *Lesson 1-11: View, move, add, rename, delete and navigate worksheet tabs.*

1 Download the sample files (if you haven't already done so).

1. Open the Safari web browser and type in the URL:

   https://TheSmartMethod.com

2. Click the *Sample Files* link on the top right of the home page.

3. Download the sample files for:
   Excel 2019 Essential Skills for Mac.

   Be sure to select the *for Mac* version of the course, as the Windows sample files may not work on a Mac.

2 Move the sample files to your Documents folder.

By default, the sample files will be downloaded to your *Downloads* folder. They will be easier to access and work with if you move them to your *Documents* folder.

1. Open Finder by clicking its icon on the Dock.

2. Click the *Downloads* folder under *Favorites*.

3. Click and drag the downloaded *AllSessions2019Essential* file into the *Documents* folder.

3 Open the sample workbook: *The Wealth of Nations*.

1. Open Excel.

2. Click *Open* on the left-hand menu bar.

3. Click: *On my Mac* in the central pane.

4. Navigate to your sample files, which should now be in the *Documents* folder.

5. Open the *AllSessions2019Essential* folder.

6. Open the *Session 1* folder.

7. Double click *The Wealth of Nations* to open the sample workbook.

4 Go to cell ZZ3 using the Name Box.

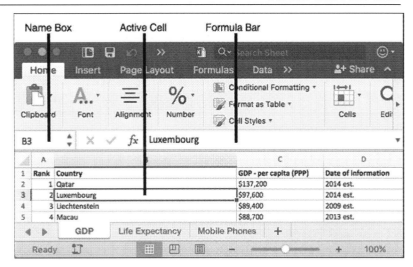

Excel uses the letter of the column and the number of the row to identify cells. This is called the *cell address*. In the above example the cell address of the active cell is B3.

In Excel 2019 there are a little over a million rows and a little over sixteen thousand columns. You may wonder how it is possible to name all of these columns with only 26 letters in the alphabet.

When Excel runs out of letters it starts using two: X,Y,Z and then AA, AB, AC etc. But even two letters is not enough. When Excel reaches column ZZ it starts using three letters: ZX, ZY, ZZ and then AAA, AAB, AAC etc.

The currently selected cell is called the *Active Cell* and has a green line around it. The Active Cell's address is always displayed in the *Name Box* and its contents are displayed in the *Formula Bar*.

You can also use the *Name Box* to move to a specific cell.

To see this in action, type **ZZ3** into the *Name Box* and then press the <Enter> key. You are teleported to cell ZZ3:

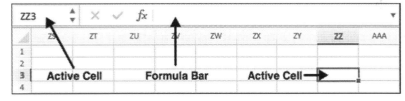

5   Return to cell A1 by pressing **<Ctrl>+<Home>** (↖).

See sidebar if you can't find the *Ctrl* key on your keyboard.

6   Go to the end of the worksheet by pressing **<Ctrl>+<End>** (↘).

7   Use the Scroll Bars.

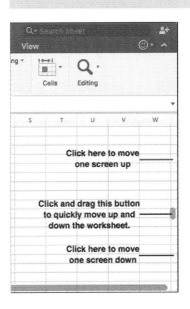

There are two scroll bars for the Excel window, which appear when you move the mouse cursor close to the edges of the screen.

The vertical scroll bar runs from top to bottom of the window and allows you to quickly move up and down the worksheet.

The horizontal scroll bar is at the bottom of the window and allows you to move to the left and right in wide worksheets. See sidebar for how the scroll bars work.

Lesson 1-8: Save a workbook to a local file

1   Open *The Wealth of Nations* from your sample files folder (if it isn't already open).

2   Save the workbook.

When you are editing a workbook, the changes you make are only held in the computer's memory. If there is a power cut or your computer crashes, you will lose any work that has been done since the last save.

For this reason, you should get into the habit of regularly saving your work.

Even though you haven't changed this workbook, save it by clicking the *Save* button on the *Quick Access Toolbar* at the top left of the screen.

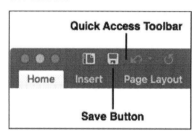

3   Save the workbook with a different name.

1. Click: ⌘→File→Save As.

If you are signed into a OneDrive, the following dialog appears:

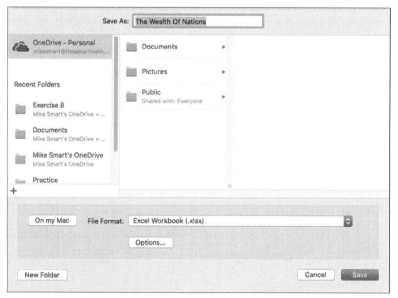

Saving to a OneDrive enables you to store your files online (see facing page sidebar).

2. If the OneDrive dialog appears, click the *On my Mac* button.

The Wealth of Nations

note

OneDrive and Cloud Computing

The *Save As* dialog allows you to save your workbook to a OneDrive:

A OneDrive can be thought of as a "disk drive in the sky".

It is just like the Documents folder on your computer but exists on a Microsoft server many miles away, accessed via the Internet.

The OneDrive can be very useful when you need to access your files from several different computers.

A OneDrive also provides an easier way to share files with others.

The OneDrive is part of a completely new way of working called *Cloud Computing*.

Support for Cloud Computing was first added in the Excel 2013 release.

Because Cloud Computing is such an involved (and complex) subject I have devoted an entire session to it in: *Session Eight: Cloud Computing*.

I advise you not to jump ahead to the last session at this stage in your learning, as this session will be difficult to understand until you have completed the earlier sessions.

This allows you to save the workbook to your own computer instead of your OneDrive.

3. Click the drop-down arrow to the right of the *File Format* drop-down list.

4. A list appears showing a large number of different file types:

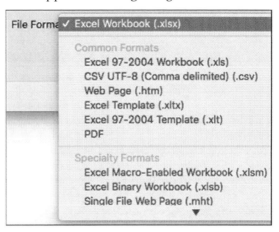

Most of the time you'll want to use the default format: *Excel Workbook* but there may be times when you'll need to save in one of the other formats. You'll learn all about the most important formats (and when you should use them) in the next lesson: *Lesson 1-9: Understand common file formats.* For now, you'll stay with the default: *Excel Workbook* format.

5. Click inside the *Save As* box.

6. Type: **The Wealth of Nations Copy**

7. Click the *Save* button.

Notice that the name of the workbook in the title bar (at the top of the window) has now changed, indicating that you are now viewing the new workbook that you have just saved.

Lesson 1-9: Understand common file formats

1   Open a new blank workbook.

You learned how to do this in: *Lesson 1-2: Start Excel and open a new blank workbook.*

2   View the file formats supported by Excel.

1.   Click ⌘→File→Save As.

2.   Click the drop-down arrow to the right of the *File Format* list.

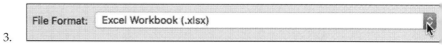

3.

A list appears showing all of the different file formats supported by Excel (see sidebar).

3   Understand the most important file formats.

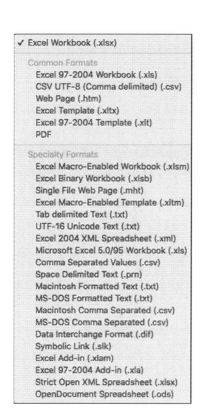

Excel Workbook (the Open XML format)

Before Office 2007 was released, every Office program stored its information on the hard disk in a completely different way. These incompatible formats are called *binary formats*. This made it very difficult to write applications that could be used together.

All of this has changed with the new file format that was first introduced in Office 2007: *Office Open XML.*

Microsoft have published exactly how this format works and given it away free to the world's developer community. This allows other programs to easily work with Excel workbook files. For example, Apple's iPhone supports Office Open XML Email attachments.

Unfortunately, the future has to co-exist with the past and there are still some people in the world (though a rapidly declining number) using pre-2007 versions of Office (97, 2000, 2002, 2003 and 2004). If you save your files in the Open XML format, only people running Office 2007/2008/2010/2011/2013/2016/2019 will be able to read them (but see the sidebar on the facing page for two potential solutions to this problem).

Excel Macro-Enabled Workbook

An Excel Macro-Enabled Workbook is simply a workbook that has program code (called VBA code) embedded within it. Macros are beyond the scope of this book, but are covered in the *Excel Expert Skills* book in this series.

While macro code is very powerful it can also be destructive, as it is extremely simple to write damaging viruses within Excel macro code.

Macro programming (also called VBA programming) is a vast subject of its own and is not useful to the vast majority of Excel users.

Versions of Excel before Excel 2007 could potentially allow a workbook to infect your machine with a macro virus because all Excel files were capable of carrying macros. Because the formats are now separate, it is easier to avoid opening potentially infected files.

Excel 97-2004 Workbook

This is the old binary format that allows users with earlier versions of Excel to open your workbooks. Some features won't work in earlier versions and if you've used those in your workbook, Excel will display a warning when you save telling you which features will be lost.

Excel Binary Workbook

An oddity in Excel 2007/2008/2010/2011/2013/2016/2019 is a binary format called: *Excel Binary Workbook.* This is a binary alternative to Open XML but it can't be read by earlier versions of Excel. The only advantage of this format is that it loads and saves more quickly than Open XML. You will only notice a speed difference when working with very large worksheets.

PDF

If you need to send a worksheet to a user who does not own a copy of Excel, you can save it in PDF (Portable Document Format). This format was invented by Adobe and is also sometimes called *Adobe Acrobat* or simply *Acrobat.*

All major web browsers can open and display PDF files. In macOS (the operating system used by Apple computers), PDF files will, by default, open using Preview. If you send a user a PDF file you can be confident that they will be able to read and print (but not change) the worksheet.

Other formats

As you can see, there are several other less commonly used formats supported by Excel 2019, but the above formats are the only ones you'll normally encounter. The most important thing to remember is that, unless there's a good reason to use a different format, you should always save documents in the default *Excel Workbook* format.

Lesson 1-10: Pin a workbook and understand file organization

1   Close down and restart Excel.

2   Pin a workbook to the *Recent Workbooks* list.

1.   Click *Recent* in the left-hand menu bar.

A list of recently opened documents appears in the right-hand pane.

The list begins with the most recently opened workbook (probably the *Wealth of Nations Copy* workbook saved in: *Lesson 1-8: Save a workbook*).

2.   Move the mouse cursor to the right of one of the files in the *Recent* list:

Notice that a pin icon  has appeared next to the workbook name.

'Pinning' a workbook can be a great time saver, as it enables any workbook that you use a lot to always be shown in the *Recent Workbooks* list. You won't have to waste time looking for them on the hard drive.

You can also view all pinned documents by clicking the *Pinned* button above the list of recent documents.

All   Pinned

3.   Click one of the pin icons. The item moves to the top of the list and a pin icon appears next to it.

4.   Double click on *The Wealth of Nations* to open the workbook.

3   Understand file organization.

By default, Excel saves all workbooks into your *Documents* folder along with other Office documents (such as Word and PowerPoint

The Wealth of Nations

note

How do I create a subfolder?

The concept of folders, subfolders and files is a very fundamental macOS (or OS X) skill rather than an Excel skill.

If you do not have basic macOS skills (an understanding of how your Mac organizes files) you would get good value from a macOS book to give you the foundation skills you need to use any Mac program.

Here's how you create a new subfolder:

1. Use *Finder* to navigate to your *Documents* folder.

2. Click: ⌘→File→New Folder.

A new folder will appear called *untitled folder*.

3. You will now be able to type: **Excel** in order to name the folder.

If this doesn't work for you, click the new folder and click: ⌘→File→Rename. You'll then be able to type: **Excel** to rename the folder.

files). This clearly is going to cause problems when you have a few hundred files.

It is better to organize yourself from the start by setting up an orderly filing system.

4　Create an *Excel* subfolder beneath your *Documents* folder.

I create a folder called *Excel* beneath the *Documents* folder. In this folder I create subfolders to store my work. You can see a screenshot of my Excel folder below (of course, your needs will be different to mine).

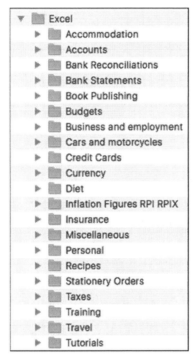

See sidebar if you don't know how to create a subfolder.

note

Changing the default number of worksheets created in new workbooks

When you open a new blank workbook in Excel 2019, one new worksheet is automatically created called *Sheet1*.

In some older versions of Excel (such as Excel 2010 for Windows), three worksheets were created called *Sheet1, Sheet2* and *Sheet3*.

My opinion is that this is a change for the better, as it keeps things neater. Most of my workbooks only need one worksheet.

But if you long for the "good old days" here's how you can make Excel 2019 mimic Excel 2010 (and earlier versions) at start-up:

1. Click:

🍎→Excel→Preferences

2. Click *General.*

3. Enter the number of sheets required in the *Sheets in new workbooks* box:

Sheets in new workbooks: 3

Lesson 1-11: View, move, add, rename, delete and navigate worksheet tabs

When you save an Excel file onto your hard disk, you are saving a single workbook containing one or more worksheets. You can add as many worksheets as you need to a workbook.

There are two types of worksheet. Regular worksheets contain cells. Chart sheets, as you would expect, each contain a single chart. You'll be exploring charts in depth in: **Session Five: Charts and Graphics**.

1   Open *The Wealth of Nations* from your sample files folder (if it isn't already open).

2   Move between worksheets.

Look at the tabs in the bottom left corner of your screen. Notice that this sample workbook contains three worksheets. Click on each tab in turn to view each worksheet.

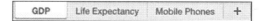

3   Add a new worksheet.

1.   Click the *New Sheet* button (the plus sign next to *Mobile Phones*).

   ➕ A new tab appears named *Sheet1*.

2.   Double-click the *Sheet1* tab.

3.   Type the word **Population** followed by the **<Enter>** key.

4   Move a worksheet's tab.

1.   Click on the *Population* tab (you may have to do this twice).

2.   Hold the mouse button down and drag to the left or right. As you drag, you'll notice an icon of a page and a black arrow showing you where the tab will be placed.

3.   Release the mouse button to move the tab to the location of your choice.

5   Understand the tab scroll buttons

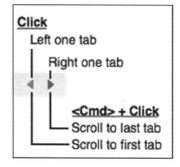

Because this workbook only has four tabs, there's no need to use the tab scroll buttons (in fact, they don't do anything when all tabs are visible). When there are more tabs than will fit on the screen, the *tab scroll buttons* are used to move between tabs.

6 **Move between worksheets using the keyboard.**

You can move between worksheets using only the keyboard by pressing the **<Cmd>+<PgUp>** (⬍) and **<Cmd>+<PgDn>** (⬍) keyboard shortcuts to cycle through all of the tabs in your workbook.

7 **Change tab colors.**

1. Right click any of the worksheet tabs. A shortcut menu appears.

   If you don't have a mouse with two buttons, **<Ctrl>+Click** will have the same effect (see sidebar).

2. Move the mouse cursor to *Tab Color* and choose any color.

   It is best practice to choose a color from the top block of *Theme Colors* rather than one of the *Standard Colors*.

   You'll discover why later, in: **Lesson 4-9: Understand themes**.

3. Repeat for the other tabs on the worksheet.

8 **Delete a worksheet.**

Right click on the *Population* tab and select *Delete* from the shortcut menu.

9 **Delete several worksheets at the same time.**

1. Hold down the **<Cmd>** key.

2. Click each tab you want to delete in turn. Don't select them all as it isn't possible to delete every worksheet in a workbook.

3. Right click any of the selected tabs and select *Delete* from the shortcut menu.

4. Click *Delete* when prompted.

Don't worry about the missing tabs. You're going to close the workbook without saving it, so you won't overwrite the original workbook.

10 **Close the workbook without saving it.**

1. Click: ⬥→File→Close.

   A dialog is displayed:

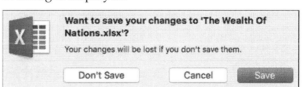

2. Click *Don't Save* so that you don't over-write the workbook.

   Because you haven't saved the workbook it will remain in its original state when you next open it.

Lesson 1-12: Use the Ribbon

The Ribbon provides fast access to hundreds of Excel features.

The sheer breadth of Excel features can seem overwhelming. This book will gently introduce all of the most important features, one at a time.

By the end of the book you'll be really comfortable and productive with the Ribbon.

1   Start Excel and open a new blank workbook.

You learned how to do this in: *Lesson 1-2: Start Excel and open a new blank workbook.*

2   Use Ribbon tabs.

Each Ribbon tab has its own toolkit available to you. By far the most important tab is the *Home* tab which has buttons for all of the most common and useful features.

Click each tab in turn and view the buttons. The screenshot below has the *Insert* tab selected. Don't worry if the buttons seem cryptic at the moment. Most of them will make complete sense by the end of this book (and if you later go on to complete the *Expert Skills* course, Excel will have no mysteries left at all).

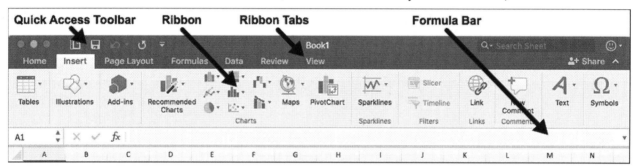

3   Display Ribbon group names.

The Ribbon is divided into several groups of icons. Each group has its own name, but these names are hidden by default. Displaying the group names makes it much easier to find what you are looking for.

note

Contextual tabs

Sometimes Excel will show you even more tabs.

For example, in: *Session Five: Charts and Graphics,* you'll learn how to create charts.

When you click on a chart, two new tabs appear called *Chart Design* and *Format*.

These new tabs provide access to a range of features relating to charts.

1.   Click: ⌘→Excel→Preferences.

The *Excel Preferences* dialog appears.

2.   Click *View*.

3.   In the *In Ribbon, Show* group, click *Group Titles*.

4.   Close the *Excel Preferences* dialog.

4   Type the word **Test** into any blank cell and then press the **<Enter>** key on the keyboard once.

Notice how the Active Cell moves to the cell beneath.

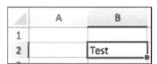

5 Make the cell with the word *Test* into the active cell.

Click once on the word *Test* or use the arrow keys on the keyboard to navigate back to the cell. Be very careful not to double-click, otherwise Excel will think that you want to edit the cell.

6 Click the *Home* tab on the Ribbon and focus upon the *Font* group (it's the second panel from the left). Try clicking each of the buttons and you will see the word *Test* change to reflect your choices.

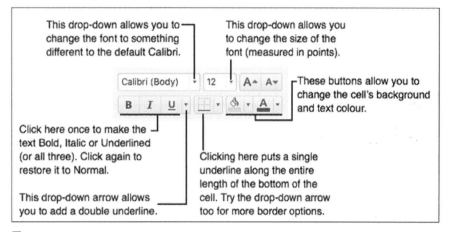

7 Minimize the Ribbon.

Click a second time on the *Home* Ribbon tab.

Notice how the Ribbon is now minimized in order to save screen space (though the *Formula Bar* is still visible).

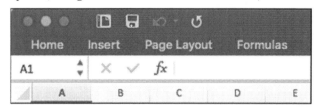

You can always minimize the Ribbon by clicking a second time on the currently selected tab.

8 Bring back the Ribbon.

Click on any tab to bring back the Ribbon.

9 Close Excel without saving changes.

1. Click: ⌘→File→Close or click the red cross ⦿ in the top left corner.

2. When asked if you want to save your changes, click the *Don't Save* button.

Lesson 1-13: Understand Ribbon components

The whole is more than the sum of its parts.
Aristotle, Greek critic, philosopher, physicist & zoologist
(384 BC – 322 BC)

The Ribbon is made up of several different controls.

Command group

Similar actions are grouped into a cluster. For example, every control relating to numbers is clustered into the *Number* group.

Normal button

Simply executes a command when clicked. The *Bold* button on the *Home* tab is a good example.

Menu button

This type of button has a little down-arrow on it. It will display a drop-down menu when clicked.

Split button

This is the hardest button to understand because these buttons look almost the same as the *Menu* button. When you hover the mouse cursor over a split button, the icon and drop-down arrow highlight separately as different "buttons within a button".

A good example is the *Underline* button on the *Home* tab.

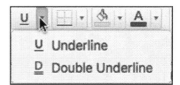

Clicking the icon part of a split button (the U) will perform the default action of the button (in this case a single underline). Clicking the arrow part of the button will display a drop-down list of further choices (in this case the choice between a single and double underline).

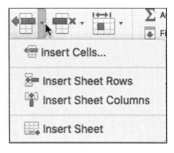

Drop down list

I often shorten this to simply "Drop Down" in this book. A drop down is a simple menu listing several choices.

If you see an ellipsis (…) after a drop down list item, this means that a dialog will be displayed after you click, offering further choices.

Drop down gallery

This is a little like a drop-down list but has graphics to visually demonstrate the effect of each choice.

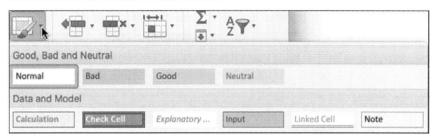

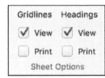

Check box

A little square box that you can click to switch an option on or off.

In this example (from the *Page Layout* Ribbon tab) you are able to switch the gridlines on and off for the screen display and/or the printout.

Lesson 1-14: Customize the Quick Access Toolbar and preview the printout

You can customize the *Quick Access Toolbar* to suit your own special requirements. In this lesson, you'll add some useful buttons to the *Quick Access Toolbar* to save a few clicks when accessing common commands.

The *Quick Access Toolbar* is one of the keys to being really productive with Excel. This lesson will introduce you to the main features.

1 Open *The Wealth of Nations* from your sample files folder.

2 Preview how the *Life Expectancy* worksheet will look when printed.

1. Click the *Life Expectancy* tab at the bottom of the worksheet.

2. Click: ⌘→File→Print.

The *Print* dialog appears.

The *Print* dialog displays a huge number of print-related features. A preview of how the page will look when it is printed is displayed on the left-hand side of the dialog.

3. Click the *Next Page* and *Previous Page* buttons to move through the print preview.

Notice there's a button to the bottom-left of the preview pane that allows you to cycle through each page:

4. Click the *Cancel* button at the bottom right of the dialog to return to the workbook.

3 Add a *Print* button to the Quick Access Toolbar.

Printing is a very useful feature and you'll probably use it a lot. Every time you print, however, it is going to take two clicks of the mouse. Wouldn't it be better if you could open the *Print* dialog with just one click?

1. Click the *Customize Quick Access Toolbar button* (see sidebar).

2. Click the *Print* item in the drop-down list.

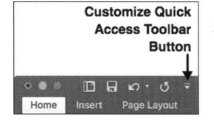

Customize Quick Access Toolbar Button

The Wealth of Nations

note

Not all Excel commands can be added to the Quick Access Toolbar

Customizing the Quick Access Toolbar is a relatively new feature in *Excel for Mac* and isn't quite as comprehensive as in *Excel for Windows*.

Many Excel commands cannot yet be added to the Quick Access Toolbar, but this can be expected to change in the future as Microsoft continue to release updates.

tip

The Quick Access Toolbar is one of the keys to being really productive with Excel 2019.

Always try to minimize the number of mouse clicks needed to do common tasks.

If you find yourself forever changing tabs to use a button, change two clicks into one by adding the button to the Quick Access Toolbar.

All of those extra clicks add up to a lot of time over the weeks and years.

A new button now appears on the Quick Access Toolbar. You are now able to *Print* your work with a single click of the mouse.

4   Add a *Copy* button to the Quick Access Toolbar.

A *More Commands...* option is available when you click the *Customize Quick Access Toolbar* button. This enables you to add any of Excel's commands to the toolbar.

1. Click the *Customize Quick Access Toolbar* button.

2. Click the *More Commands…* item in the dropdown list.

    A dialog appears, showing all of Excel's available commands on the left and the commands on the *Quick Access Toolbar* on the right.

3. Click *Copy* in the left-hand pane of the dialog.

4. Click the right arrow in the middle of the dialog.

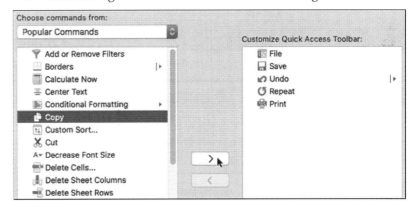

5. Click *Save.*

    A *Copy* button is added to the Quick Access Toolbar.

5   Remove the *Copy* button from the Quick Access Toolbar.

1. Click the *Customize Quick Access Toolbar* button and click *More Commands* from the dropdown list.

2. Click *Copy* in the right-hand pane of the dialog and then click the left arrow button in the middle of the dialog.

3. Click *Save.*

Lesson 1-15: Understand views

Views provide different ways to look at your worksheet.

Excel 2019 has three main views. They are:

View	Icon	What it is used for
Normal		This is the view you've been using until now. It's the view most users use all of the time when they are working with Excel.
Page Layout		This view allows you to see (almost) exactly what the printout will look like. Unlike running a *Print Preview,* you are able to edit cells just as you can in *Normal* view.
Page Break Preview		A page break indicates when the printer should advance onto a new sheet of paper. If you progress to the Essential Skills course in this series, you'll use this view in: *Lesson 7 5: Insert, delete and preview page breaks,* to make sure that the page breaks in the right place.

note

Page Break Preview is only available in Excel 365

The *Page Break Preview* feature has been added to *Excel for Mac* since it was first released.

New feature updates are only provided to Excel 365 users, so this option will not be available if you are not using Excel 365.

If you are using Excel 365 and still don't have this feature, you just need to update to the latest version.

You saw how to update Excel in: *Lesson 1-3: Check that your Excel version is up to date.*

1   Open the *Wealth of Nations* sample workbook (if it isn't already open).

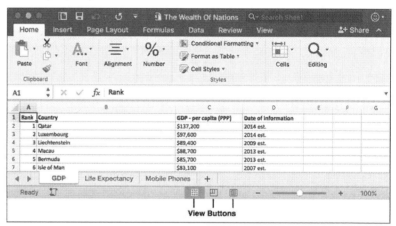

You can change views in two ways:

1.   By clicking one of the View buttons at the bottom of the window (see above).

2.   By clicking one of the buttons on the Ribbon's *View* tab (see below).

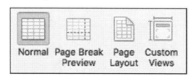

The Wealth of Nations

2 View the GDP worksheet in *Page Layout* view.

1. Click on the *GDP* tab.

2. Select *Page Layout* view by clicking:
   View→Workbook Views→Page Layout.

The worksheet is displayed in *Page Layout* view. You are able to see (almost) exactly what will be printed. Headers, footers and margins are all shown.

You are also able to edit the worksheet.

You may wonder why Excel users don't use *Page Layout* view all of the time when editing worksheets. While some users may prefer to do this, most will want to see the maximum amount of data possible on screen and so will prefer the *Normal* view.

3 Select *Page Break Preview* view.

Click: View→Workbook Views→Page Break Preview.

The worksheet is displayed in *Page Break Preview* view.

This view zooms out, showing the breaks between pages as blue dotted lines:

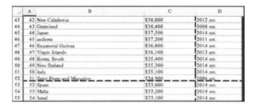

It is possible to click and drag the dotted lines to change the place where the page breaks.

4 Return to *Normal* view.

Click: View→Workbook Views→Normal.

Lesson 1-16: Hide and Show the Formula Bar and Ribbon

Most desktop computers have large display screens. The space taken by the Ribbon and Formula Bar isn't usually a problem.

As you'll discover in: **Session Eight: Cloud Computing**, it is now possible to run Excel 2019 on tablet computers (and even on Smartphones). These devices often have a very small display screen, meaning that the Ribbon and Formula Bar take up too much valuable screen space.

When screen space is limited, you may wish to hide the Formula Bar, Ribbon, or even both, in order to maximize the number of cells visible on the screen.

1   Open *The Wealth of Nations* from your sample files folder (if it isn't already open) and click the *Life Expectancy* tab.

Notice that the *Ribbon* and *Formula Bar* are taking up space that could be used to display the contents of the worksheet.

Consider the screen below:

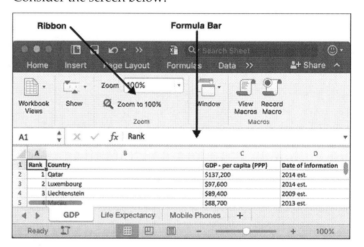

This is the type of smaller screen that you might see on a small tablet device or Smartphone.

Only five rows are visible, making the worksheet difficult to work with. Hiding the Ribbon, Formula Bar, or both, will free up some valuable screen space.

1   Hide the Formula Bar.

Click: View→Show→Formula Bar.

The Formula Bar vanishes:

The Wealth of Nations

2   Reduce the Ribbon display to only show tabs.

In: *Lesson 1-12: Use the Ribbon,* you learned how to hide the Ribbon by clicking the selected Ribbon tab a second time.

You can now see as much of the worksheet as possible, which can be very useful on smaller screens.

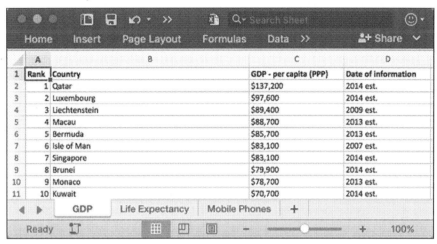

3   Restore the Ribbon and the Formula Bar.

1. Click any of the Ribbon tabs.

   The Ribbon is restored.

2. Click: View→Show→Formula Bar.

   The Formula Bar is restored.

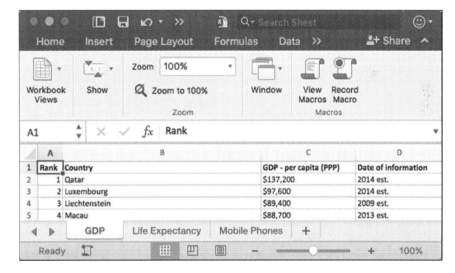

note

The screenshots shown in this lesson may differ from those you see on your screen

The Excel 2019 help system is delivered online. This means that Microsoft are able to constantly correct and update help topics.

For this reason, the information you see on your screen may differ from the screenshots shown in this lesson.

Lesson 1-17: Use the help search system

Excel 2019 for Mac not only provides information about Excel features, but also enables you to execute Ribbon commands directly from inside the help system. This can be a huge time saver.

1 Open the *Wealth of Nations* from your sample files folder (if it isn't already open).

2 Click ⌘→Help and click inside the *Search* box.

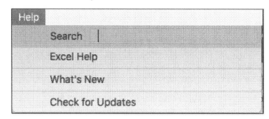

When you click inside the *Search* box, a flashing cursor appears and you are able to type a question.

3 Ask Excel how you can save a file.

You learned how to save a file in: *Lesson 1-8: Save a workbook to a local file.* In that lesson you clicked the *Save* button on the *Quick Access Toolbar.*

Imagine that you have forgotten how to save a file.

Type **Save** into the *Search* box.

Excel displays a menu of choices, showing every command that contains the word *Save.*

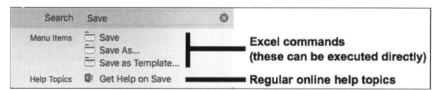

Notice that the list is delineated into two sections. The first section contains commands. The second has the type of regular help topics that you are used to reading in traditional help systems.

4 Execute the Save command directly from the search.

Click the *Save* command at the top of the menu:

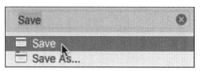

In a traditional help system, you would have expected to see some text explaining how the *Save* command works. Instead the command is executed immediately. The workbook is saved in exactly the same way it would have been if you had clicked the *Save* button on the *Quick Access Toolbar.*

The Wealth of Nations

You can see that two other commands are also available:

- *Save As.* You learned how to use the *Save As* command in: *Lesson 1-8: Save a workbook to a local file.*

- *Save As Template.* You're going to learn about templates later, in: **Lesson 3-14: Create a template**.

You can see how useful help search is when you can't remember where a command is situated on the Ribbon and want to execute the command as quickly as possible.

You can also see that it could be dangerous to execute commands that you don't understand.

Fortunately, Excel also offers regular help that you can read as a reference.

5   Read the Excel help topics relating to the Save command.

Click: ⌘→Help→Get Help on Save.

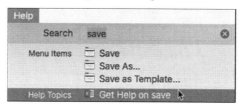

Links to several topics from the Excel 2019 reference manual are shown. You can click on any of these links to read Microsoft's own help topics about *Save* related features.

note

You need an Internet connection to use Excel 2019's help features

In previous versions of Excel, it was possible to access offline help when no Internet connection was available.

Support for offline help has been dropped from Excel 2019. If you have no Internet connection, you will not be able to access Excel's help features.

Note that you must be connected to the internet in order to view the Excel help topics (see sidebar).

Session 1: Exercise

In this exercise you'll try to remember the name of each of the Excel screen elements. The answers are on the next page so you might want to recap by turning the page for a little revision before you start.

Keep trying until you are able to name each of the screen elements from memory. You'll be seeing this terminology during the remainder of the book, so it's important that you can correctly identify each element.

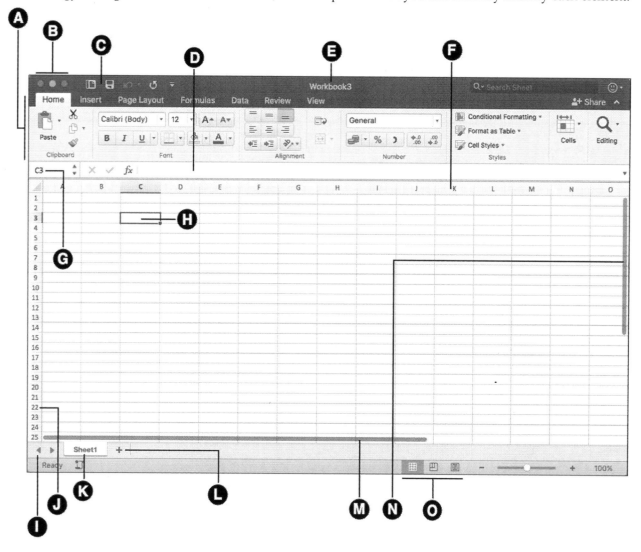

If you need help slide the page to the left

Session 1: Exercise answers

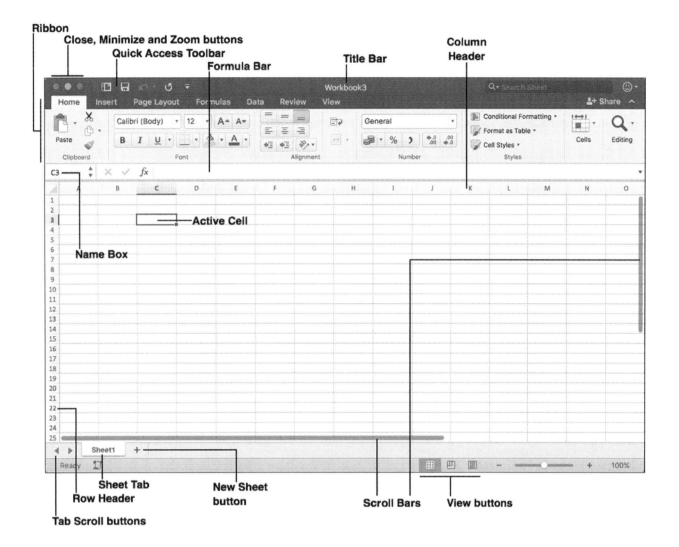

2

Session Two: Doing Useful Work with Excel

> Only those who have the patience to do simple things perfectly ever acquire the skill to do difficult things easily.
>
> *Unknown author*

Now that you've mastered the basics, you are ready to do really useful work with this amazing tool. In this session you will learn to use all of Excel's basic features properly. This will put you way ahead of anybody that hasn't been formally trained in Excel best practice. You'll be doing simple things, but you'll be doing them perfectly!

Even after years of daily use, many users are unable to properly use Excel's fundamental features. They often reach their goal, but get there in a very inefficient way, simply because they were never taught how to do things correctly. By the end of this session you'll be astonished with how well you are working with Excel.

Session Objectives

By the end of this session you will be able to:

- Enter text and numbers into a worksheet
- Create a new workbook and view two workbooks at the same time
- Use AutoSum to quickly calculate totals
- Select a range of cells and understand Smart Tags
- Enter data into a range and copy data across a range
- Select adjacent and non-adjacent rows and columns
- Select non-contiguous cell ranges and view summary information
- AutoSelect a range of cells
- Re-size rows and columns
- Use AutoSum to sum a non-contiguous range
- Use AutoSum to quickly calculate averages
- Create your own formulas
- Create functions using Formula AutoComplete
- Use AutoFill for text and numeric series
- Use AutoFill to adjust formulas
- Use AutoFill options
- Speed up your AutoFills and create a custom fill series
- Understand linear and exponential series
- Use Flash Fill to split and concatenate text
- Use the zoom control
- Print out a worksheet

Lesson 2-1: Enter text and numbers into a worksheet

Excel beginners tend to reach for the mouse far too often. One of the keys to productivity with Excel is to avoid using the mouse when entering data. In this lesson you'll quickly populate a worksheet without using the mouse at all.

1 Open the sample file: *First Quarter Sales and Profit.*

	A	B	C	D
1	Sales and Profit Report - First Quarter 2016			
2				
3		Jan	Feb	Mar
4	New York	22,000	29,000	19,000
5	Los Angeles			
6	London			
7	Paris			
8	Munich			

2 Notice the difference between values and text.

Cells can contain values or text. Values can be numbers, dates or formulas (more on formulas later).

Excel usually does a great job of recognizing when there are values in a cell and when there is text. The giveaway is that text is always (by default) left aligned in the cell and values are right aligned.

Look at the numbers on this worksheet. Notice how they are all right aligned. This lets you know that Excel has correctly recognized them as values and will happily perform mathematical operations using them.

3 Save a value into a cell.

1. Type the value **42000** into cell B5. Notice that the mouse cursor is still flashing in the cell.

At this stage the value has not been saved into the cell.

If you change your mind, you can still undo the value by pressing the **<ESC>** key at the top left of your keyboard or by clicking the *Cancel button* ⊠ on the left-hand side of the Formula Bar.

2. Decide that you want to keep this value in the cell by either pressing the **<Enter>**, **<Tab>** or an **<Arrow>** key on the keyboard, or by clicking the *Confirm button* ✓ on the left-hand side of the Formula Bar.

4 Enter a column of data without using the mouse.

When you enter data into a column, there's no need to use the mouse. Press the **<Enter>** key after each entry and the active cell moves to the cell beneath. Try this now with the following January sales data:

First Quarter Sales and Profit

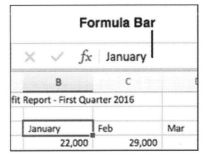

1. Type **18,000** into cell B6.

2. Press the **<Enter>** key to move to cell B7.

3. Do the same to enter the following values into the next two cells.

	A	B	C	D
1	Sales and Profit Report - First Quarter 2016			
2				
3		Jan	Feb	Mar
4	New York	22,000	29,000	19,000
5	Los Angeles	42,000		
6	London	18,000		
7	Paris	35,000		
8	Munich	12,000		

5   **Enter a row of data without using the mouse.**

You can also enter a row of data without using the mouse.

1. Click in cell C5.

2. Type **39,000** and then press the **<Tab> (→)** key.

   The <Tab> key is on the left-hand side of the keyboard above the <Caps Lock> key. Notice how pressing the <Tab> key saves the value into the cell and then moves one cell to the right.

3. Type **43,000** into cell D5 and press the **<Enter>** key.

   You magically move to cell C6, as Excel assumes that you want to begin entering data into the next row.

6   **Complete the table without using the mouse.**

By using the **<Tab>** or **<Enter>** key in the right place you should be able to complete the table now without using the mouse:

	A	B	C	D
1	Sales and Profit Report - First Quarter 2016			
2				
3		Jan	Feb	Mar
4	New York	22,000	29,000	19,000
5	Los Angeles	42,000	39,000	43,000
6	London	18,000	20,000	22,000
7	Paris	35,000	26,000	31,000
8	Munich	12,000	15,000	13,000

7   **Change the text in cell B3 to January.**

1. Double-click cell B3. Notice that there is now a flashing cursor in the cell.

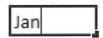

2. Type **uary** on the keyboard to change *Jan* to *January*.

3. Press the **<Enter>** key.

8   **Change the text in cell B3 back to Jan using the formula bar.**

Click once in cell B3 and then change the text in the formula bar back to **Jan** (see sidebar).

9   **Save your work as *First Quarter Sales and Profit-2*.**

Lesson 2-2: Create a new workbook and view two workbooks at the same time

tip

Other ways of creating a new workbook

- Use the keyboard shortcut <Cmd>+<N>.

- Click the File button on the Quick Access Toolbar to return to the Excel start screen.

See more details of how this is done in: *Lesson 1-2: Start Excel and open a new blank workbook.*

1   Open Excel and create a new blank workbook.

    1. Close any open Excel windows and re-open Excel.

    2. Double click the *Blank Workbook* template to create a new workbook.

       Excel helpfully creates a workbook, unimaginatively named *Book1*. If you already have a workbook open called *Book1*, the new workbook will be called *Book2...* and so on.

       Notice that *Book1* is displayed on the *Title Bar*.

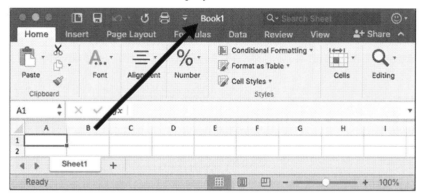

2   Maximize the window without entering Full Screen view.

    Hold the **<Alt>** key and click the green *Zoom* button at the top of the Excel window to maximize the window without entering Full Screen view.

    It's important that you are not in Full Screen view, as you cannot view full screen windows side by side. You learned about Full Screen view in: *Lesson 1-6: Understand Full Screen view.*

3   Create another new workbook and maximize it.

    1. Click: →File→New Workbook.

    2. A new blank workbook called *Book2* is displayed in the workbook window.

    3. **<Alt>+Click** the *Zoom* button to maximize the window.

       You could be forgiven for thinking that nothing has happened but you can see that the *Title Bar* now says: *Book2,* showing that you are now looking at a different workbook.

4   Use the Dock to move between workbooks.

    Right click the Excel icon on the Dock at the bottom of the screen.

note

Finding a workbook when many are open

As well as using the Dock, you can also switch windows using the Menu Bar and macOS's *Mission Control*.

To switch windows with Excel's Menu Bar, click ⌘→Window. You'll then see a list of all open workbooks and can click to switch between them.

To access Mission Control, press the <F3> key on your keyboard.

Mission Control allows you to switch between all open windows, not just Excel windows.

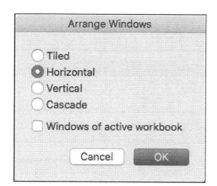

A shortcut menu is displayed, showing both *Book1* and *Book2*.

Try clicking *Book1* and *Book2* to switch between them. Both workbooks are empty so you won't see any difference in the cells, but you should see the name changing in the *Title Bar*.

See sidebar for other methods of switching windows.

5   Display both *Book1* and *Book2* at the same time.

In order to view two workbooks at the same time, they must not be in Full Screen view. If either window is in Full Screen view, you must exit this view using the skills you learned in: *Lesson 1-6: Understand Full Screen view.*

1.   Click: ⌘→Window→Arrange.

     The *Arrange Windows* dialog is displayed.

2.   Choose the *Horizontal* arrangement and click the *OK* button.

     Both workbooks are now shown, one above the other. Each window occupies exactly half of your screen:

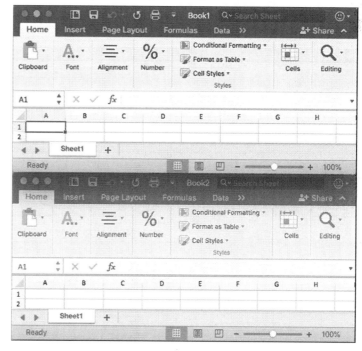

Notice that, as you click each workbook window, the *Title Bar* and the *Close/Minimize/Zoom* buttons light up to show that this is the active window.

6   Close *Book2* and maximize *Book1* to restore the display to a single workbook.

If you've forgotten how to do this, refer back to *Lesson 1-5: Minimize, re-size, move and close the Excel window* and *Lesson 1-6: Understand Full Screen view.*

anecdote

I ran an Excel course for a small company in London a couple of years ago.

The boss had sent his two office staff to learn a little more about Excel.

Before the course began I asked the delegates how long they had been using Excel. They told me that they'd been using it for two years to do all of their office reports.

When I showed them AutoSum they gasped in delight. "This will save us hours" they told me.

I was curious how they had been doing their reports before.

Believe it or not, they had been adding up all of the figures in each column with a calculator and then manually typing the totals at the bottom of each column.

In this case the boss had given them Excel as he had heard it was very good. Unfortunately, he had not initially seen the need to train the staff in its use.

With no training it seemed quite logical to them to use it like a word processor and the boss had still been delighted that his staff were using such impressive technology.

Lesson 2-3: Use AutoSum to quickly calculate totals

Excel's *AutoSum* feature is a really useful and fast way to add the values in a range of cells together.

1   Open *First Quarter Sales and Profit-2* from your sample files folder.

2   In cell A9, type the word **Total** followed by the **<Tab>** key.

The active cell moves to the right and is now in cell B9:

	A	B	C	D
7	Paris	35,000	26,000	31,000
8	Munich	12,000	15,000	13,000
9	Total			

3   Click: Home→Editing→AutoSum Σ

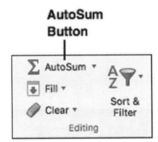

AutoSum Button

Something interesting has happened to the worksheet:

	A	B	C	D
1	Sales and Profit Report - First Quarter 2016			
2				
3		Jan	Feb	Mar
4	New York	22,000	29,000	19,000
5	Los Angeles	42,000	39,000	43,000
6	London	18,000	20,000	22,000
7	Paris	35,000	26,000	31,000
8	Munich	12,000	15,000	13,000
9	Total	=SUM(B4:B8)		

Excel has placed a *marquee* around the number range that AutoSum has guessed you want to work with. The pattern of dots that marks the boundary of the marquee is called the *marching ants*.

The marching ants surround all of the numbers in the column above, up to the first blank cell or text cell (in this case, up to the word Jan).

=SUM(B4:B8) is your first glimpse of an Excel *Formula*. Formulas always begin with an equals sign. This formula is using the SUM function to compute the Sum (or total) of the values in cells B4 to B8.

4   Press the **<Enter>** key or click the AutoSum button Σ once more to display the total January sales:

First Quarter Sales and Profit-2

	A	B	C	D
3		Jan	Feb	Mar
4	New York	22,000	29,000	19,000
5	Los Angeles	42,000	39,000	43,000
6	London	18,000	20,000	22,000
7	Paris	35,000	26,000	31,000
8	Munich	12,000	15,000	13,000
9	Total	129,000		

5   Type the word **Total** into cell E3 and press the **<Enter>** key once.

The active cell moves down one row and is now in cell E4.

	A	B	C	D	E
3		Jan	Feb	Mar	Total
4	New York	22,000	29,000	19,000	
5	Los Angeles	42,000	39,000	43,000	

6   Use AutoSum to calculate sales for New York.

1.   Click: Home→Editing→AutoSum.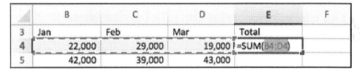

This time AutoSum correctly guesses that you want to sum the values to the left of cell E4:

	B	C	D	E	F
3	Jan	Feb	Mar	Total	
4	22,000	29,000	19,000	=SUM(B4:D4)	
5	42,000	39,000	43,000		

2.   Press the **<Enter>** key, or click the AutoSum button once more.

	A	B	C	D	E
1	Sales and Profit Report - First Quarter 2016				
2					
3		Jan	Feb	Mar	Total
4	New York	22,000	29,000	19,000	70,000
5	Los Angeles	42,000	39,000	43,000	
6	London	18,000	20,000	22,000	
7	Paris	35,000	26,000	31,000	
8	Munich	12,000	15,000	13,000	
9	Total	129,000			

7   Save your work as *First Quarter Sales and Profit-3*.

Lesson 2-4: Select a range of cells and understand Smart Tags

1   Open *First Quarter Sales and Profit-3* from your sample files folder (if it isn't already open).

2   Observe the formula behind the value in cell B9.

Click once on cell B9 or move to it with the arrow keys on your keyboard.

Look at the *formula bar* at the top of the screen. Notice that the cell displays the *value* of a calculation and the formula bar shows the *formula* used to calculate the value:

B9		×	✓	*fx*	=SUM(B4:B8)

	A	B	C	D
8	Munich	12,000	15,000	13,000
9	Total	129,000		128,000
10				
11		**Value**	**Formula**	

note

You can also delete cell contents using the mouse

Pressing the <Delete> key is the fastest way to delete cell contents.

You can also delete the contents of a cell using the mouse. To do this:

1. Right-click the cell.

2. Click *Clear Contents* from the shortcut menu.

3   Delete the contents of cell B9.

Press the <Delete> key on your keyboard.

4   Change the word *Total* in cell A9 to **USA Sales** and press the <Tab> key once.

The cursor moves to cell B9.

8	Munich	12,000
9	USA Sales	

5   Select cells B4:B5 with your mouse.

When the mouse cursor is hovered over a selected cell, there are three possible cursor shapes:

Cursor	What it does
✛ 1.6	The white cross (Select) cursor appears when you hover over the center of the active cell. You can then click and drag to select a range of cells.
1.6 ✛	The black cross (AutoFill) cursor appears when you hover over the bottom right-hand corner of the active cell. You'll be covering AutoFill later in this session.
🖐 1.6	The hand (Move) cursor appears when you hover over one of the edges of the cell (but not the bottom right corner).

First Quarter Sales and Profit-3

note

Selecting cells with the keyboard

To select cells with the keyboard hold down the **<Shift>** key and then use the **<Arrow>** keys to select the range needed.

note

Selecting a large range of cells with the <Shift>-click technique

If you need to select a very large range of cells it is sometimes useful to use this technique:

1. Click the cell in the top left corner of the required range.

2. If necessary, use the scroll bars to make the bottom right corner of the required range visible.

3. Hold down the **<Shift>** key.

4. Click in the bottom right corner of the required range.

Beginners often have difficulty selecting cells and end up moving them or AutoFilling them by mistake.

Position the mouse at the center of cell B4 so that you see the white cross (Select) cursor. When you see the white cross, hold down the left mouse button and drag down to cell B5. You have now selected cells B4 and B5 (in Excel terminology you'd say that you have selected the *range* B4:B5).

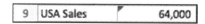

◢	A	B
3		Jan
4	New York	22,000
5	Los Angeles	42,000

6   Display total USA sales in cell B9.

Because you have selected only the cells containing USA sales (cells B4:B5), AutoSum can be used to show the value of the selected cells.

Click the AutoSum button Σ to display the total value of the selected cells.

USA sales are shown in cell B9.

9	USA Sales	64,000

Notice the small green triangle at the top left of cell B9. This is Excel's way of saying: "I think you may have made a mistake".

7   Inspect a potential error using a Smart Tag.

1. Click once on cell B9 to make it the active cell.

    An *Exclamation Mark* icon appears ⚠️. This is called a *Smart Tag*.

2. Hover the mouse cursor over the Smart Tag.

    A tip box pops up telling you what Excel thinks you may have done wrong (see below). Of course, in this case, everything is fine. The Smart Tag thinks that perhaps you didn't want to total just the USA sales – but the Smart Tag is mistaken!

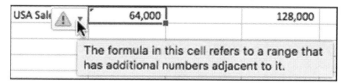

8   Examine the remedial actions suggested by the Smart Tag.

1. Hover the mouse cursor over the Smart Tag icon ⚠️.

2. Click the drop-down arrow that appears.

    A list of possible remedial actions is displayed. In this case you can choose *Ignore Error* to remove the green triangle from the corner of the cell.

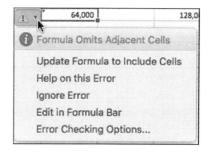

9   Save your work as *First Quarter Sales and Profit-4*.

Lesson 2-5: Enter data into a range and copy data across a range

Now that you have mastered the technique of selecting cells, you can use it to speed up data entry.

When you select a range of cells prior to entering data, Excel knows that all data entered belongs in that range. Several key combinations are then available to greatly speed up data entry.

1 Open a new workbook and save it as *Data Range Test*.

2 Select cells B2:D4.

> You learned how to do this in: *Lesson 2-4: Select a range of cells and understand Smart Tags.*

3 Type: **London.**

> The text appears in cell B2, the top left cell in the range selected.

4 Press the **<Enter>** key.

> The cursor moves to cell B3 as it normally would.

5 Type: **Paris** followed by the **<Enter>** key.

> The cursor moves to cell B4 as it normally would.

6 Type: **New York** followed by the **<Enter>** key.

> This time something new happens. The cursor doesn't move to cell B5 as you might expect, but jumps to cell C2 instead.

7 Type: **150,000** followed by the **<Enter>** key.

> The value appears in cell C2 and Excel moves down the column again to cell C3.

8   Press the **<Enter>** key without entering a value to leave C3 blank.

The cursor moves down the column to cell C4.

9   Type **225,000** followed by the **<Enter>** key.

The cursor jumps to cell D2.

10   Press **<Shift>+<Enter>** twice to change your mind about leaving the value for Paris blank.

1. Press **<Shift>+<Enter>** to move backwards to the value for New York.

2. Press **<Shift>+<Enter>** a second time and you are back to the Paris cell.

	A	B	C	D	E
1					
2		London	150,000		
3		Paris			
4		New York	225,000		
5					

11   Type **180,000** followed by the **<Tab>** key.

<Tab> moves you across the range, to cell D3.

	A	B	C	D	E
1					
2		London	150,000		
3		Paris	180,000		
4		New York	225,000		
5					

You can now appreciate how to use the technique of <Enter>, <Tab>, <Shift>+<Tab> and <Shift>+<Enter> to save a lot of time when entering a whole table of data.

12   Select cells D2:D4.

13   Type **50%** but don't press the <Enter> or <Tab> keys.

The challenge this time is to place the same value into cells D3 and D4 without having to type the value two more times.

14   Press **<Cmd>+<Enter>**.

The value is replicated into all of the other cells in the selected range.

	A	B	C	D	E
1					
2		London	150,000	50%	
3		Paris	180,000	50%	
4		New York	225,000	50%	
5					

15   Click the Save button to save the *Data Range Test* workbook.

---

note

Entering the % symbol

On most Mac keyboards, the % symbol is entered by pressing: <Shift>+<5>.

Lesson 2-6: Select adjacent and non-adjacent rows and columns

1 Open *First Quarter Sales and Profit-4* from your sample files folder (if it isn't already open).

2 Select all of column A.

Hover the mouse cursor over the letter *A* at the top of the column. The column header lights up and the mouse cursor changes to a black down arrow:

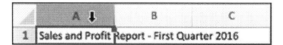

	A ↓	B	C
1	Sales and Profit Report - First Quarter 2016		

Click to select the entire column. The column becomes slightly shaded and a green line surrounds all of the cells.

	A	B	C	D
1	Sales and Profit Report - First Quarter 2016			
2				
3		Jan	Feb	Mar
4	New York	22,000	29,000	19,000

3 Click: Home→Font→Bold to bold face the column.

Because the whole column was selected, all of the values become bold faced.

	A	B	C	D
1	Sales and Profit Report - First Quarter 2016			
2				
3		Jan	Feb	Mar
4	New York	22,000	29,000	19,000
5	Los Angeles	42,000	39,000	43,000
6	London	18,000	20,000	22,000

4 Click: Home→Font→Bold once more to change the type in column A back to normal.

5 Select all of row 4.

1. Hover the mouse cursor over the number on the left-hand side of row 4. The number button lights up and the mouse cursor changes to a black arrow pointing across the row:

3		Jan
⇒	New York	22,000
5	Los Angeles	42,000

2. Click to select the row.

6 Select columns B and C.

Hover the mouse cursor over the letter at the top of column B until you see the black down arrow. When you see the arrow, click and drag to the right to select columns B and C.

First Quarter Sales and Profit-4

	A	B	C	D
1	Sales and Profit	Report - First Quarter 2016		
2				
3		Jan	Feb	Mar
4	New York	22,000	29,000	19,000

7   Select rows 6 and 7.

1. Hover over the number at the left of row 6 until you see the black arrow pointing across the row.

2. When you see the arrow, click and drag down to row 7 to select both rows.

	A	B	C
5	Los Angeles	42,000	39,000
6	London	18,000	20,000
7	Paris	35,000	26,000

8   Select columns A, B, C, D and E without dragging the mouse.

Sometimes you will need to select a large number of adjacent columns or rows. You could drag across them, but it is often easier to use the following technique:

1. Select column A.

2. Hold down the **<Shift>** key.

3. Select column E.

Columns A to E are selected.

	A	B	C	D	E
1	Sales and Profit	Report - First Quarter 2016			
2					
3		Jan	Feb	Mar	Total
4	New York	22,000	29,000	19,000	70,000

9   Select rows 4 and 6.

Perhaps you need to perform an operation on two non-adjacent rows. To select rows 4 and 6 you need to:

1. Select row 4.

2. Hold down the **<Cmd>** key on the keyboard.

3. Select row 6.

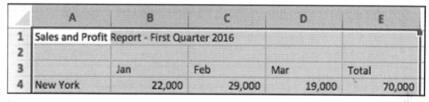

	A	B	C	D
3		Jan	Feb	Mar
4	New York	22,000	29,000	19,000
5	Los Angeles	42,000	39,000	43,000
6	London	18,000	20,000	22,000
7	Paris	35,000	26,000	31,000

Lesson 2-7: Select non-contiguous cell ranges and view summary information

Non-contiguous is a very impressive word! It simply means a range of cells that is split across two or more blocks of cells in different parts of the worksheet.

Non-contiguous ranges can be selected using both the mouse and keyboard. The keyboard method may seem a little involved at first but you'll find it much faster once you have the hang of it.

1 Open *First Quarter Sales and Profit-4* from your sample files folder (if it isn't already open).

2 Select the contiguous range B4:D8 with the keyboard.

When you need to select a contiguous range with the keyboard here's how it's done:

1. Use the arrow keys on the keyboard to navigate to cell B4.

2. Hold down the **<Shift>** key on the keyboard

3. Still holding the **<Shift>** key down, use the arrow keys on the keyboard to navigate to cell D8.

The contiguous range B4:D8 is selected.

	A	B	C	D	E
1	Sales and Profit Report - First Quarter 2016				
2					
3		Jan	Feb	Mar	Total
4	New York	22,000	29,000	19,000	70,000
5	Los Angeles	42,000	39,000	43,000	
6	London	18,000	20,000	22,000	
7	Paris	35,000	26,000	31,000	
8	Munich	12,000	15,000	13,000	
9	USA Sales	64,000		128,000	

First Quarter Sales and Profit-4

3 Select the non-contiguous range B4:B8,D4:D8 using the mouse.

1. Select the range B4:B8 using the mouse.

2. Hold down the **<Cmd>** key and select the range D4:D8 using the mouse.

The non-contiguous range B4:B8,D4:D8 is selected:

	A	B	C	D	E
1	Sales and Profit Report - First Quarter 2016				
2					
3		Jan	Feb	Mar	Total
4	New York	22,000	29,000	19,000	70,000
5	Los Angeles	42,000	39,000	43,000	
6	London	18,000	20,000	22,000	
7	Paris	35,000	26,000	31,000	
8	Munich	12,000	15,000	13,000	
9	USA Sales	64,000		128,000	

note

Where is the Fn key?

The Fn key may be in a different place depending upon the keyboard you are using.

On smaller keyboards, the Fn button is usually in the lower left corner, next to the Ctrl and Cmd keys.

On larger keyboards, the Fn key is on the right side of the keyboard in the group of buttons above the arrow keys.

note

If Fn+F8 doesn't work

The F1-F12 keys at the top of your keyboard are called *function keys*. By default, these are configured to perform actions within macOS (OS X).

Holding the Fn key allows you to override these actions and use the standard functions of these keys, enabling them to work with the features of Excel and other applications.

It's possible to configure macOS to allow these to work as standard function keys by default. If this is the case on your Mac, you can just press F8 alone, without holding Fn.

✓ Average
✓ Count
   Numerical Count
✓ Minimum
✓ Maximum
✓ Sum

4 Select the same non-contiguous range with the keyboard.

This is a little more involved than using the simple <Shift>+<Arrow keys> method used earlier.

Here's how it's done:

1. Use the arrow keys on the keyboard to navigate to cell B4.

2. Press <Fn>+<F8> (F8 is on the very top row of your keyboard).

   See sidebar if you can't find the Fn key or if something unexpected happens when you do this.

3. Use the arrow keys to navigate to cell B8.

4. Press <Fn>+<Shift>+<F8>.

5. Use the arrow keys to navigate to cell D4.

6. Press <Fn>+<F8>.

7. Use the arrow keys to navigate to cell D8.

8. Press <Fn>+<Shift>+<F8>.

The non-contiguous range B4:B8,D4:D8 is selected:

	A	B	C	D	E
1	Sales and Profit Report - First Quarter 2016				
2					
3		Jan	Feb	Mar	Total
4	New York	22,000	29,000	19,000	70,000
5	Los Angeles	42,000	39,000	43,000	
6	London	18,000	20,000	22,000	
7	Paris	35,000	26,000	31,000	
8	Munich	12,000	15,000	13,000	
9	USA Sales	64,000		128,000	

5 Obtain total sales figures for January and March using the status bar.

The status bar contains summary information for the currently selected range.

Look at the bottom right of your screen. You can see the average sales and total sales (sum of sales) for January and March:

Average: 25,700   Count: 10   Sum: 257,000

6 View the maximum and minimum sales for January and March using the status bar.

Right-click the status bar and click *Maximum* and *Minimum* from the pop-up menu (see sidebar).

The status bar now also displays maximum and minimum values.

Average: 25,700   Count: 10   Min: 12,000   Max: 43,000   Sum: 257,000

7 Close the workbook without saving.

Lesson 2-8: AutoSelect a range of cells

When data is arranged in a block (as it is in the Sales Report used in this lesson) it is referred to as a *Range*.

You will often want to select a row or column of cells within a range, or even the entire range.

You can select ranges by using any of the techniques covered so far but this could be very time consuming if the range encompassed hundreds, or even thousands, of rows and columns.

In this lesson you'll learn how to select range rows, range columns and entire ranges with a few clicks of the mouse.

1   Open *Sales Report* from your sample files folder.

This report contains a single block of cells in the range A3 to E19.

	A	B	C	D	E
1	Weekly Sales Report				
2					
3	Invoice No	Date	Customer	Country	Total
4	10918	10 March 2016	Bottom-Dollar Markets	Canada	1,700.81
5	10917	10 March 2016	Romero y tomillo	Spain	429.92
6	10926	10 March 2016	Ana Trujillo Emparedados y helados	Mexico	604.42
7	10929	11 March 2016	Frankenversand	Germany	1,380.33
8	10934	11 March 2016	Lehmanns Marktstand	Germany	587.50
9	10939	11 March 2016	Magazzini Alimentari Riuniti	Italy	749.05
10	10939	11 March 2016	Magazzini Alimentari Riuniti	Italy	749.05
11	10925	12 March 2016	Hanari Carnes	Brazil	558.29
12	10944	12 March 2016	Bottom-Dollar Markets	Canada	1,204.75
13	10923	12 March 2016	La maison d'Asie	France	879.83
14	10937	13 March 2016	Cactus Comidas para llevar	Argentina	757.64
15	10947	13 March 2016	B's Beverages	UK	258.50
16	10933	13 March 2016	Island Trading	UK	1,081.71
17	10938	14 March 2016	QUICK-Stop	Germany	3,209.95
18	10949	14 March 2016	Bottom-Dollar Markets	Canada	5,195.85
19	10945	14 March 2016	Morgenstern Gesundkost	Germany	287.88
20					
21	This report excludes sales to Asia and South Africa.				

Range

2   Select all cells within the range to the right of cell A7.

1.   Click in cell A7 to make it the active cell.

2.   Hover over the right-hand border of cell A7 until you see the hand cursor shape.

7	1092⟨🖑⟩1 March 2016
8	10934 11 March 2016

3.   When you see this cursor shape, hold down the **<Shift>** key and double-click.

All cells to the right of A7, but within the range, are selected.

7	10929 11 March 2016 Frankenversand	Germany	1,380.33

3   Select all cells within the range except the header row.

1.   Click in cell A4 to make it the active cell.

Sales Report

note

Other ways to AutoSelect a range

Using the keyboard

Here's how you would select the entire range in the Weekly Sales Report (excluding the header row) using the keyboard method.

Make cell A4 the active cell by navigating to it with the <Arrow> keys.

1. Press: <Cmd>+<Shift>+ <DownArrow>

   Cells A4:A19 are selected.

2. Press: <Cmd>+<Shift>+ <RightArrow>

   The entire range (excluding the header row) is selected.

Using shortcut keys

The shortcut keys method is the fastest way to select the entire range *including* the header row.

1. Click anywhere inside the range.

2. Press: <Cmd>+<A>

   The entire range (including the header row) is selected.

From the Menu Bar

The Menu Bar method isn't as powerful as the other methods, but does provide a way to select the current range (described as the *region* in the dialog).

Make sure that the active cell is within the range.

1. Click:

   →Edit→Find→Go To…

   The *Go To* dialog is displayed.

2. Click *Special…*

   The *Go To Special* dialog is displayed.

3. Click the *Current Region* option button and then click the *OK* button.

2. Hover over the right-hand border of cell A4 until you see the hand cursor shape.

4	1091...
5	10917 10

3. When you see this cursor shape, hold down the **<Shift>** key and double-click.

   All cells to the right of cell A4, but within the range, are selected.

4. Hover over the bottom border of the selected cells until you see the hand cursor shape.

Date	Customer
10 March 2016	Bottom-Dollar Markets
10 March 2016	Romero y tomillo

5. When you see this cursor shape, hold down the **<Shift>** key and double-click.

   The entire range (except the header row) is selected.

	A	B	C	D	E
1	Weekly Sales Report				
2					
3	Invoice No	Date	Customer	Country	Total
4	10918	10 March 2016	Bottom-Dollar Markets	Canada	1,700.81
5	10917	10 March 2016	Romero y tomillo	Spain	429.92
6	10926	10 March 2016	Ana Trujillo Emparedados y helados	Mexico	604.42
7	10929	11 March 2016	Frankenversand	Germany	1,380.33
8	10934	11 March 2016	Lehmanns Marktstand	Germany	587.50
9	10939	11 March 2016	Magazzini Alimentari Riuniti	Italy	749.05
10	10939	11 March 2016	Magazzini Alimentari Riuniti	Italy	749.05
11	10925	12 March 2016	Hanari Carnes	Brazil	558.29
12	10944	12 March 2016	Bottom-Dollar Markets	Canada	1,204.75
13	10923	12 March 2016	La maison d'Asie	France	879.83
14	10937	13 March 2016	Cactus Comidas para llevar	Argentina	757.64
15	10947	13 March 2016	B's Beverages	UK	258.50
16	10933	13 March 2016	Island Trading	UK	1,081.71
17	10938	14 March 2016	QUICK-Stop	Germany	3,209.95
18	10949	14 March 2016	Bottom-Dollar Markets	Canada	5,195.85
19	10945	14 March 2016	Morgenstern Gesundkost	Germany	287.88
20					
21	This report excludes sales to Asia and South Africa.				

You can also use this technique to select cells to the left of the active cell or above the active cell.

4 Close the workbook without saving.

Lesson 2-9: Re-size rows and columns

note

Why are you calling the pound sign a hash?

In the USA and Canada, the hash symbol is called the **pound sign** or the **number sign**.

In different USA/Canada regions the single symbol has different names because it can be used to denote a number (as in contestant #5) or as a weight (as in 3# of butter).

Throughout this book I will refer to the # as a hash because that is the term used in most other English-speaking countries.

note

Making several columns or rows the same size

Sometimes you will want to make several columns exactly the same width.

To do this, select the columns that you want to resize and then click and drag the intersection of any of the selected columns.

When the mouse button is released, this will make each of the selected columns exactly the same width.

First Quarter Sales and Profit-4

1 Open *First Quarter Sales and Profit-4* from your sample files folder (if it isn't already open).

Notice that columns B, C, D and E are far too wide for their contents. It would be useful to make them narrower to keep the worksheet compact.

2 Re-size column B so that it is just wide enough to contain the January sales figures.

Hover over the line separating the letters B and C until you see the *re-size* cursor shape:

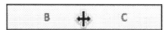

When you see this shape, keep the mouse still and then click and drag to the left. Column B will re-size as you drag. Make it narrower so that the values just fit in the column. Notice that the column width is displayed in points and pixels as you drag.

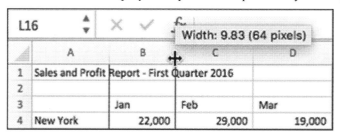

3 Re-size column B so that it is too narrow to contain the January sales figures.

Notice that when the column isn't wide enough to contain the contents, hash signs are shown instead of values (if you're used to hashes being called **pound signs** or **number signs** see the sidebar).

	A	B	C	D
1	Sales and Profit Report - First Quarter 2016			
2				
3		Jan	Feb	Mar
4	New York	######	29,000	19,000

4 Automatically re-size column B so that it is a perfect fit for the widest cell in the column.

1. Hover over the line separating the letters B and C until you see the re-size cursor shape:

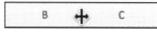

2. When you see this shape, double-click to automatically re-size column B.

5 Automatically re-size every column in the worksheet in one operation.

note

Other ways to re-size rows and columns

You can also re-size rows and columns using the Ribbon.

Click: Home→Cells→Format.

A drop-down menu appears.

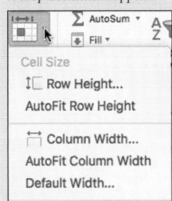

You can use the *Row Height* and *Column Width* options to set the row or column to a specific number of centimeters or inches (depending on your Excel settings).

You can also use the *AutoFit Row Height* and *AutoFit Column Width* options to automatically size the row or column (you achieved this more efficiently with a double-click in the lesson).

Default Width… allows you to set a new width for all columns, but this will not affect columns that have already been manually resized.

You can also resize rows and columns using the following Menu Bar commands:

🍎→Format→Row→Height
🍎→Format→Column→Width

---

1. Select every cell in the worksheet by clicking the *select all* button in the top left corner of the worksheet (you can also do this by clicking in any blank cell and then pressing <Cmd>+<A>).

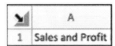

2. Hover over the intersection of any two columns until you see the re-size cursor shape 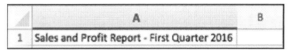 and then double-click.

Every column is now perfectly sized.

Notice that AutoFit has done its job rather too well. Column A is now wide enough to accommodate all of the text in cell A1.

	A	B
1	Sales and Profit Report - First Quarter 2016	

6 Automatically re-size column A so that it is only wide enough to contain the longest city name (Los Angeles).

1. Select cells A4:A9.

2. Click: Home→Cells→Format→AutoFit Column Width.

This time the column is automatically sized so that it is wide enough to contain all of the text in the selected cells.

	A	B	C	D	E
1	Sales and Profit Report - First Quarter 2016				
2					
3		Jan	Feb	Mar	Total
4	New York	22,000	29,000	19,000	70,000
5	Los Angeles	42,000	39,000	43,000	

Notice that the text has spilled over from cell A1 into the adjoining columns B, C, D and E. This always happens when a cell contains text and the adjacent cells are empty.

7 Manually size row 3 so that it is about twice as tall as the other rows.

Do this in exactly the same way as you re-sized the columns but, this time, hover between the intersection of rows 3 and 4 until you see the re-size cursor shape, and then click and drag downwards.

1	Sales and Profit Report - First Quarter 2016
2	Height: 15.00 (15 pixels)
3	Jan Feb Mar
4	New York 22,000 29,000 19,000

8 Auto-resize row 3 so that it is the same size as the other rows again.

1. Hover over the line separating the numbers 3 and 4 until you see the re-size cursor shape.

2. When you see this shape, double-click to automatically re-size row 3.

9 Close Excel without saving.

Lesson 2-10: Use AutoSum to sum a non-contiguous range

In: *Lesson 2-7: Select non-contiguous cell ranges and view summary information,* you learned how to view the sum of January and March sales using the status bar. But how can you put that value onto the worksheet?

Now that you have the hang of selecting non-contiguous ranges, you can use this skill in conjunction with your AutoSum skills to create a formula that will calculate the total of a non-contiguous range.

1 Open *First Quarter Sales and Profit*-4 from your sample files folder (if it isn't already open).

2 Enter the text **Jan/Mar Sales** in cell A10 and press the **<Tab>** key.

The active cell moves to cell B10.

3 Re-size column A so that it is wide enough to contain the text.

1. Hover over the line separating the letters A and B until you see the re-size cursor shape:

2. When you see this shape, keep the mouse still and then click and drag to the right. Column A will re-size as you drag. Make it wider so that the words *Jan/Mar Sales* comfortably fit in the column:

	A	B	C	D
1	Sales and Profit Report - First Quarter 2016			
2				
3		Jan	Feb	Mar
4	New York	22,000	29,000	19,000
5	Los Angeles	42,000	39,000	43,000
6	London	18,000	20,000	22,000
7	Paris	35,000	26,000	31,000
8	Munich	12,000	15,000	13,000
9	USA Sales	64,000		
10	Jan/Mar Sales			

4 Use AutoSum to calculate the total sales for January and March in cell B10.

1. Click Home→Editing→Σ (the AutoSum button).

An AutoSum appears in cell B10, but it isn't anything like what you want yet. AutoSum guesses that you want to sum the USA Sales total.

8	Munich	12,000	15,000	13,000
9	USA Sales	64,000		
10	Jan/Mar Sales	=SUM(B9)		
11				

2. Select the range B4:B8 with the mouse.

First Quarter Sales and Profit-4

3. Hold down the **<Cmd>** key and select the range D4:D8 with the mouse.

Notice that the non-contiguous range **B4:B8,D4:D8** is shown in the AutoSum's formula:

	A	B	C	D	E
1	Sales and Profit Report - First Quarter 2016				
2					
3		Jan	Feb	Mar	Total
4	New York	22,000	29,000	19,000	70,000
5	Los Angeles	42,000	39,000	43,000	
6	London	18,000	20,000	22,000	
7	Paris	35,000	26,000	31,000	
8	Munich	12,000	15,000	13,000	
9	USA Sales	64,000			
10	Jan/Mar Sales	=SUM(B4:B8,D4:D8			
11					

4. Press the **<Enter>** key or click the AutoSum button ∑ again to show the sales for January and March in cell B10.

	A	B	C	D	E
1	Sales and Profit Report - First Quarter 2016				
2					
3		Jan	Feb	Mar	Total
4	New York	22,000	29,000	19,000	70,000
5	Los Angeles	42,000	39,000	43,000	
6	London	18,000	20,000	22,000	
7	Paris	35,000	26,000	31,000	
8	Munich	12,000	15,000	13,000	
9	USA Sales	64,000			
10	Jan/Mar Sales	257,000			
11					

5 Save your work as *First Quarter Sales and Profit-5*.

Lesson 2-11: Use AutoSum to quickly calculate averages

Excel's *AutoSum* feature isn't only restricted to addition. It is also able to compute averages and maximum/minimum values.

In this lesson you'll use AutoSum to calculate the average sales for each month.

1   Open *First Quarter Sales and Profit-5* from your sample files folder (if it isn't already open).

2   Delete cells E3:E4.

   Select cells E3 and E4 and press the **<Delete>** key on your keyboard.

3   Type the word **Average** in cell E3 and press the **<Enter>** key.

   The cursor moves to cell E4.

	A	B	C	D	E
3		Jan	Feb	Mar	Average
4	New York	22,000	29,000	19,000	

4   Use AutoSum to create a formula that will show the average New York sales in cell E4.

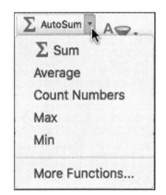

   1.   Click: Home→Editing→AutoSum→Drop down arrow (see sidebar).

        A drop-down menu is displayed, showing all of the different ways in which AutoSum can operate upon a range of cells.

   2.   Click *Average*.

        Excel generates an AVERAGE function and inserts the cell range B4:D4. This is exactly what you want:

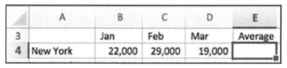

   3.   Press the **<Enter>** key or click the AutoSum button 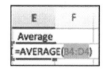 again to see the average sales for New York:

		Jan	Feb	Mar	Average
3		Jan	Feb	Mar	Average
4	New York	22,000	29,000	19,000	23,333

5   Type the word: **Maximum** into cell F3 and then press the **<Enter>** key.

6   Use AutoSum to create a formula in cell F4 that will show the Maximum New York sales for this period.

   1.   Place an AutoSum in cell F4, but this time choose *Max* from the drop-down menu.

        This time you have a small problem. AutoSum is including the average value (23,333) in the calculation.

First Quarter Sales and Profit-5

	B	C	D	E	F
	Jan	Feb	Mar	Average	Maximum
1	22,000	29,000	19,000	23,333	=MAX(B4:E4)

2. Select cells B4:D4 with the mouse

The marquee now covers the correct cells and the average value in cell E4 is no longer included.

3		Jan	Feb	Mar	Average	Maximum
4	New York	22,000	29,000	19,000	23,333	=MAX(B4:D4

Notice that the MAX function is now working with the range B4:D4.

3. Press the **<Enter>** key or click the AutoSum button Σ once more to see the maximum sales the New York office managed during the first quarter of the year:

3		Jan	Feb	Mar	Average	Maximum
4	New York	22,000	29,000	19,000	23,333	29,000

7 Change the words *USA Sales* in cell A9 back to **Sales** and press the **<Tab>** key.

8 Press the **<Fn>+<F2>** keys on the keyboard (or double-click cell B9) to bring back the marquee (shown as a blue box).

9 Adjust the marquee using click and drag so that all offices are included in the Sales total.

Notice that there is a small blue square on each corner of the range. These are called *sizing handles*.

1. Hover the mouse cursor over the bottom right (or bottom left) sizing handle until the cursor shape changes to a double headed arrow. It is really important that you see the double headed arrow and not the hand or white cross.

4	22,000
5	42,000
6	18,000

2. When you see the double headed arrow, click and drag with the mouse down to cell B8.

3. Release the mouse button.

4. Press the **<Enter>** key or click the AutoSum button Σ again.

	A	B
3		Jan
4	New York	22,000
5	Los Angeles	42,000
6	London	18,000
7	Paris	35,000
8	Munich	12,000
9	Sales	129,000
10	Jan/Mar Sales	257,000

10 Save your work as *First Quarter Sales and Profit-6*.

tip

Another way to bring back the blue box showing a range is to click the range in the *Formula Bar*.

Lesson 2-12: Create your own formulas

The AutoSum tool is very useful for quickly inserting SUM(), AVERAGE(), COUNT(), MAX() and MIN() formulas into cells. Many Excel users never get any further with their formulas than this.

In this session you'll create your own formulas without the use of AutoSum. You'll be amazed at how easy it is.

1 Open *First Quarter Sales and Profit*-6 from your sample files folder (if it isn't already open).

2 Select cells A10:B10 and press the **<Delete>** key once.

The previous contents of cells A10:B10 are removed.

3 Type the word **Costs** into cell A11 and **Profit** into cell A12.

4 Type the value **83,000** into cell B11 and press the **<Enter>** key to move down to cell B12.

11	Costs	83,000
12	Profit	

5 Enter a formula into cell B12 to compute the profit made in January.

1. Type: **=B9-B11** into cell B12.

2. Press the **<Enter>** key.

The profit for January is displayed:

9	Sales	129,000
10		
11	Costs	83,000
12	Profit	46,000

6 Enter the formula again using the mouse to select cell references.

The method that you have just used to enter the formula works just fine but it isn't the best method. Sooner or later you will make a mistake. For example, you could easily type =**B8-B11**, resulting in an incorrect answer.

To eliminate such errors, you should always select cell references visually rather than simply typing them in. You can visually select cells using either the mouse or the keyboard. First you'll use the mouse method.

1. Click in cell B12 and press the **<Delete>** key on the keyboard to clear the old formula.

2. Press the equals **<=>** key on the keyboard.

3. Click once on the value 129,000 in cell B9.

4. Press the minus **<->** key on the keyboard.

5. Click once on the value 83,000 in cell B11.

6. Press the **<Enter>** key on the keyboard.

First Quarter Sales and Profit-6

If you followed the above steps carefully you will see that you have created the same formula but with a much lower possibility of making a mistake.

7   Enter the formula again using the visual keyboard technique.

The very best Excel experts hardly use the mouse. You waste valuable seconds every time you reach for the mouse.

Here's the expert technique of visual selection via keyboard:

1.   Use the arrow keys to navigate to cell B12 and then press the **<Delete>** key on the keyboard to clear the old formula.

2.   Press the **<=>** key on the keyboard.

3.   Press the **<Up Arrow>** key three times to move to cell B9.

4.   Press the **<->** key on the keyboard.

5.   Press the **<Up Arrow>** key once to move to cell B11.

6.   Press the **<Enter>** key on the keyboard.

8   Type **10% Bonus** into cell B13.

This employer is very generous and pays the staff ten percent of all profits as an incentive bonus.

In cell A13 type the words: **10% Bonus** and then press the **<Tab>** key on the keyboard to move to cell B13.

9   Enter a formula that uses the multiplication operator.

The multiplication operator is not an X as you might expect but an asterisk (*). The other Excel operators are shown in the sidebar.

You need to press **<Shift>+<8>** to enter an asterisk. If you are using a full-size keyboard with a numeric keypad at the right-hand side you can also use the numeric keypad's **<*>** key.

Whichever key you use you'll still see an asterisk in the formula.

Use either the *mouse selection* technique or the *visual keyboard* technique to enter the formula shown below into cell B13 and then press the **<Enter>** key to see how much bonus was earned:

=B12*0.1

	A	B
11	Costs	83,000
12	Profit	46,000
13	10% Bonus	=B12*0.1

Note that multiplying a value by 0.1 calculates ten percent of the value. You'll learn more about calculating percentages later, in: *Lesson 4-3: Format numbers using built-in number formats.*

11	Costs	83,000
12	Profit	46,000
13	10% Bonus	4,600

10   Save your work as *First Quarter Sales and Profit-7.*

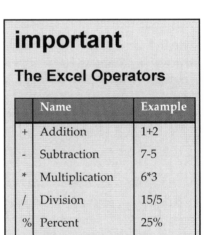

important

The Excel Operators

	Name	Example
+	Addition	1+2
-	Subtraction	7-5
*	Multiplication	6*3
/	Division	15/5
%	Percent	25%
^	Exponentiation	4^2

note

Excel automatically adds closing brackets to functions

If you type:

=SUM(B4:B5

... and then press the **<Enter>** key, Excel will automatically add the closing bracket for you resulting in:

=SUM(B4:B5)

First Quarter Sales and Profit-7

Lesson 2-13: Create functions using Formula AutoComplete

1 Open *First Quarter Sales and Profit-7* from your sample files folder (if it isn't already open).

2 Type the words **USA Sales** into cell A15 and **European Sales** into cell A16.

The text *European Sales* may have spilled over into column B if column A isn't wide enough to contain it.

3 If necessary, re-size column A so that it is wide enough for the words *European Sales* to fit within the column.

You learned how to do this in: *Lesson 2-9: Re-size rows and columns.*

4 Click into cell B15 and type **=S** into the cell.

Something amazing happens:

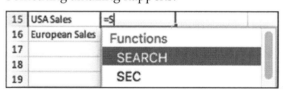

A list appears showing every function in the Excel function library beginning with S. This feature is called *Formula AutoComplete* (if AutoComplete didn't display as expected see the facing-page sidebar).

You've already encountered the SUM(), AVERAGE() and MAX() functions courtesy of AutoSum.

You may be pleased (or dismayed) to know that there are over 300 functions in the Excel function library. The good news is that most untrained Excel users only ever get to understand SUM() and AVERAGE()!

When you typed =S Excel listed all functions beginning with S.

5 Continue typing: **=SU**

Notice that the list now only shows functions beginning with SU and look... there's the *SUM()* function that you need, three down in the list.

You could simply click on it with the mouse, but let's work like an Excel pro and do it with the keyboard.

6 Press the **<Down Arrow>** key to move the cursor over the SUM function.

7 Complete the formula to display the syntax box.

Complete the formula by pressing the **<Tab>** key.

Alternatively, type **M(** to finish the formula manually.

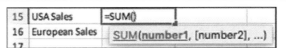

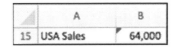
Notice that a little box has appeared beneath the function. This box displays the *Syntax* of the SUM function (see sidebar for more information).

8   Select the cells that you need to sum (cells B4:B5) with the mouse or keyboard.

If you want to be a real pro you should select them with the keyboard. To do this:

1.   Press the **<Up Arrow>** key repeatedly until you reach cell B4.

2.   Hold down the **<Shift>** key and press the **<Down Arrow>** key once to select cells B4:B5.

3.   Press the **<Enter>** key.

The total USA sales are displayed in cell B15.

	A	B
15	USA Sales	64,000

If you typed the formula in manually, you might notice that Excel automatically added a closing bracket when you pressed the <Enter> key (see sidebar facing page).

9   Use the same technique to create a SUM() function in cell B16 to show the total European sales (cells B6:B8).

1.   Click in cell B16.

2.   Type **=SU**

3.   Press the **<Down Arrow>** key to move the cursor over the SUM function.

4.   Press the **<Tab>** key to automatically enter the SUM function into cell B16.

5.   Select the range B6:B8.

6.   Press the **<Enter>** key.

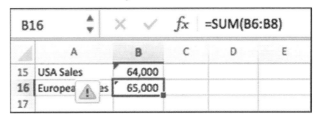

The formula should now be: **=SUM(B6:B8)**

10   Save your work as *First Quarter Sales and Profit-8.*

Lesson 2-14: Use AutoFill for text and numeric series

1   Open *First Quarter Sales and Profit-8* from your sample files folder (if it isn't already open).

2   Delete the text **Feb** and **Mar** from cells C3:D3.

Select cells C3:D3 and then press the **<Delete>** key on your keyboard.

3   Make B3 the active cell

Click once inside cell B3. Notice that there is a green border around the cell and a spot on the bottom right-hand corner. This is the AutoFill handle. If you don't see it, refer to the sidebar.

4   Hover over the AutoFill handle with your mouse until the cursor shape changes to a black cross.

Many of my students have great difficulty with this when they try it for the first time.

- You don't want the hand: 🖑 – that would move the cell.

- You don't want the white cross: ✥ – that would select the cell.

- You want the black cross: ✚ – the AutoFill cursor.

5   When the black cross cursor is visible, hold down the mouse button and drag your mouse to the right to AutoFill the other months: **Feb** and **Mar**.

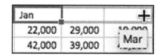

Notice the tip that appears as you drag, previewing the month that will appear in each cell.

When you release the mouse button, the name of each month appears in cells C3 and D3.

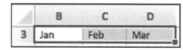

6   Type: **Monday** into cell A18 and AutoFill down to cell A24 to show the days of the week.

(If you are not using an English language version of Excel you will need to type **Monday** in your own language).

First Quarter Sales and Profit-8

7   In cell B18 type the number **1** and in cell B19 type the number **2**.

8   Select cells B18 and B19.

9   AutoFill down to B24 to create sequential numbers:

	A	B
18	Monday	1
19	Tuesday	2
20	Wednesday	3

10   In cell C18 type **9** and in cell C19 type **18**.

11   Select cells C18 and C19.

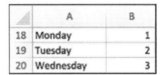

12   AutoFill down to B24 to create the nine times table.

	A	B	C
18	Monday	1	9
19	Tuesday	2	18
20	Wednesday	3	27

13   Use AutoFill to create sequential dates.

1.   Type **01-Jan-16** into cell D18.

2.   Type **02-Jan-16** into cell D19.

3.   Select cells D18:D19.

4.   AutoFill down to D24 to create sequential dates.

14   Use AutoFill to quickly copy text.

Sometimes you will want to duplicate the value from one cell into many others to the right of, left of, beneath, or above the active cell.

When a cell containing text is the active cell and it isn't defined as a *fill series* (the built-in fill series are days of the week and months of the year), AutoFill will simply duplicate the contents of the cell.

Type the text **Adjusted** into cell E18 and then AutoFill it down as far as cell E24.

The same text is now shown in each of the cells:

	A	B	C	D	E
18	Monday	1	9	01-Jan-16	Adjusted
19	Tuesday	2	18	02-Jan-16	Adjusted
20	Wednesday	3	27	03-Jan-16	Adjusted
21	Thursday	4	36	04-Jan-16	Adjusted
22	Friday	5	45	05-Jan-16	Adjusted
23	Saturday	6	54	06-Jan-16	Adjusted
24	Sunday	7	63	07-Jan-16	Adjusted

15   Save your work as *First Quarter Sales and Profit-9*.

Lesson 2-15: Use AutoFill to adjust formulas

AutoFill can save you a lot of time when extending or copying text and number sequences. But the story's not over yet.

AutoFill's ability to copy and adjust formulas is one of the most powerful tools in Excel's impressive toolbox.

1 Open *First Quarter Sales and Profit-9* from your sample files folder (if it isn't already open).

2 Consider the formula in cell B9.

Click onto cell B9 and view the formula displayed in the formula bar (the formula bar is at the top right of the screenshot below).

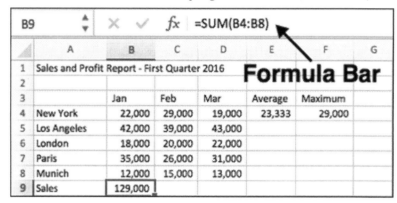

The formula is *=SUM(B4:B8)*. AutoSum created it for you in: *Lesson 2-3: Use AutoSum to quickly calculate totals*. The formula uses the SUM() function to add together the values in the range B4:B8.

Think about the formula that would work in cell C9 (the total sales for February). It would be: *=SUM(C4:C8)*. Similarly the formula that would work in cell D9 (the total sales for March) would be *=SUM(D4:D8)*.

As you move to the right, all that is needed is to increment the letter for each cell reference in the formula and you'll get the right answer every time.

AutoFill is very clever and realizes this. When you AutoFill a cell containing a formula to the right, AutoFill increments the letters in each cell reference.

Most of the time that is exactly what you want.

Later, in *Lesson 3-11: Understand absolute and relative cell references,* and *Lesson 3-12: Understand mixed cell references* you'll learn how to fine-tune the way in which AutoFill adjusts cell references. This will allow you to implement some more advanced AutoFill techniques.

3 AutoFill cell B9 to the right as far as cell D9.

You learned how to do this in: *Lesson 2-14: Use AutoFill for text and numeric series.*

First Quarter Sales and Profit-9

You may see a row of hashes in cell C9 and/or D9. This is because the value may be too wide to fit in the cell. If this is the case, AutoFit the column using the skills learned in: *Lesson 2-9: Re-size rows and columns.*

The correct answers for *Feb* and *Mar* sales are shown on the worksheet. Click on the *Feb* total cell (C9) and look at the formula in the formula bar.

C9		×	✓	*fx*	=SUM(C4:C8)	
	A	B	C	D	E	
1	Sales and Profit Report - First Quarter 2016					
2						
3		Jan	Feb	Mar	Average	
4	New York	22,000	29,000	19,000	23,333	
5	Los Angeles	42,000	39,000	43,000		
6	London	18,000	20,000	22,000		
7	Paris	35,000	26,000	31,000		
8	Munich	12,000	15,000	13,000		
9	Sales	129,000	129,000	128,000		

You can see that AutoFill has done its job perfectly, creating the sum of the values in cells C4:C8. The five branches have sold exactly the same amount in both January and February, but a little less in March.

4 Consider the formula in cell E4.

Click onto cell E4 and view the formula displayed in the formula bar.

E4		×	✓	*fx*	=AVERAGE(B4:D4)	
	A	B	C	D	E	
1	Sales and Profit Report - First Quarter 2016					
2						
3		Jan	Feb	Mar	Average	
4	New York	22,000	29,000	19,000	23,333	
5	Los Angeles	42,000	39,000	43,000		
6	London	18,000	20,000	22,000		

The formula is *=AVERAGE(B4:D4)*. AutoSum created it for you in: *Lesson 2-11: Use AutoSum to quickly calculate averages.*

Think about the formula that would work in cell E5 (the average sales for Los Angeles). It would be: *=AVERAGE(B5:D5)*. Similarly the formula that would work in cell E6 (the average sales for London) would be *=AVERAGE(B6:D6)*.

As you move downward, all that is needed is to increment the number for each cell reference in the formula. This is exactly what AutoFill will do.

E	F
Average	Maximum
23,333	29,000
41,333	43,000
20,000	22,000
30,667	35,000
13,333	15,000

5 AutoFill cell E4 down to E8 to see the average sales for each branch.

6 AutoFill cell F4 down to F8 to view the maximum sales for each branch.

7 Save your work as *First Quarter Sales and Profit-10.*

Lesson 2-16: Use AutoFill options

Sometimes AutoFill begins to misbehave and actually gets in the way of efficient work by wrongly anticipating what you need.

1   Open *First Quarter Sales and Profit-10* from your sample files folder (If it isn't already open).

2   Populate cells F18 to F24 with sequential dates beginning with 1-Jan-16 using AutoFill.

    1.   In cell F18, type the date: **1-Jan-16**

    2.   AutoFill cell F18 down as far as cell F24.

       The cells are populated with sequential dates:

	A	B	C	D	E	F
18	Monday	1	9	01-Jan-16	Adjusted	01-Jan-16
19	Tuesday	2	18	02-Jan-16	Adjusted	02-Jan-16
20	Wednesday	3	27	03-Jan-16	Adjusted	03-Jan-16
21	Thursday	4	36	04-Jan-16	Adjusted	04-Jan-16
22	Friday	5	45	05-Jan-16	Adjusted	05-Jan-16
23	Saturday	6	54	06-Jan-16	Adjusted	06-Jan-16
24	Sunday	7	63	07-Jan-16	Adjusted	07-Jan-16

3   Populate cells G18 to G24 with the date *31-Mar-16* using the AutoFill Smart Tag.

    1.   In cell G18 type the date: **31-Mar-16**

    2.   AutoFill down as far as cell G24.

       At some time, you'll need to add transaction dates to a worksheet and will have four or five entries with the same date.

       AutoFill is perfect for eliminating the need to re-type the date for each transaction, but its insistence upon incrementing the date every time could be very frustrating.

       Fortunately, you can change the default behavior.

    3.   Click the Auto Fill Options Smart Tag ⊞ at the bottom right corner of the filled cells.

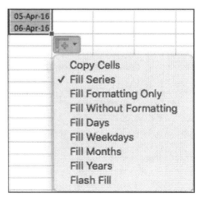

    4.   Click *Copy Cells* to tell AutoFill not to increment the date.

4   Understand AutoFill options.

The *Fill Formatting* options will be covered later in: *Session Four: Making Your Worksheets Look Professional.*

Here's what the other options will do:

Copy Cells	Fill Series	Fill Days	Fill Weekdays	Fill Months	Fill Years
This is what you just did. The first cell is copied to the other cells.	The default for dates that include the day. The date increments by one day at a time.	The date increments by one day at a time.	Because 1st April 2016 was a Friday, the weekend days are omitted and the series jumps from 1st April to 4th April.	Normally this would show the same day number for each month. In this example, there are only 30 days in three of the months so 30th is shown instead of 31st.	The same calendar day is shown for each subsequent year.
31-Mar-16 31-Mar-16 31-Mar-16 31-Mar-16 31-Mar-16 31-Mar-16 31-Mar-16	31-Mar-16 01-Apr-16 02-Apr-16 03-Apr-16 04-Apr-16 05-Apr-16 06-Apr-16	31-Mar-16 01-Apr-16 02-Apr-16 03-Apr-16 04-Apr-16 05-Apr-16 06-Apr-16	31-Mar-16 01-Apr-16 04-Apr-16 05-Apr-16 06-Apr-16 07-Apr-16 08-Apr-16	31-Mar-16 30-Apr-16 31-May-16 30-Jun-16 31-Jul-16 31-Aug-16 30-Sep-16	31-Mar-16 31-Mar-17 31-Mar-18 31-Mar-19 31-Mar-20 31-Mar-21 31-Mar-22

You'll also notice the *Flash Fill* option. Flash Fill is a new feature in Excel 2019 for Mac, and you'll look at it in depth later in this session.

5   Populate cells F18 to F24 with sequential dates using a right-click AutoFill.

1.   Click on cell F18 to make it the active cell.

2.   AutoFill down to cell F24, but this time hold down the right mouse button instead of the left mouse button.

When you release the mouse button, you are instantly presented with the AutoFill options (see sidebar).

This method is preferred to the Smart Tag method because it is faster (one click instead of two).

3.   Click: *Fill Series* or *Fill Days.*

In this example *Fill Series* and *Fill Days* produce exactly the same result.

6   Save your work as *First Quarter Sales and Profit-11.*

Lesson 2-17: Speed up your AutoFills and create a custom fill series

In this lesson you're going to learn some advanced AutoFill techniques that will massively speed up your efficient use of the AutoFill feature.

1 Open *First Quarter Sales and Profit*-11 (if it isn't already open).

2 Use an AutoFill double-click to populate cells G19:G24 with sequential dates.

1. Delete the contents of cells G18:G24.

2. Type: **31-Mar-16** into cell G18.

	A	B	C	D	E	F	G
18	Monday	1	9	01-Jan-16	Adjusted	01-Jan-16	31-Mar-16
19	Tuesday	2	18	02-Jan-16	Adjusted	02-Jan-16	
20	Wednesday	3	27	03-Jan-16	Adjusted	03-Jan-16	
21	Thursday	4	36	04-Jan-16	Adjusted	04-Jan-16	
22	Friday	5	45	05-Jan-16	Adjusted	05-Jan-16	
23	Saturday	6	54	06-Jan-16	Adjusted	06-Jan-16	
24	Sunday	7	63	07-Jan-16	Adjusted	07-Jan-16	

3. Double click the AutoFill handle to automatically fill cells G19:G24.

Hover over the AutoFill handle (the black spot at the bottom right hand corner of cell G18). When you are sure that you have the correct black cross cursor shape, double click to automatically fill down to the end of the range.

	A	B	C	D	E	F	G
18	Monday	1	9	01-Jan-16	Adjusted	01-Jan-16	31-Mar-16
19	Tuesday	2	18	02-Jan-16	Adjusted	02-Jan-16	01-Apr-16
20	Wednesday	3	27	03-Jan-16	Adjusted	03-Jan-16	02-Apr-16
21	Thursday	4	36	04-Jan-16	Adjusted	04-Jan-16	03-Apr-16
22	Friday	5	45	05-Jan-16	Adjusted	05-Jan-16	04-Apr-16
23	Saturday	6	54	06-Jan-16	Adjusted	06-Jan-16	05-Apr-16
24	Sunday	7	63	07-Jan-16	Adjusted	07-Jan-16	06-Apr-16

3 Create a custom list containing the values: *North, South, East* and *West.*

1. Click: ⌘→Excel→Preferences→Custom Lists.

   The *Custom Lists* dialog appears.

2. Click in the *List entries* box and add four custom list entries: **North, South, East** and **West**, pressing the **<Enter>** key between each item.

First Quarter Sales and Profit-11

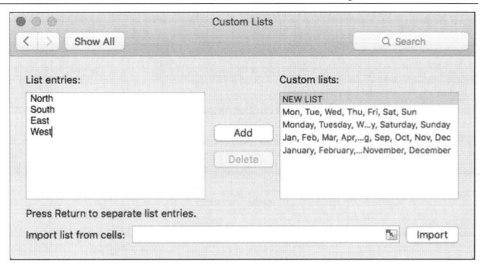

3. Click the *Add* button to add the new custom list.

4. Click the *Close* button to close the *Custom Lists* dialog.

4 Use the newly-created custom list.

Type **North** into any cell and AutoFill down.

As you AutoFill, the custom list entries appear in the worksheet.

5 Delete the North, South, East, West... cells from the worksheet.

6 Save your work as *First Quarter Sales and Profit-12*.

important

A synonym is a word you use when you can't spell the other one.

Baltasar Gracián
(Philsopher 1601-1658)

Excel uses different terminology in various menus, dialog boxes and task panes that mean the same thing (in the context of this lesson):

Series, *Forecast* and *Trend* mean the same thing.

Growth and *Exponential* also mean the same thing.

In this lesson I'll consistently use the terminology *Series* and *Exponential*.

note

Excel can calculate a linear series when the step values of cells are not equal

Excel calculates a linear series (AutoFill also calls this a *fill series*) using this formula:

Start Value + Step Value

Sometimes you may need to produce linear series values from a series of numbers that have different step values. For example, consider this range:

	A	B
2	Value	Step Value
3	1	
4	2.1	1.1
5	2.9	0.8
6	4.1	2.3

In this case Excel will use a more complex mathematical operation (called the *least-squares algorithm*) to determine the correct step value to use. In the above example, Excel would calculate a step value of 1.01.

Rabbit Population

Lesson 2-18: Understand linear and exponential series

Linear series

In: *Lesson 2-14: Use AutoFill for text and numeric series*, you used AutoFill's *Fill Series* method to automatically create these numeric series:

	A	B	C
18	Monday	1	9
19	Tuesday	2	18
20	Wednesday	3	27

These are both examples of *Linear* series.

Imagine that you had originally selected cells B1:B2 before AutoFilling column B:

	B
1	9
2	18
3	

To calculate a linear series Excel first identifies the *step value*. The linear series in column B has a *step value* of nine (18-9=9).

When you use AutoFill to *Fill Series*, Excel adds the *step value* to the *start value* (the number shown in the previous cell).

After you have AutoFilled down to cell B3, the value shown in cell B3 will thus be twenty-seven (18 (the start value) +9 (the step value) = 27)

This is an example of a very simple linear series. Excel is also able to calculate a linear series even when the step values of the selected cells are not equal (see sidebar).

Exponential (or Growth) series

An exponential series is calculated by *multiplying* (rather than adding) the *start value* by the *step value*. This type of series is usually referred to as an *exponential* (rather than linear) series. Excel also uses the term *growth series* as a synonym for *exponential series* (see sidebar).

Here's an example:

- A truly excellent restaurant opens in town. On the first day they only have one customer but the customer is so delighted by the food, service and value that the customer tells two friends.

- The next day the two friends eat there and the restaurant has two diners.

- The two friends are also so pleased with their experience that they each also tell two friends. On the third day the restaurant has four diners.

note

Here's how you could have used the Ribbon to complete this lesson:

1. Enter the value **200** into cell B4.

2. Select cells B4:B51.

3. Click: Home→Editing→ Fill→Series…

The *Series* dialog appears.

4. Enter the following values into the *Series* dialog:

Note that the value: **1.2** is used because an exponential (growth) series multiplies each *start value* by the *step value*.

trivia

According to an old legend, the inventor of the game of Chess presented his new game to a powerful king. The king was so pleased with the game that he offered the inventor any reasonable reward.

The inventor asked for one grain of rice for the first square on the chessboard, two for the second, four for the third… and so on for each square on the chessboard.

The king thought the inventor was foolish to ask for such a simple gift. Much later he found that there was not enough rice in the entire world to fulfil the inventor's request.

With the Excel skills you have learned in this lesson, you should easily be able to model the King's dilemma and discover exactly how many grains of rice would have been needed (about 18.5 Quintillion).

You can see that the restaurant owner might expect that this trend will continue and that each day the number of diners will double (in Excel's terminology, the *step value* is 2). Eventually, of course, the restaurant will become full and the trend will have to end (in Excel's terminology the number of seats in the restaurant is the *stop value*).

In this lesson you will model this type of exponential series.

1 Open *Rabbit Population* from your sample files folder.

2 If the rabbit population of an island increases at the rate of 20% per month, use an exponential progression to calculate how a newly introduced community of 200 rabbits will grow in four years.

1. Type the value: **200** into cell B4 to set the rabbit population at the beginning of the period.

2. Type the value: **240** into cell B5 to set the rabbit population after one month.

3. Select the range B4:B5.

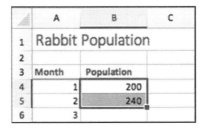

Hold down the right-click mouse button on the AutoFill handle at the bottom-right of the selected range and drag down to AutoFill to cell B51.

4. Click *Growth Trend* on the shortcut menu. Note that this is the shortcut menu's synonym for: *Exponential Series*.

5. After four years (48 months) the 200 rabbits will have grown to a population of a little over a million.

	A	B
49	46	731,452
50	47	877,743
51	48	1,053,291

3 Save your work as *Rabbit Population-1.*

note

You can also Flash Fill more quickly by using the AutoFill handle

The *AutoFill handle* is the small black dot on the bottom-right corner of the active cell (or range of cells).

In: *Lesson 2-16: Use AutoFill options*, you learned that if you right-click and drag the AutoFill handle you are presented with *AutoFill options*:

Copy Cells
Fill Series
Fill Formatting Only
Fill Without Formatting

Fill Days
Fill Weekdays
Fill Months
Fill Years

Linear Trend
Growth Trend
Flash Fill
Series...

You can use the *Flash Fill* item on the *AutoFill options* list to request a Flash Fill.

This will do the same as clicking:

Home→Editing→Fill→Flash Fill

You'll find that this method is faster than using the Ribbon.

This method is also the preferred way to provide Flash Fill with more than one example result for more complex problems (you'll do this in: *Lesson 2-20: Use multiple example Flash Fill to concatenate text*).

Phone Book-1

Lesson 2-19: Use Flash Fill to split text

Here are two examples of international telephone numbers.

+44 (0)113-4960227 (a UK telephone number)
+356 (0)2138-3393 (a Maltese telephone number)

The *country code* (or international dialing code) is shown as a + symbol followed by one or more numbers. The *NDD* (National Direct Dialing prefix) is shown in brackets. This is the access code used to make a call within the relevant country but is omitted when calling from outside the country. The *Area Code* consists of the numbers after the closing bracket but before the hyphen.

In this lesson, you'll use *Flash Fill* to split telephone numbers into the *Country Code, Area Code* and *Phone Number* like this:

	A	B	C	D	E
3	Company	Telephone	Country Code	Area Code	Phone Number
4	Books A Million	+44 (0)113-4960227	+44	113	4960227
5	Maltese Books	+356 (0)2138-3393	+356	2138	3393
6	Bargain Bookstore	+44 (0)115-4960498	+44	115	4960498

In Mac Excel versions prior to Excel 2019 you had to use some very complex formulas to split this type of text. With the new *Flash Fill* feature, you can achieve the same result in seconds.

1   Open *Phone Book-1* from your sample files folder.

2   Extract the *Country Code* from the telephone number in column B and place it into column C.

If you were to type **+44** into cell C4, Excel would interpret it as a positive number and display the result as 44 (without the plus sign).

In order to signal to Excel that you want the plus sign to be displayed, you will need to indicate that +44 should be regarded as text rather than as a number.

You discovered the technique for doing this in: *Lesson 2-1: Enter text and numbers into a worksheet.*

If an apostrophe is placed before a number, Excel will regard it as text.

1.   Type: **'+44** into cell C4 (an apostrophe followed by **+44**).

2.   Press: **<Enter>**

3.   Making sure that the active cell is in one of the cells that will be Flash Filled (i.e. anywhere in the range C3:C18), click:

Home→Editing→Fill→Flash Fill

You can also find Flash Fill on the Data tab, under:

Data→Data Tools→Flash Fill

note

The difference between Flash Fill and a formula-based solution

There are two ways to solve the problem posed in this lesson:

1. Use Flash Fill

This is the method used in this lesson. Flash Fill provides a fast and simple solution.

2. Use complex formulas

Only expert Excel users could construct the complex formulas required to split the telephone numbers contained in the sample file without the use of Flash Fill.

In the *Expert Skills* book in this series you will solve exactly the same problem presented in this lesson without Flash Fill.

Complex formulas are used instead, to provide a formula-based solution.

Advantage of a formula-based solution

The results of a Flash Fill do not automatically update when the source data changes.

This means that if you changed the telephone number in column B you would then need to Flash Fill three times to update columns C, D and E.

Formula results automatically update whenever the source cells change.

This means that if you changed the telephone number in the formula-based solution, the *Country Code, Area Code* and *Phone Number* would automatically update.

Alternatively, you could also use the shortcut keys: **<Ctrl>+<E>** to Flash Fill. **<Cmd>+<E>** will not have the same effect, as the Mac version of Excel uses **<Cmd>+<E>** as the shortcut to center a cell.

The country code is extracted into the remaining cells in column C.

	A	B	C
3	Company	Telephone	Country Code
4	Books A Million	+44 (0)113-4960227	+44
5	Maltese Books	+356 (0)2138-3393	+356
6	Bargain Bookstore	+44 (0)115-4960498	+44

Notice that Excel has placed a green triangle in the top-left corner of each cell. Excel thinks you may have made an error but, of course, the value is fine. If you want to remove the green triangles, use the method you learned in: *Lesson 2-4: Select a range of cells and understand Smart Tags.*

3   Extract the *Area Code* from the telephone number in column B and place it into column D.

Use the same method as you did for the country code. The first area code you need to type is: **'113**

Even though there is no plus sign, it is still useful to include the apostrophe as it will prevent Excel from re-formatting numbers (see next step for more on this).

4   Extract the *Phone Number* from the telephone number in column B and place it into column E.

Use the same method as you did for the country code. The first telephone number is: **'4960227**

In this case you must use a leading apostrophe to prevent Excel from re-formatting large numbers. For example, the telephone number: *20180948* would be displayed as *2E+07* if you didn't include the apostrophe.

The *Country Code, Area Code* and *Phone Number* are now extracted for every international telephone number:

	A	B	C	D	E
3	Company	Telephone	Country Code	Area Code	Phone Number
4	Books A Million	+44 (0)113-4960227	+44	113	4960227
5	Maltese Books	+356 (0)2138-3393	+356	2138	3393
6	Bargain Bookstore	+44 (0)115-4960498	+44	115	4960498

5   Save your work as *Phone Book-2.*

note

Flash Fill doesn't understand mathematics

Consider this problem:

	A	B
1	100	101
2	1120	1121
3	180	
4	149	

You could be forgiven for thinking that Flash Fill could populate cells B3 and B4 with the numbers 181 and 150. In order to produce this result Flash Fill would have to detect a mathematical relationship between the numbers in columns A and B.

Because Flash Fill doesn't understand mathematics, it will always see the problem as a textual one and will produce this result:

	A	B
1	100	101
2	1120	1121
3	180	181
4	149	141

Flash Fill has used the logic "replace the last character displayed in column A with 1" and not "Add one to the value displayed in column A".

Lesson 2-20: Use multiple example Flash Fill to concatenate text

Understand concatenation

Here is an example of splitting text:

	A	B	C
3	Name	First Name	Last Name
4	Jessica Sagan	Jessica	Sagan
5	Stephen Bell	Stephen	Bell

In the above example, the text: *Jessica Sagan* was split into two separate words: *Jessica* and *Sagan*. You saw how to do this using Flash Fill in: *Lesson 2-19: Use Flash Fill to split text*

Concatenation is exactly the opposite of splitting. The two separate words *Jessica* and *Sagan* can be concatenated to produce the single word: *Jessica Sagan*. This is an example of very simple concatenation.

In this lesson, you'll perform some very advanced concatenation using *Flash Fill*.

1 Open *Client Names-1* from your sample files folder.

This workbook contains a list of very inconsistently formatted client names:

	A	B	C	D
3	Last	Middle	First	
4	Sagan	Elizabeth	Jessica	
5	Bell	p	Stephen	
6	jennings		John	

You want to clean up this data so that client names are consistently formatted like this:

	A	B	C	D
3	Last	Middle	First	**Formatted Name**
4	Sagan	Elizabeth	Jessica	Sagan, Jessica E.
5	Bell	p	Stephen	Bell, Stephen P.
6	jennings		John	Jennings, John
7	Simpson	Jane	Meryl	Simpson, Meryl J.
8	hawking		Alfred	Hawking, Alfred
9	Ashe	m	Lucille	Ashe, Lucille M.

For Flash Fill to automate this task you will need to tell Flash Fill what is needed by providing more than one example.

2 Type: **Formatted Name** into cell D3 and bold face the text.

(Excel will probably bold-face the text automatically).

It is important that the header text in row 3 is bold faced.

Client Names-1

When Flash Fill sees different formatting in the first row the row is assumed to be a header row. Flash Fill then excludes the value in the header row from its logic, providing more reliable results.

3 Provide a single example result in cell D4.

Type: **Sagan, Jessica E.** into cell D4.

4 Flash Fill cells D5:D9 based upon the example result in cell D4.

	A	B	C	D
3	Last	Middle	First	Formatted Name
4	Sagan	Elizabeth	Jessica	Sagan, Jessica E.
5	Bell	p		Stephen	Bell, Stephen T.
6	jennings		John	jennings, John O.
7	Simpson	Jane	Meryl	Simpson, Meryl E.
8	hawking		Alfred	hawking, Alfred L.
9	Ashe	m	Lucille	Ashe, Lucille U.

You learned how to do this in: *Lesson 2-19: Use Flash Fill to split text.*

Excel completes the task but the results are not what you wanted (see sidebar).

With only one example, Flash Fill has completely misunderstood the requirement.

5 Provide two example results in cells D4 and D5.

1. Delete the names in cells D5:D9.

2. Provide another example of the correct result (in cell D5).

	A	B	C	D
3	Last	Middle	First	Formatted Name
4	Sagan	Elizabeth	Jessica	Sagan, Jessica E.
5	Bell	p		Stephen	Bell, Stephen P.
6	jennings		John	

6 Flash Fill cells D6:D9 based upon the example results in cells D4 and D5.

1. Select cells D4:D9.

2. Click: Home→Editing→Fill→Flash Fill.

This time Flash Fill has done a better job (see sidebar).

	A	B	C	D
3	Last	Middle	First	Formatted Name
4	Sagan	Elizabeth	Jessica	Sagan, Jessica E.
5	Bell	p		Stephen	Bell, Stephen P.
6	jennings		John	
7	Simpson	Jane	Meryl	Simpson, Meryl J.
8	hawking		Alfred	
9	Ashe	m	Lucille	Ashe, Lucille M.

Notice the two blank results (for *John Jennings* and *Alfred Hawking*).

Flash Fill doesn't yet understand how to treat clients without a middle name. The blank spaces are Flash Fill's way of asking you for yet another example.

7 Provide another example result in cell D6.

	A	B	C	D
3	Last	Middle	First	Formatted Name
4	Sagan	Elizabeth	Jessica	Sagan, Jessica E.
5	Bell	p		Stephen	Bell, Stephen P.
6	jennings		John	Jennings, John
7	Simpson	Jane	Meryl	Simpson, Meryl J.
8	hawking		Alfred	Hawking, Alfred
9	Ashe	m	Lucille	Ashe, Lucille M.

1. Type: **Jennings, John** into cell D6.

2. Press the **<Enter>** key.

3. Select cells D4:D9.

4. Click: Home→Editing→Fill→Flash Fill.

This time Flash Fill has completed the task successfully (see sidebar).

8 Save your work as *Client Names-2*.

note

Flash Fill in Excel for Windows

While Excel 2019 is the first Mac version of Excel to include Flash Fill, this feature has been available in the Windows version of Excel since Excel 2013.

The Windows version of Excel also includes an automatic Flash Fill feature, which automatically tries to apply Flash Fill features 'as you type'.

You can see more about the differences between the Windows and Mac versions of Excel 2019 in: *Appendix A: Differences between the Windows and Mac versions of Excel 2019.*

Lesson 2-21: Use Flash Fill to solve common problems

Flash Fill (introduced to the Mac version of Excel in Excel 2019) is one of Excel's most useful features. It isn't possible to over-state how useful this tool is. I find myself using Flash Fill almost every day to solve a huge number of different problems.

This lesson gives examples of many everyday tasks that I have found can be quickly and simply completed using Flash Fill. I've also included all of the examples in the sample file: *Flash Fill Examples.*

In the following examples, Flash Fill filled the shaded cells.

Split text

Full Name	First Name	Last Name
Jessica Elizabeth Sagan	Jessica	Sagan
Stephen Bell	Stephen	Bell
John Paul Jennings	John	Jennings

Extract initials from names

Name	Initials
Jessica Elizabeth Sagan	JES
Stephen Bell	SB
John Paul Jennings	JPJ

Remove title from names

Full Name	Short Name
Miss Jessica Elizabeth Sagan	Jessica Sagan
Mr Stephen Bell	Stephen Bell
Mr John Paul Jennings	John Jennings

Add commas (a useful name format for alphabetical sorting)

Name	Sort Name
Jessica Elizabeth Sagan	Sagan, Jessica
Stephen Bell	Bell, Stephen
John Paul Jennings	Jennings, John

Concatenate text

First Name	Middle Name	Last Name	Full Name
Jessica	Elizabeth	Sagan	Jessica Elizabeth Sagan
Stephen		Bell	Stephen Bell
John	Paul	Jennings	John Paul Jennings

Concatenate text and insert extra text

First Name	Middle Name	Last Name	Full Name
Jessica	Elizabeth	Sagan	First Name: Jessica, Last Name: Sagan
Stephen		Bell	First Name: Stephen, Last Name: Bell
John	Paul	Jennings	First Name: John, Last Name: Jennings

Flash Fill Examples

Change capitalization

Mixed Case	Title Case
jessica elizabeth sagan	Jessica Elizabeth Sagan
stephen Bell	Stephen Bell
john Paul jennings	John Paul Jennings

Extract the day, month or year from a date

In all the date based examples note that the *Date* column is formatted as a date. You will learn how to format cells as dates later in: *Lesson 4-1: Format dates.*

Date	Day	Date	Month	Date	Year
19th January 2013	19	19th January 2013	January	19th January 2013	2013
5th August 1967	5	5th August 1967	August	5th August 1967	1967
20th September 1999	20	20th September 1999	September	20th September 1999	1999

Extract the day/month from a date

Date	Day/Month
19th January 2013	19th January
5th August 1967	5th August
20th September 1999	20th September

Extract domain names from e-mail addresses

E-mail address	Domain
Mary@QuiteContrary.com	QuiteContrary.com
Humpty@Dumpty.com	Dumpty.com
Jack@Nimble.com	Nimble.com

Format telephone numbers

Name	Tel (unformatted)	Tel (formatted)
Books A Million	1134960227	(113) 496-0227
Bargain Bookstore	1154960498	(115) 496-0498
Books for Less	1164960593	(116) 496-0593

note

Can my mouse be used to zoom?

The first Apple mouse to include a scroll wheel was the Mighty Mouse, first released in 2005. If you are using an Apple mouse from before 2005, you won't be able to zoom in and out using the mouse.

Apple's most recent mouse (the Magic Mouse) does not include a scroll wheel, but instead allows you to scroll by holding your finger on the mouse's surface and then moving it in the direction that you wish to scroll.

Any other mouse that has a scroll wheel should allow you to zoom as shown in this lesson. You do not need to use an Apple mouse.

note

If mouse zooming doesn't work

You might find that mouse zooming doesn't work, even though you have a Magic Mouse or a mouse with a scroll wheel. This may be due to a bug in Excel for Mac.

Excel sometimes gets confused over whether you are trying to scroll within the workbook or trying to scroll through items in menus on the Ribbon.

If this happens to you, you should be able to fix the problem by quitting and restarting Excel.

You saw how to do this in: *Lesson 1-5: Minimize, re-size, move and close the Excel window.*

First Quarter Sales and Profit-12

Lesson 2-22: Use the zoom control

Zooming is used to magnify or reduce the worksheet. If you have a lot of rows in a worksheet and have good eyes, you might want to zoom out sometimes to see more of the worksheet on one screen.

1 Open *First Quarter Sales and Profit-12* from your sample files folder.

2 Zoom in and out of the worksheet using the mouse.

The fastest way to zoom a worksheet is by using the mouse, if your mouse has this ability (see sidebar).

To zoom using the mouse, hold down the **<Ctrl>** key on the keyboard and roll the mouse wheel to zoom in and out.

3 Zoom in and out of a worksheet using the zoom control.

The zoom control is at the bottom right of your screen.

Click and drag on the zoom control slider to zoom in and out of your worksheet. You can also zoom by clicking the plus and minus buttons on either side of the Zoom control.

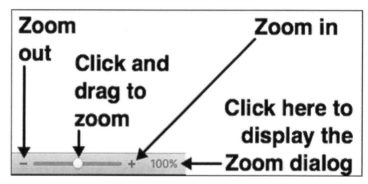

4 Use the Zoom dialog to make cells A3:D9 fill the screen.

1. Select cells A3:D9.

	A	B	C	D	E
2					
3		Jan	Feb	Mar	Average
4	New York	22,000	29,000	19,000	23,333
5	Los Angeles	42,000	39,000	43,000	41,333
6	London	18,000	20,000	22,000	20,000
7	Paris	35,000	26,000	31,000	30,667
8	Munich	12,000	15,000	13,000	13,333
9	Sales	129,000	129,000	128,000	

2. Click on the right hand side of the zoom bar.

Zoom level. Click to open the Zoom dialog box.

The *Zoom* dialog is displayed.

3. Select the *Fit Selection* option button.

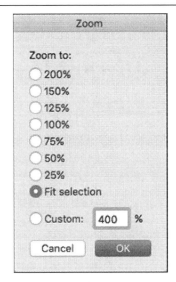

4. Click the *OK* button.

    The worksheet is zoomed so that the selected cells completely fill the screen.

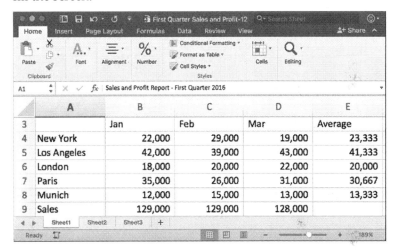

5   Zoom back to 100% using the Ribbon.

    You'll probably find the zoom bar to be the quickest and most convenient way to zoom, but you can also zoom using the Ribbon.

    Click: View→Zoom→Zoom to 100%.

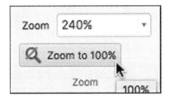

    The screen is restored to normal size.

Lesson 2-23: Print out a worksheet

You aren't going to explore every option for preparing and printing a worksheet in this lesson. Printing is such a huge subject that this course devotes a whole session to it in: *Session Seven: Printing Your Work.*

This lesson only aims to teach you the bare minimum skills you need to put your work onto paper.

1   Open *First Quarter Sales and Profit-12* from your sample files folder (if it isn't already open).

	A	B	C	D	E	F	G
1	Sales and Profit Report - First Quarter 2016						
2							
3		Jan	Feb	Mar	Average	Maximum	
4	New York	22,000	29,000	19,000	23,333	29,000	
5	Los Angeles	42,000	39,000	43,000	41,333	43,000	
6	London	18,000	20,000	22,000	20,000	22,000	
7	Paris	35,000	26,000	31,000	30,667	35,000	
8	Munich	12,000	15,000	13,000	13,333	15,000	
9	Sales	129,000	129,000	128,000			
10							
11	Costs	83,000					
12	Profit	46,000					
13	10% Bonus	4,600					
14							
15	USA Sales	64,000					
16	European Sales	65,000					
17							
18	Monday	1	9	01-Jan-16	Adjusted	01-Jan-16	31-Mar-16
19	Tuesday	2	18	02-Jan-16	Adjusted	02-Jan-16	01-Apr-16
20	Wednesday	3	27	03-Jan-16	Adjusted	03-Jan-16	02-Apr-16
21	Thursday	4	36	04-Jan-16	Adjusted	04-Jan-16	03-Apr-16
22	Friday	5	45	05-Jan-16	Adjusted	05-Jan-16	04-Apr-16
23	Saturday	6	54	06-Jan-16	Adjusted	06-Jan-16	05-Apr-16
24	Sunday	7	63	07-Jan-16	Adjusted	07-Jan-16	06-Apr-16

2   Click: →File→Print.

The *Print* dialog appears, showing a preview of how the document will print. By default, a simplified version of the dialog is shown.

3   Click *Show Details* to show the complete Print dialog.

The complete dialog is shown, enabling you to access more printing options.

If the complete dialog is already visible, the *Show Details* button will be replaced by a *Hide Details* button.

First Quarter Sales and
Profit-12

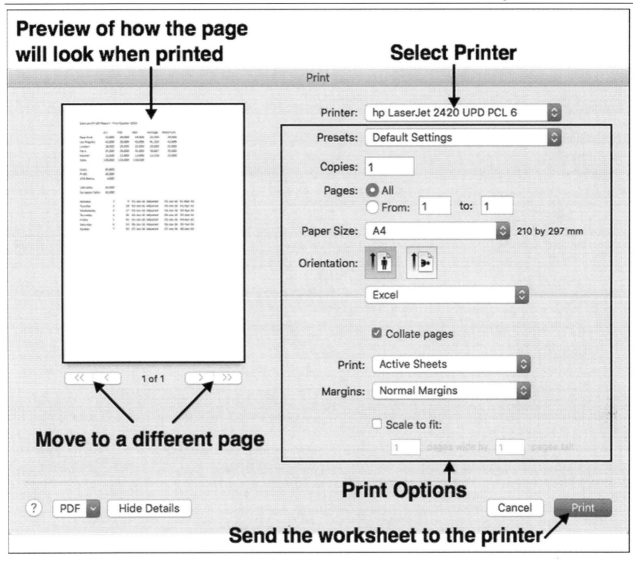

Preview of how the page will look when printed

Select Printer

Move to a different page

Print Options

Send the worksheet to the printer

4   Print the worksheet.

Click the *Print* button:

The page is printed on the selected printer.

Session 2: Exercise

1 Open a new blank workbook.

2 Use AutoFill to put the three months Jan, Feb, and Mar into cells A4:A6.

3 Using only the keyboard, add the following data:

	A	B	C	D	E
1	Profit Analysis				
2					
3		London	Paris	New York	Average
4	Jan	2,500	3,100	2,300	
5	Feb	2,200	2,700	2,600	
6	Mar	2,100	2,600	2,800	
7	Total				

4 Use AutoSum to compute London's total profit for Jan/Feb/Mar in cell B7.

5 Use AutoSum to compute the average January profit in cell E4.

6 Use AutoFill to extend the London total in cell B7 to the Paris and New York totals in cells C7 and D7.

7 Use AutoFill to extend the January average profit in cell E4 to the February and March average profits in cells E5 and E6.

8 Select all of column A and all of column E (at the same time) and bold face the values in them.

9 Select rows 3 and row 7 (at the same time) and bold face the values in them.

	A	B	C	D	E
1	**Profit Analysis**				
2					
3		**London**	**Paris**	**New York**	**Average**
4	**Jan**	2,500	3,100	2,300	**2,633**
5	**Feb**	2,200	2,700	2,600	**2,500**
6	**Mar**	2,100	2,600	2,800	**2,500**
7	**Total**	**6,800**	**8,400**	**7,700**	

10 Select cells B4:B6 and cells D4:D6 at the same time and then read the total London and New York sales figure for Jan, Feb and March from the summary information displayed on the status bar.

11 Select cells B4:D6 and zoom the selection so that these cells fill the screen.

12 Save your work as *Exercise2-End*.

If you need help slide the page to the left

Session 2: Exercise answers

These are the questions that students find the most difficult to answer:

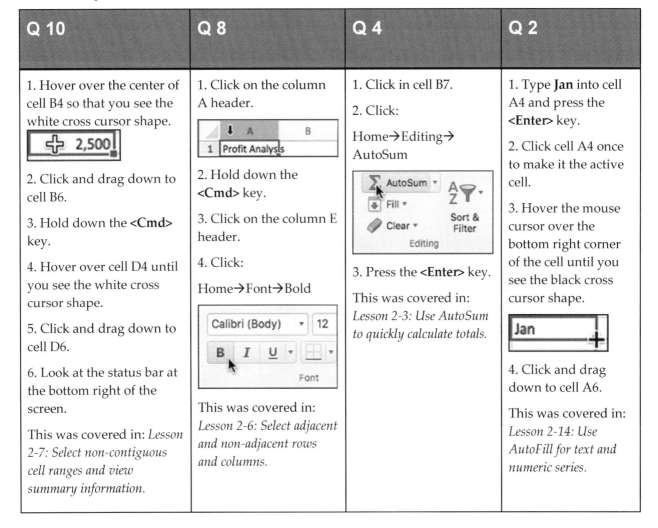

Q 10	Q 8	Q 4	Q 2
1. Hover over the center of cell B4 so that you see the white cross cursor shape.	1. Click on the column A header.	1. Click in cell B7.	1. Type **Jan** into cell A4 and press the **<Enter>** key.
2. Click and drag down to cell B6.	2. Hold down the **<Cmd>** key.	2. Click: Home→Editing→ AutoSum	2. Click cell A4 once to make it the active cell.
3. Hold down the **<Cmd>** key.	3. Click on the column E header.	3. Press the **<Enter>** key.	3. Hover the mouse cursor over the bottom right corner of the cell until you see the black cross cursor shape.
4. Hover over cell D4 until you see the white cross cursor shape.	4. Click: Home→Font→Bold	This was covered in: *Lesson 2-3: Use AutoSum to quickly calculate totals.*	
5. Click and drag down to cell D6.			4. Click and drag down to cell A6.
6. Look at the status bar at the bottom right of the screen.			This was covered in: *Lesson 2-14: Use AutoFill for text and numeric series.*
This was covered in: *Lesson 2-7: Select non-contiguous cell ranges and view summary information.*	This was covered in: *Lesson 2-6: Select adjacent and non-adjacent rows and columns.*		

If you have difficulty with the other questions, here are the lessons that cover the relevant skills:

1   Refer to: Lesson 1-2: Start Excel and open a new blank workbook.

3   Refer to: Lesson 2-1: Enter text and numbers into a worksheet.

5   Refer to: Lesson 2-3: Use AutoSum to quickly calculate totals.

6   Refer to: Lesson 2-15: Use AutoFill to adjust formulas.

7   Refer to: Lesson 2-15: Use AutoFill to adjust formulas.

9   Refer to: Lesson 2-6: Select adjacent and non-adjacent rows and columns.

11   Refer to: Lesson 2-22: Use the zoom control.

12   Refer to: Lesson 1-8: Save a workbook to a local file.

Session Three: Taking Your Skills to the Next Level

One only gets to the top rung of the ladder by steadily climbing up one at a time, and suddenly all sorts of powers, all sorts of abilities which you thought never belonged to you – suddenly become within your own possibility.

Margaret Thatcher,
Prime Minister of the United Kingdom from 1979-1990

After mastering all of the techniques covered in session two, you're already able to do useful work with the world's most powerful business tool, but of course, you're only on the first rung of a very long ladder.

While you are now able to do the simple things well, there are a few more insights you need to really get Excel working.

Most of the skills covered in this session will take your powers beyond those of casual Excel users.

Session Objectives

By the end of this session you will be able to:

- Insert and delete rows and columns
- Use AutoComplete and fill data from adjacent cells
- Cut, copy and paste
- Cut, copy and paste using drag and drop
- Use Paste Values
- Increase/decrease decimal places displayed
- Transpose a range
- Use Undo and Redo
- Insert, View and Print cell comments
- Understand absolute, relative and mixed cell references
- Understand templates
- Create a template
- Use a template
- Freeze columns and rows
- Split the window into multiple panes
- Check spelling

Lesson 3-1: Insert and delete rows and columns

1 Open *The World's Fastest Cars* from your sample files folder.

	A	B	C	D	E	F	G
1	The World's Fastest Cars						
2							
3	Make	Model	Top Speed (MPH)	0-60	BHP	Price (USD)	Country
4	Ferrari	F12 Berlinetta	227	3.1	730	330,000	Italy
5	Lamborghini	Aventador Super Veloce	217	2.8	690	493,095	Italy
6	Aston Martin	V12 Vantage S	205	3.7	565	123,695	UK
7	Ferrari	488 GTB	205	2.9	661	242,737	Italy
8	Lamborghini	Huracán	202	2.5	602	237,250	Italy
9	Porsche	911 Turbo S Sport+	197	3.1	560	241,105	Germany
10	Aston Martin	Vanquish Volante	197	3.8	568	299,000	UK
11	Mercedes	SLS AMG Black Series	196	3.5	622	275,000	Germany
12	Lotus	Evora 400	186	4.1	400	89,900	UK
13	Tesla	Model S P90D	155	2.6	762	130,700	USA

A worksheet opens, showing some of the fastest cars in the world.

The list does not, however, show the true fastest production car in the world (when this book was written in 2018): the *Bugatti Veyron Super Sport*. There may be an even faster car by the time you read this book. You need to insert a row above row 4 to add the new car to the list.

2 Insert a blank row above row 4.

Right-click the row header button [4] and click *Insert* from the shortcut menu.

3 Add the following data to the new row:

3	Make	Model	Top Speed (MPH)	0-60	BHP	Price (USD)	Country
4	Bugatti	Veyron Super Sport	268	2.4	1,184	1,700,000	Germany
5	Ferrari	F12 Berlinetta	227	3.1	730	330,000	Italy

4 If the text is bold-faced, restore it to normal.

You learned how to do this in: *Lesson 2-6: Select adjacent and non-adjacent rows and columns.*

5 Add a column to the left of column A.

Adding columns is just like adding rows.

Right-click on the column header [A] and then click *Insert* from the shortcut menu.

A blank column appears on the left hand side of the worksheet:

	A	B	C	D
1		The World's Fastest Cars		
2				
3		Make	Model	Top Speed (MPH)
4		Bugatti	Veyron Super Sport	268
5		Ferrari	F12 Berlinetta	227
6		Lamborghini	Aventador Super Veloce	217

6 Delete the newly-inserted Column A.

note

Other ways of inserting and deleting rows and columns

The right-click method, described in this lesson, is the fastest and most intuitive way to insert rows and columns, but there are three additional methods.

To insert rows or columns:

Click: ⌘→Insert→Rows or ⌘→Insert→Columns.

OR

Click: Home→Cells→Insert (drop down list)

OR

Press <Cmd>+<Shift>+<+>

(and then select *Entire row* or *Entire column*).

To delete rows or columns:

Click: ⌘→Edit→Delete.

(and then select *Entire row* or *Entire column*).

OR

Click: Home→Cells→Delete (drop down list)

OR

Press <Cmd>+<->

(and then select *Entire row* or *Entire column*).

The World's Fastest Cars

Deleting is just like adding. Right-click on the column header 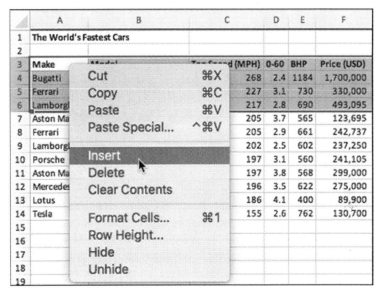 but, this time, select *Delete* from the shortcut menu.

7   Insert four rows above row 3.

Nearly every Excel user does this by inserting a single row four times until they learn the correct technique.

1. Select the four rows 3:6 by clicking and dragging across the row header buttons.

2. Right-click anywhere in the selected area.

3. Click *Insert* from the shortcut menu.

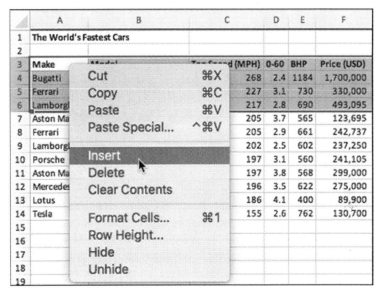

Four blank rows are inserted.

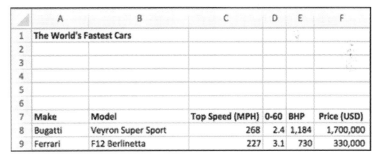

8   Delete the four newly-inserted rows.

1. Select the four rows that you want to delete (by clicking and dragging the mouse cursor over row headers 3, 4, 5 and 6).

2. Right-click anywhere in the selected area.

3. Click *Delete* from the shortcut menu.

9   Save your work as: *The World's Fastest Cars-2*.

Lesson 3-2: Use AutoComplete and fill data from adjacent cells

1   Open *The World's Fastest Cars-2* from your sample files folder (if it isn't already open).

	A	B	C	D	E	F	G
1	The World's Fastest Cars						
2							
3	Make	Model	Top Speed (MPH)	0-60	BHP	Price (USD)	Country
4	Bugatti	Veyron Super Sport	268	2.4	1,184	1,700,000	Germany
5	Ferrari	F12 Berlinetta	227	3.1	730	330,000	Italy
6	Lamborghini	Aventador Super Veloce	217	2.8	690	493,095	Italy
7	Aston Martin	V12 Vantage S	205	3.7	565	123,695	UK
8	Ferrari	488 GTB	205	2.9	661	242,737	Italy
9	Lamborghini	Huracán	202	2.5	602	237,250	Italy
10	Porsche	911 Turbo S Sport+	197	3.1	560	241,105	Germany
11	Aston Martin	Vanquish Volante	197	3.8	568	299,000	UK
12	Mercedes	SLS AMG Black Series	196	3.5	622	275,000	Germany
13	Lotus	Evora 400	186	4.1	400	89,900	UK
14	Tesla	Model S P90D	155	2.6	762	130,700	USA

2   Type the letter **F** into cell A15.

Notice that Excel guesses that you want to type *Ferrari* into the cell. This is because the word Ferrari appears above it in the column.

If this doesn't happen, somebody has switched AutoComplete off. See the sidebar to find out how to switch it back on.

	A	B	C	D	E	F	G
13	Lotus	Evora 400	186	4.1	400	89,900	UK
14	Tesla	Model S P90D	155	2.6	762	130,700	USA
15	Ferrari						

3   Press the **<Tab>** key to accept the guess.

4   Enter **LaFerrari** for the model and **217** for the top speed.

	A	B	C	D	E	F	G
14	Tesla	Model S P90D	155	2.6	762	130,700	USA
15	Ferrari	LaFerrari	217	2.6	950	1,690,000	Italy

5   Use the *Fill* command to enter **2.6** into cell D15.

The Ferrari has the same 0-60 time as the Tesla P90D. Instead of typing **2.6** into the cell, you can use the *Fill* command.

1.   Click in cell D15.

2.   Click: Home→Editing→Fill→Down.

note

If AutoComplete doesn't work, somebody has switched it off

It's almost certain that AutoComplete will be enabled on any computer that you work on. It is such a useful feature that you'd never want to disable it.

If AutoComplete doesn't work for you it's because somebody has switched it off.

Bring it back like this:

1. Click: ⌘→Excel→Preferences.

2. Click *AutoComplete*.

3. Make sure that *AutoComplete the closest match while I type* is checked.

The World's Fastest Cars-2

note

You can also Fill Down and Fill Right, using keyboard shortcuts and the Menu Bar

The following shortcut key combinations can be used for the *Fill Down* and *Fill Right* commands:

<Cmd>+<D>	Fill Down
<Cmd>+<R>	Fill Right

Unfortunately, there is no simple shortcut key combination for *Fill Up* or *Fill Left*.

Fill options are also available from the ■→Edit→Fill menu.

Notice that there are also *Right, Up* and *Left* options. These can be used to copy values from adjacent cells in any direction.

6   Enter **950** for the BHP value and **1,690,000** for the price.

7   Right-click in cell G15 and choose *Pick From Drop-down List...* from the shortcut menu.

A unique list of all countries that currently exist in column G is displayed.

	A	B	C	D	E	F	G	H
1	The World's Fastest Cars							
2								
3	Make	Model	Top Speed (MPH)	0-60	BHP	Price (USD)	Country	
4	Bugatti	Veyron Super Sport	268	2.4	1,184	1,700,000	Germany	
5	Ferrari	F12 Berlinetta	227	3.1	730	330,000	Italy	
6	Lamborghini	Aventador Super Veloce	217	2.8	690	493,095	Italy	
7	Aston Martin	V12 Vantage S	205	3.7	565	123,695	UK	
8	Ferrari	488 GTB	205	2.9	661	242,737	Italy	
9	Lamborghini	Huracán	202	2.5	602	237,250	Italy	
10	Porsche	911 Turbo S Sport+	197	3.1	560	241,105	Germany	
11	Aston Martin	Vanquish Volante	197	3.8	568	299,000	UK	
12	Mercedes	SLS AMG Black Series	196	3.5	622	275,000	Germany	
13	Lotus	Evora 400	186	4.1	400	89,900	UK	
14	Tesla	Model S P90D	155	2.6	762	130,700	USA	
15	Ferrari	LaFerrari	217	2.6	950	1,960,000		
16							Germany	
17							Italy	
18							UK	
19							USA	
20								

8   Click *Italy* to automatically enter the country.

9   Save your work as *The World's Fastest Cars-3*.

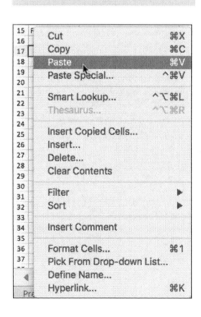

The World's Fastest Cars-3

Lesson 3-3: Cut, copy and paste

1   Open *The World's Fastest Cars-3* from your sample files folder (if it isn't already open).

2   Click cell A1 to make it the active cell.

3   Copy the text from cell A1 to the clipboard.

The clipboard is a container for copied text and is common to all of Microsoft Office. When you ask Excel to copy, Excel takes the value in cell A1 (in this case text) and places a copy of it onto the clipboard. The existing contents of cell A1 remain unaltered.

The clipboard is useful because you can later paste the clipboard's contents back into the worksheet (or into any other Office document such as a PowerPoint presentation, Word document or Outlook Email).

There are several ways to copy, but these two are the quickest:

EITHER

Right click and select *Copy* from the shortcut menu.

OR

Press **<Cmd>+<C>** on the keyboard.

The slowest methods are either to click:

Home→Clipboard→Copy or →Edit→Copy.

4   Click cell A17 to make it the active cell.

5   Paste the copied text into cell A17.

There are also several ways to paste, but these two are the quickest:

EITHER

Right click cell A17 and then select *Paste* from the shortcut menu (see sidebar).

OR

Click cell A17 and then press **<Cmd>+<V>** on the keyboard.

The slowest methods are either to click:

Home→Clipboard→Paste or →Edit→Paste.

The text appears in cell A17.

14	Tesla	Model S P90D		155
15	Ferrari	LaFerrari		217
16				
17	**The World's Fastest Cars**			

6   Edit the text in cell A17 to read:
The World's Fastest Italian Cars

You learned how to do this in: *Lesson 2-1: Enter text and numbers into a worksheet.*

7   Select all of row 5 and copy it to the clipboard.

Selecting an entire row was covered in: *Lesson 2-6: Select adjacent and non-adjacent rows and columns.*

8   Select all of row 19 and paste into it.

The contents of row 5 are copied to row 19.

17	The World's Fastest Italian Cars			
18				
19	Ferrari	F12 Berlinetta	227	3.1

9   Use the same technique to paste row 6 into row 20.

10   Cut the text from the range A8:G9 to place it onto the clipboard.

When you cut text, the text is copied from the source cell(s) to the clipboard. If you then paste the text to a new location, the text is automatically deleted from the source cells(s).

1. Select the range A8 to G9.

2. Cut the range to place it onto the clipboard.

   There are several ways to cut, but these two are the quickest:

   EITHER

   Right click and select *Cut* from the shortcut menu.

   OR

   Press **<Cmd>+<X>**.

   The slowest methods are to click:

   Home→Clipboard→Cut or →Edit→Cut.

11   Click in cell A21 to make it the active cell.

12   Paste the cut range into the range beginning in cell A21.

The cut text appears with the top left hand corner in cell A21.

7	Aston Martin	V12 Vantage S		205	3.7	565	123,695	UK
8								
9								
10	Porsche	911 Turbo S Sport+		197	3.1	560	241,105	Germany
11	Aston Martin	Vanquish Volante		197	3.8	568	299,000	UK
12	Mercedes	SLS AMG Black Series		196	3.5	622	275,000	Germany
13	Lotus	Evora 400		186	4.1	400	89,900	UK
14	Tesla	Model S P90D		155	2.6	762	130,700	USA
15	Ferrari	LaFerrari		217	2.6	950	1,960,000	Italy
16								
17	The World's Fastest Italian Cars							
18								
19	Ferrari	F12 Berlinetta		227	3.1	730	330,000	Italy
20	Lamborghini	Aventador Super Veloce		217	2.8	690	493,095	Italy
21	Ferrari	488 GTB		205	2.9	661	242,737	Italy
22	Lamborghini	Huracán		202	2.5	602	237,250	Italy
23								

13   Save your work as *The World's Fastest Cars-4.*

Lesson 3-4: Cut, copy and paste using drag and drop

1   Open *The World's Fastest Cars-4* from your sample files folder (if it isn't already open).

2   Move cells A21:G22 to cells A8:G9 using drag and drop.

1.   Select cells A21:G22.

2.   Hover the mouse cursor over the green border surrounding the range until you see the hand cursor shape.

20	Lamborghini	Aventador Sup	217	2.8	690	493,095	Italy
21	Ferrari	488 GTB	205	2.9	661	242,737	Italy
22	Lamborghini	Huracán	202	2.5	602	237,250	Italy
23							

It is very important that you see the hand and not the white cross or AutoFill cursor shape.

If you do not see a hand icon, somebody may have switched the drag and drop facility off. See sidebar for how to bring it back.

3.   Click and drag the selected cells, dropping them to their previous location (beginning at cell A8).

You'll see a green outline showing where the cells will be dropped. Move them to the location shown in the screenshot below.

7	Aston Martin	V12 Vantage S	205	3.7	565	123,695	UK
8							
9							
10	Porsche	911 Turbo S Sp	197	3.1	560	241,105	Germany
11	Aston Martin	Vanquish Vola		3.8	568	299,000	UK

4.   Release the mouse button.

The contents of the cells are moved back to A8:G9.

7	Aston Martin	V12 Vantage S	205	3.7	565	123,695	UK
8	Ferrari	488 GTB	205	2.9	661	242,737	Italy
9	Lamborghini	Huracán	202	2.5	602	237,250	Italy
10	Porsche	911 Turbo S Sp	197	3.1	560	241,105	Germany

3   Copy cells A8:G9 to cells A22:G23 using right-click drag and drop.

1.   Select cells A8:G9.

2.   Hover the mouse cursor over the green border surrounding the range until you see the hand cursor shape.

3.   Right-click and drag the rectangle to rows 21 and 22.

4.   Release the mouse button.

Several options are presented (see sidebar).

5.   Click *Copy Here* from the shortcut menu.

This time the contents of the cells are copied rather than moved.

Move Here
Copy Here
Copy Here as Values Only
Copy Here as Formats Only
Link Here
Create Hyperlink Here

Shift Down and Copy
Shift Right and Copy
Shift Down and Move
Shift Right and Move

Cancel

The World's Fastest Cars-4

17	The World's Fastest Italian Cars						
18							
19	Ferrari	F12 Berlinetta	227	3.1	730	330,000	Italy
20	Lamborghini	Aventador Sup	217	2.8	690	493,095	Italy
21	Ferrari	488 GTB	205	2.9	661	242,737	Italy
22	Lamborghini	Huracán	202	2.5	602	237,250	Italy

note

Another way to copy cells via drag and drop

Hover over the border of the selected cells with the **<Alt>** key held down. You will see the mouse cursor shape change to a hand with a plus sign.

You can now drag and drop (holding the left mouse button down) to copy the cells to a new location.

4 Copy the contents of row 15 to row 23 using right-click drag and drop.

17	The World's Fastest Italian Cars						
18							
19	Ferrari	F12 Berlinetta	227	3.1	730	330,000	Italy
20	Lamborghini	Aventador Sup	217	2.8	690	493,095	Italy
21	Ferrari	488 GTB	205	2.9	661	242,737	Italy
22	Lamborghini	Huracán	202	2.5	602	237,250	Italy
23	Ferrari	LaFerrari	217	2.6	950	1,960,000	Italy

5 Rename Sheet1 to: **World Cars**

You learned how to rename worksheet tabs in: *Lesson 1-11: View, move, add, rename, delete and navigate worksheet tabs.*

6 Add a new worksheet and name it: **Italian Cars**

You learned how to add new worksheets in: *Lesson 1-11: View, move, add, rename, delete and navigate worksheet tabs.*

◄ ► World Cars | Italian Cars | +

7 Move cells A17:G23 from the *World Cars* worksheet to cells A1:G7 on the *Italian Cars* worksheet.

1. Select cells A17:G23 on the *World Cars* worksheet.

2. Cut the cells and paste them into cell A1 of the *Italian Cars* worksheet.

8 Insert one blank row above row 3 on the *Italian Cars* worksheet.

You learned how to do this in: *Lesson 3-1: Insert and delete rows and columns.*

9 Copy the titles from row 3 of the *World Cars* worksheet to row 3 of the *Italian Cars* worksheet.

	A	B	C	D	E	F	G
1	The World's Fastest Italian Cars						
2							
3	Make	Model	Top Speed (MPH)	0-60	BHP	Price (USD)	Country
4	Ferrari	F12 Berlinetta	227	3.1	730	330,000	Italy
5	Lamborghini	Aventador Super Veloce	217	2.8	690	493,095	Italy
6	Ferrari	488 GTB	205	2.9	661	242,737	Italy
7	Lamborghini	Huracán	202	2.5	602	237,250	Italy
8	Ferrari	LaFerrari	217	2.6	950	1,960,000	Italy

10 Resize all columns on the *Italian Cars* worksheet so that they are wide enough to display their contents.

You learned how to do this in: *Lesson 2-9: Re-size rows and columns.*

11 Save your work as *The World's Fastest Cars-5.*

Lesson 3-5: Use Paste Values and increase/decrease decimal places displayed

1 Open *The World's Fastest Cars-5* from your sample files folder (if it isn't already open).

2 Select the *World Cars* worksheet and add a new column to the left of column D.

Right click on the column D header and click *Insert* from the shortcut menu.

3 Rename cell C3 from *Top Speed (MPH)* to *MPH*.

4 Type **KM/H** into cell D3.

5 Re-size column C so that it is just wide enough for the contents.

This skill was covered in: *Lesson 2-9: Re-size rows and columns.*

6 Given that one mile=1.609344 Km, enter a formula into cell D4 to convert MPH into KM/H.

This skill was covered in: *Lesson 2-12: Create your own formulas.*

The correct formula is: **=C4*1.609344**

The Bugatti's top speed is now displayed in Kilometers per hour.

	A	B	C	D	E	F
3	Make	Model	MPH	KM/H	0-60	BHP
4	Bugatti	Veyron Super Sport	268	431.304192	2.4	1,184

7 AutoFill the formula in cell D4 down to the bottom of the list (cell D15).

This skill was covered in: *Lesson 2-15: Use AutoFill to adjust formulas.*

	A	B	C	D	E	F
3	Make	Model	MPH	KM/H	0-60	BHP
4	Bugatti	Veyron Super Sport	268	431.304192	2.4	1,184
5	Ferrari	F12 Berlinetta	227	365.321088	3.1	730

The worksheet is giving the right answers, but you're not really interested in seeing speeds to six decimal places. It would be nice to simply show whole numbers (also called integers) in the same way that values are shown for MPH.

8 Use the *Decrease Decimal* button to format the values in column D to display as whole numbers.

1. Select cells D4:D15.

2. Click the Home→Number→Decrease Decimal button [.00 →.0] six times.

The World's Fastest Cars-5

note

Other ways to paste values

Using the Smart Tag

If you perform a regular *paste* and then suddenly realize that you really wanted to *paste values*, you don't need to start again.

Notice that a Smart Tag is displayed at the bottom right corner of the pasted cells.

You can click the Smart Tag to change the paste to *Values Only*.

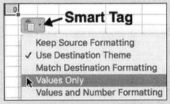

Using the Menu Bar

1. Click:
⌘→Edit→Paste Special.

2. Click *Values*.

3. Click *OK*.

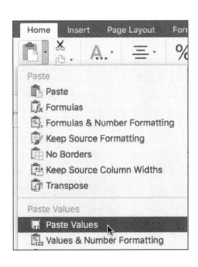

9   Make column D narrower to make things neater.

This skill was covered in: *Lesson 2-9: Re-size rows and columns.*

10   Copy cells D4:D15 to cells D17:D28 using copy and paste.

1.   Select cells D4:D15.

2.   Right-click anywhere in the selected range and then click *Copy* from the shortcut menu.

3.   Right-click cell D17 and click *Paste* from the shortcut menu.

Unexpectedly, all of the values are pasted as zeros.

	A	B	C	D	E
16					
17				0	
18				0	

11   Inspect the formula in cell D17.

Click cell D17 and look at the formula displayed in the Formula Bar at the top of the screen:

f_x | =C17*1.609344

It is now clear why the value was correctly calculated as zero.

When you paste a formula, Excel will, by default, adjust the formula in exactly the same way it does when you AutoFill.

12   Undo the previous paste.

Click the undo button [↶] on the Quick Access Toolbar.

You are going to learn a lot more about the undo button later in: *Lesson 3-7: Use Undo and Redo.*

13   Copy and paste again, this time using Paste Values.

Copy cells D4:D15, then click in cell D17 and click:
Home→Clipboard→Paste drop down→Paste Values.

This time the values within the cells (rather than the formulas used to calculate the values) are pasted.

	A	B	C	D	E	F
15	Ferrari	LaFerrari	217	349	2.6	950
16						
17				431		
18				365		

14   Delete the values in cells D17:D28.

Select cells D17:D28 and press the <**Delete**> key.

15   Save your work as *The World's Fastest Cars-6.*

Lesson 3-6: Transpose a range

Paste Values is the most used special pasting option, but there's another that is often very useful.

If a worksheet has many columns but few rows it may become impossible to print. In this case you may wish to reverse the arrangement so that the worksheet has many rows but few columns.

Transposing allows you to do this automatically.

1   Open *The World's Fastest Cars-6* from your sample files folder (if it isn't already open).

2   Add a new worksheet and name it: *Transposed.*

   This skill was covered in: *Lesson 1-11: View, move, add, rename, delete and navigate worksheet tabs.*

3   Select and copy the range A3:H15 on the *World Cars* worksheet.

	A	B	C	D	E	F	G	H
2								
3	Make	Model	MPH	KM/H	0-60	BHP	Price (USD)	Country
4	Bugatti	Veyron Super Sport	268	431	2.4	1,184	1,700,000	Germany
5	Ferrari	F12 Berlinetta	227	365	3.1	730	330,000	Italy
6	Lamborghini	Aventador Super Veloce	217	349	2.8	690	493,095	Italy
7	Aston Martin	V12 Vantage S	205	330	3.7	565	123,695	UK
8	Ferrari	488 GTB	205	330	2.9	661	242,737	Italy
9	Lamborghini	Huracán	202	325	2.5	602	237,250	Italy
10	Porsche	911 Turbo S Sport+	197	317	3.1	560	241,105	Germany
11	Aston Martin	Vanquish Volante	197	317	3.8	568	299,000	UK
12	Mercedes	SLS AMG Black Series	196	315	3.5	622	275,000	Germany
13	Lotus	Evora 400	186	299	4.1	400	89,900	UK
14	Tesla	Model S P90D	155	249	2.6	762	130,700	USA
15	Ferrari	LaFerrari	217	349	2.6	950	1,960,000	Italy
16								

4   Select cell A3 on the *Transposed* worksheet.

5   Click: Home→Clipboard→ Paste (drop down list)→Transpose.

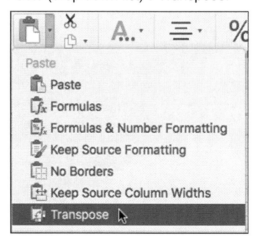

The cells are pasted in a rather interesting way. The columns have now become rows and the rows have become columns.

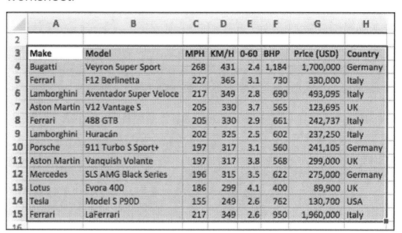

The World's Fastest Cars-6

	A	B	C	D	E	F	G	H	I	J	K	L	M
1													
2													
3	Make	Bugatti	Ferrari	Lamborghini	Aston Martin	Ferrari	Lamborghini	Porsche	Aston Martin	Mercedes	Lotus	Tesla	Ferrari
4	Model	Veyron Super	F12 Berlinetta	Aventador Su	V12 Vantage S	488 GTB	Huracán	911 Turbo S S	Vanquish Vol:	SLS AMG Blac	Evora 400		Model S P90D	LaFerrari
5	MPH	268	227	217	205	205	202	197	197	196	186	155	217
6	KM/H	431	365	349	330	330	325	317	317	315	299	249	349
7	0-60	2.4	3.1	2.8	3.7	2.9	2.5	3.1	3.8	3.5	4.1	2.6	2.6
8	BHP	1,184	730	690	565	661	602	560	568	622	400	762	950
9	Price (USD)	1,700,000	330,000	493,095	123,695	242,737	237,250	241,105	299,000	275,000	89,900	130,700	1,960,000
10	Country	Germany	Italy	Italy	UK	Italy	Italy	Germany	UK	Germany	UK	USA	Italy

Notice also that the width of the columns has not been maintained.

Many of the cells in row 4 are too small to display the model names.

6   Automatically size all columns in one operation.

1. Select every cell in the workbook by clicking the *Select All* button in the top left corner of the worksheet:

2. Hover the mouse cursor over the intersection of any two columns until you see the *re-size* cursor shape  and then double-click.

Every column is now perfectly sized.

	A	B	C	D
1				
2				
3	Make	Bugatti	Ferrari	Lamborghini
4	Model	Veyron Super Sport	F12 Berlinetta	Aventador Super Veloce
5	MPH		268	227	217
6	KM/H		431	365	349

7   Save your work as *The World's Fastest Cars-7.*

Lesson 3-7: Use Undo and Redo

Excel's (fantastically useful) *Undo* feature enables you to reverse an action when you have made a mistake.

It is only possible to undo the previous 100 actions.

Sometimes you may undo an action and then change your mind. Redo will step through the operations in reverse, in effect "undoing the undo"!

1 Close any workbooks that are open and then re-open Excel.

> Excel keeps tabs on the last 100 actions taken. By closing and re-opening Excel you'll clear the existing list of actions available for undo.

2 Open *The World's Fastest Cars-7* from your sample files folder and select the *World Cars* worksheet.

3 Type **UK Cars** into cell A17 and bold face the text.

4 Copy row 3 into row 19.

5 Copy row 7 into row 20.

6 Copy row 11 into row 21.

7 Copy row 13 into row 22.

> The worksheet should now look like this:

	A	B	C	D	E	F	G	H
1	The World's Fastest Cars							
2								
3	**Make**	**Model**	**MPH**	**KM/H**	**0-60**	**BHP**	**Price (USD)**	**Country**
4	Bugatti	Veyron Super Sport	268	431	2.4	1,184	1,700,000	Germany
5	Ferrari	F12 Berlinetta	227	365	3.1	730	330,000	Italy
6	Lamborghini	Aventador Super Veloce	217	349	2.8	690	493,095	Italy
7	Aston Martin	V12 Vantage S	205	330	3.7	565	123,695	UK
8	Ferrari	488 GTB	205	330	2.9	661	242,737	Italy
9	Lamborghini	Huracán	202	325	2.5	602	237,250	Italy
10	Porsche	911 Turbo S Sport+	197	317	3.1	560	241,105	Germany
11	Aston Martin	Vanquish Volante	197	317	3.8	568	299,000	UK
12	Mercedes	SLS AMG Black Series	196	315	3.5	622	275,000	Germany
13	Lotus	Evora 400	186	299	4.1	400	89,900	UK
14	Tesla	Model S P90D	155	249	2.6	762	130,700	USA
15	Ferrari	LaFerrari	217	349	2.6	950	1,960,000	Italy
16								
17	**UK Cars**							
18								
19	**Make**	**Model**	**MPH**	**KM/H**	**0-60**	**BHP**	**Price (USD)**	**Country**
20	Aston Martin	V12 Vantage S	205	330	3.7	565	123,695	UK
21	Aston Martin	Vanquish Volante	197	317	3.8	568	299,000	UK
22	Lotus	Evora 400	186	299	4.1	400	89,900	UK

8 Click the Undo button on the Quick Access Toolbar.

> The Lotus details disappear from row 22.

9 Click the Redo button on the Quick Access Toolbar.

> The Lotus details re-appear in row 22.

---

note

Using the keyboard to undo and redo

It is well worth remembering the undo keyboard shortcut:

<Cmd>+<Z>

I use it all of the time. It is also the undo shortcut for the other Office applications.

You'll use the Redo action far less, but for completeness it is:

<Cmd>+<Y>

The World's Fastest Cars-7

---

10   Click the drop-down arrow to the right of the Undo button on the Quick Access Toolbar.

A drop-down menu appears showing all of the actions that have taken place (or the previous 100 actions if more than 100 actions have taken place) since the workbook was opened.

11   Click the Bold action to undo 5 actions.

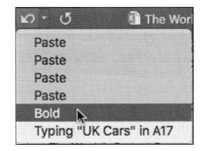

Only the text *UK Cars* remains on the worksheet and it is no longer bold faced.

14	Tesla	Model S P90D	155	249
15	Ferrari	LaFerrari	217	349
16				
17	UK Cars			
18				

12   Click the Redo button on the Quick Access Toolbar.

The Redo button redoes the *Bold* action and *UK Cars* is bold-faced again.

13   Click the Redo button 4 times to redo all of your actions.

The worksheet reverts to its former state.

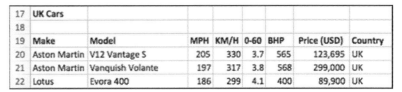

17	UK Cars							
18								
19	Make	Model	MPH	KM/H	0-60	BHP	Price (USD)	Country
20	Aston Martin	V12 Vantage S	205	330	3.7	565	123,695	UK
21	Aston Martin	Vanquish Volante	197	317	3.8	568	299,000	UK
22	Lotus	Evora 400	186	299	4.1	400	89,900	UK

14   Delete rows 17 to 22.

15   Save your work as *The World's Fastest Cars-8*.

Lesson 3-8: Insert cell comments

1   Open *The World's Fastest Cars-8* from your sample files folder (if it isn't already open) and select the *World Cars* worksheet.

2   Using Microsoft Word (not Excel), open *Car Descriptions* from your sample files folder.

1.   Open Microsoft Word.

2.   Click *Open* and open *Car Descriptions* from your sample files folder.

3   Return to Excel without closing Word.

You will notice two buttons on the Dock at the bottom of the screen (see sidebar).

Click the button with the Excel logo to return to Excel.

4   Set up the name that will appear in the comment box.

Whenever you enter a comment, your name is added to the top.

This allows other users to identify the source of each comment if you later distribute the workbook.

1.   Click: ⌘→Excel→Preferences.

2.   Click *General*.

3.   In the *Personalize* category, type your name into the *User name* box.

Personalize	
User name:	Mike Smart

4.   Close the *General* dialog.

5   Quit and restart Excel.

The new *User name* setting won't take effect until you close and reopen Excel.

Note that you must completely quit Excel – simply closing all open Excel windows will not have the desired effect.

Quitting Excel was covered in: *Lesson 1-5: Minimize, re-size, move and close the Excel window (sidebar).*

6   Re-open *The World's Fastest Cars-8*.

7   Copy the text for the Mercedes SLS from the Word document.

1.   Return to Word.

2.   Click and drag across the Mercedes SLS text with the mouse cursor.

3.   Right-click within the selected text and click *Copy* from the shortcut menu.

note

Excel uses your log in user name by default

If you don't set up your user name as described, Excel will use your macOS log-in user name instead (your Apple ID).

This is the reason you'll often see cryptic user names (like JSmith93) in other people's worksheets.

Car Descriptions

The World's Fastest Cars-8

note

Other ways to insert a comment

Click: Review→Comments→ New Comment.

OR

Press: **<Shift>+<Fn>+<F2>**

OR

Click:
🍎→Insert→New Comment

note

If the comments stay visible

If the comments stay visible when you click away from them, it's because you have the *Show All Comments* setting enabled.

To disable *Show All Comments*, click:

Review→Comments→ Show All Comments

You'll learn more about *Show All Comments* in *Lesson 3-9: View cell comments*.

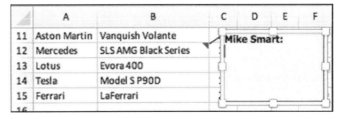

8 Add the comment text to the Mercedes SLS model cell (cell B12).

1. Return to Excel.

2. Right-click cell B12 and click *Insert Comment* from the shortcut menu.

A comment box with your name at the top is shown next to cell B12.

	A	B	C	D	E	F
11	Aston Martin	Vanquish Volante				
12	Mercedes	SLS AMG Black Series	Mike Smart:			
13	Lotus	Evora 400				
14	Tesla	Model S P90D				
15	Ferrari	LaFerrari				

3. Paste into the comment box.

The text that you copied from the Word document appears in the box.

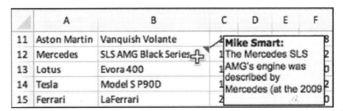

9 Enlarge the comment box, using the sizing handles, so that all text is visible.

The sizing handles are the small blue dots that appear on the corners and edges of the comment box. When you hover over a sizing handle, the cursor shape changes to a double headed arrow.

1. Hover carefully over the bottom-right sizing handle until you see the double-headed arrow cursor shape.

2. Click and drag the sizing handles to re-size the comment box.

10 Click anywhere in the worksheet.

The comment disappears, but a small red triangle has appeared in the top right corner of the cell (see sidebar if the comment doesn't disappear).

11 Add two more comments for the Tesla and Ferrari 488 GTB.

12 Save your work as *The World's Fastest Cars-9*.

Lesson 3-9: View cell comments

1   Open *The World's Fastest Cars-9* from your sample files folder (if it isn't already open) and select the *World Cars* worksheet.

Cells with comments show a small red triangle in their top right-hand corner.

2   View the comment behind a single cell.

Hover the mouse cursor over any of the cells with a red triangle. The cell comment is displayed.

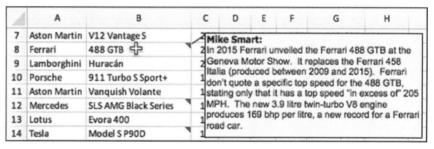

3   View all of the comments in a worksheet at the same time.

Click: Review→Comments→Show All Comments.

Every comment on the worksheet is displayed.

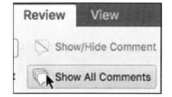

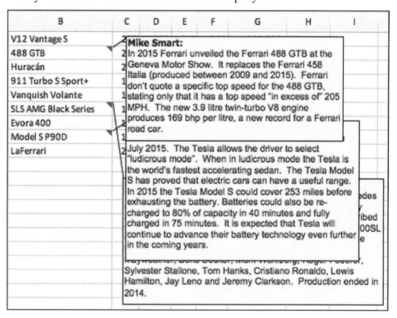

Unfortunately, the comments overlap so you are unable to read them all at the same time. It is possible to view each comment by clicking it, as this brings the window to the front, but it isn't very elegant.

4   Move and re-size the comments so that they do not overlap.

Click a comment and then hover anywhere on the border *but not on a sizing handle* until you see the four-headed arrow icon. When you see the four-headed arrow, click and drag to move the comment.

The World's Fastest Cars-9

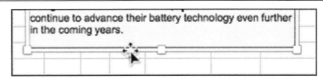

	A	B	C	D E F G H I J K
1	The World's Fastest Cars			
2				**Mike Smart:**
3	Make	Model	MPH	In 2015 Ferrari unveiled the Ferrari 488 GTB at the Geneva Motor Show. It
4	Bugatti	Veyron Super Sport	268	replaces the Ferrari 458 Italia (produced between 2009 and 2015). Ferrari don't quote a specific top speed for the 488 GTB, stating only that it has a top speed
5	Ferrari	F12 Berlinetta	227	"in excess of" 205 MPH. The new 3.9 litre twin-turbo V8 engine produces 169
6	Lamborghini	Aventador Super Veloce	217	bhp per litre, a new record for a Ferrari road car.
7	Aston Martin	V12 Vantage S	205	**Mike Smart:**
8	Ferrari	488 GTB	205	The Mercedes SLS AMG's engine was described by Mercedes (at the 2009
9	Lamborghini	Huracán	202	launch) as "the world's most powerful naturally aspirated production series engine". Mercedes have described this car as "the spiritual successor to the
10	Porsche	911 Turbo S Sport+	197	Mercedes-Benz 300SL Gullwing". Celebrities who have purchased the SLS
11	Aston Martin	Vanquish Volante	197	include Eddie Murphy, Arnold Schwarzenegger, Al Pacino, Floyd Mayweather,
12	Mercedes	SLS AMG Black Series	196	Boris Becker, Mark Wahlberg, Roger Federer, Sylvester Stallone, Tom Hanks, Cristiano Ronaldo, Lewis Hamilton, Jay Leno and Jeremy Clarkson. Production
13	Lotus	Evora 400	186	ended in 2014.
14	Tesla	Model S P90D	155	**Mike Smart:**
15	Ferrari	LaFerrari	217	The all electric Tesla Model S P90D was introduced in July 2015. The Tesla
16				allows the driver to select "ludicrous mode". When in ludicrous mode the Tesla is the world's fastest accelerating sedan. The Tesla Model S has proved that
17				electric cars can have a useful range. In 2015 the Tesla Model S could cover 253
18				miles before exhausting the battery. Batteries could also be re-charged to 80% of
19				capacity in 40 minutes and fully charged in 75 minutes. It is expected that Tesla
20				will continue to advance their battery technology even further in the coming years.

5 Hide all of the comments.

Click: Review→Comments→Show All Comments.

The comments disappear.

6 Make the Ferrari 488 GTB comment display all of the time.

Sometimes you will want to send somebody a worksheet and make sure that an important comment is on view when they open it.

Right click cell B8 and click *Show Comment* from the shortcut menu.

The comment remains on display all of the time (even if you are not hovering over the comment cell).

7 Hide the Ferrari 488 GTB comment.

Right click cell B8 and click *Hide Comment* from the shortcut menu.

8 Save your work as *The World's Fastest Cars-10*.

note

Other ways to show/hide comments

The right-click method is definitely the fastest, but you can also show and hide comments using the Ribbon.

To show or hide a comment:

1. Click the cell containing the comment to make it the active cell.

2. Click:

   Review→Comments→ Show/Hide Comment

Lesson 3-10: Print cell comments

One of the most common comment-related questions asked in my Excel classroom courses is: "how can I print the comments on my worksheet?" Excel can do this, but the feature is hidden away in the *Page Setup* dialog and missed by most users.

1 Open *The World's Fastest Cars-10* from your sample files folder (if it isn't already open) and select the *World Cars* worksheet.

2 Make the Tesla comment display all of the time.

Right click cell B14 and click: *Show Comment* from the shortcut menu.

3 Move the Tesla comment so that it doesn't obscure the data in the worksheet.

This was covered in: *Lesson 3-9: View cell comments.*

	A	B	C	D	E	F	G	H
1	The World's Fastest Cars							
2								
3	Make	Model	MPH	KM/H	0-60	BHP	Price (USD)	Country
4	Bugatti	Veyron Super Sport	268	431	2.4	1,184	1,700,000	Germany
5	Ferrari	F12 Berlinetta	227	365	3.1	730	330,000	Italy
6	Lamborghini	Aventador Super Veloce	217	349	2.8	690	493,095	Italy
7	Aston Martin	V12 Vantage S	205	330	3.7	565	123,695	UK
8	Ferrari	488 GTB	205	330	2.9	661	242,737	Italy
9	Lamborghini	Huracán	202	325	2.5	602	237,250	Italy
10	Porsche	911 Turbo S Sport+	197	317	3.1	560	241,105	Germany
11	Aston Martin	Vanquish Volante	197	317	3.8	568	299,000	UK
12	Mercedes	SLS AMG Black Series	196	315	3.5	622	275,000	Germany
13	Lotus	Evora 400	186	299	4.1	400	89,900	UK
14	Tesla	Model S P90D	155	249	2.6	762	130,700	USA
15	Ferrari	LaFerrari	217	349	2.6	950	1,690,000	Italy

Mike Smart:
The all electric Tesla Model S P90D was introduced in July 2015. The Tesla allows the driver to select "ludicrous mode". When in ludicrous mode the Tesla is the world's fastest accelerating sedan. The Tesla Model S has proved that electric cars can have a useful range. In 2015 the Tesla Model S could cover 253 miles before exhausting the battery. Batteries could also be re-charged to 80% of capacity in 40 minutes and fully charged in 75 minutes. It is expected that Tesla will continue to advance their battery technology even further in the coming years.

4 Tell Excel to print comments exactly as they are displayed on the worksheet.

1. Click: Page Layout→Page Setup→Page Setup.

The *Page Setup* dialog is displayed.

2. Click the *Sheet* tab.

3. Click the *Comments* drop-down and select: *As displayed on sheet.*

The World's Fastest Cars-10

note

The At end of sheet option

You might have noticed the *At end of sheet* option in *Comments* drop-down menu within the *Page Setup* dialog.

This setting is intended to print all of the worksheet's comments at the end of the page, instead of printing them as they are displayed.

Unfortunately, this feature was not functional in the Mac version of Excel at the time this book was written.

It's possible that Excel for Mac will have been updated to fix this problem by the time you read this book.

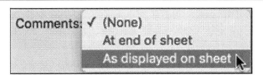

4.   Click the *OK* button.

5   Open the *Print* dialog to view the comments as they would print.

Click: ●→File→Print.

The *Print* dialog opens and displays a print preview of the worksheet in the left-hand pane.

The comments are displayed exactly as they would print.

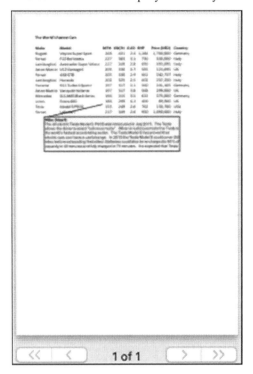

6   Click the *Cancel* button to close the *Print* dialog.

7   Hide the comment.

Right click cell B14 and click: *Hide Comment* from the shortcut menu.

8   Save your work as: *The World's Fastest Cars-11*.

Lesson 3-11: Understand absolute and relative cell references

You've seen how useful Excel's AutoFill is when copying formulas. Most of the time things work perfectly, as you normally want to increment row and column references when you AutoFill down and across.

Sometimes AutoFill can be a little too helpful when it adjusts cell references that you would like to be left alone. This lesson will illustrate the type of worksheet that requires *absolute cell references* as you convert USD (US Dollar) prices to GBP (Great Britain Pounds).

1   Open *The World's Fastest Cars-11* from your sample files folder (if it isn't already open) and select the *World Cars* worksheet.

2   Insert a column to the left of column H.

    This skill was covered in: *Lesson 3-1: Insert and delete rows and columns.*

3   Type **Price (GBP)** into cell H3.

4   Type **USD/GBP** into cell G1.

5   Type **0.66519** into cell H1.

    This was the USD/GBP exchange rate in December 2015 but it will have changed by the time you read this book.

    If you want more realism you can get the current exchange rate from http://oanda.com. If you are not in England or America it might be fun to change the exchange rate to match your own currency.

6   If necessary, adjust the number of decimal places in cell H1 to show all five decimal places.

    You learned how to do this in: *Lesson 3-5: Use Paste Values and increase/decrease decimal places displayed.*

7   Make the text in cells G1 and H1 bold.

8   Place a formula in cell H4 that will calculate the price of a Bugatti Veyron in GBP (Great Britain Pounds).

    Formulas were covered in: *Lesson 2-12: Create your own formulas.*

    The correct formula is: **=G4*H1**

    You can now see that the Bugatti costs £1,130,823 in Great Britain Pounds.

	G	H	I
1	USD/GBP	0.66519	
2			
3	Price (USD)	Price (GBP)	Country
4	1,700,000	1,130,823	Germany
5	330,000		Italy

The World's Fastest Cars-11

tip

A faster way to add those dollar signs

1. Click on the formula bar so that the cursor is touching the cell reference that you want to convert to absolute:

2. Press the **<Fn>+<F4>** keys on the keyboard. Be careful that you see two dollar signs after pressing the key.

   If you see only one dollar sign it is because you have pressed the keys twice and inadvertently created a mixed cell reference.

   You'll learn about mixed cell references later, in: *Lesson 3-12: Understand mixed cell references.*

   If this happens, just keep on pressing the **<Fn>+<F4>** keys until you see the two dollar signs again.

f_x =G4*$H$1

	G	H	I
3	Price (USD)	Price (GBP)	Country
4	1,700,000	1,130,823	Germany
5	330,000	219,513	Italy
6	493,095	328,002	Italy

9 Consider what will happen if you AutoFill this formula.

AutoFill was covered in: *Lesson 2-15: Use AutoFill to adjust formulas.*

As the formula is AutoFilled downward, the number part of each formula will be incremented like this:

	H
1	0.66519
2	
3	Price (GBP)
4	=G4*H1
5	=G5*H2
6	=G6*H3

Consider cell H5 (the price of the Ferrari F12 Berlinetta). The formula in this cell is **=G5*H2**.

AutoFill has done a wonderful job with G5. It has changed the reference from the Bugatti's price to the Ferrari F12, and that's exactly what you wanted.

But AutoFill has seriously messed up with the H2 reference. The exchange rate is always in cell H1. It never moves.

To express this in Excel terminology: G4 is a **relative reference** (i.e. you want AutoFill to adjust it) while H1 is an **absolute reference** (i.e. you want AutoFill to leave it alone).

10 Change the formula in cell H4 to make H1 into an absolute reference.

To make a reference absolute, you simply add a dollar sign in front of both the letter and number.

So: H1 becomes $H$1.

Click in cell H4 and then edit the formula (shown in the formula bar) so that it now reads:

=G4*$H$1

11 AutoFill the formula in cell H4 to the end of the list.

(AutoFill was covered in: *Lesson 2-15: Use AutoFill to adjust formulas*).

The price of each car is now displayed in both US Dollars and Great Britain Pounds.

Click on each of the GBP prices and observe the formula shown in the formula bar at the top of the screen.

In each cell Excel has adjusted the G4 part of the formula but left the H1 part of the formula alone.

12 Save your work as *The World's Fastest Cars-12.*

note

Don't worry if you're unable to understand this concept at first

In my "Essential Skills" classroom courses I've found that many students find mixed cell references a very difficult concept to understand.

I never waste a lot of time on this lesson if it is clear that some students are unable to easily follow the logic.

I'd advise that you take the same approach and don't waste a lot of time on this lesson if you find it difficult to follow.

You won't need to use mixed cell references anywhere else in the *Essential Skills* course and it's a skill that most office workers don't have.

If you do skip this lesson it's well worthwhile returning to it later, when you've completed the course and have been using Excel for a few months.

By then you will probably have encountered some of the real-world business problems that are more efficiently solved using mixed cell references.

Lesson 3-12: Understand mixed cell references

Before you tackle mixed cell references I must warn you that this subject is a bit of a brain teaser (see sidebar). The skill is well worth mastering as you'll find it extremely useful in many types of real-world worksheets.

1 Open *International Price List* from your sample files folder.

This worksheet will calculate the price of each car in five different currencies. The exchange rates are shown in row 4.

These were the exchange rates in December 2015 but will have changed by the time you read this book. If you would like more realism you can obtain the current exchange rates from http://oanda.com.

2 Add a formula to cell D6 that will calculate the UK price of a Bugatti Veyron.

Formulas were covered in: *Lesson 2-12: Create your own formulas.*

The correct formula is: **=C6*D4**

You can see that the Veyron costs £1,130,823.

	C	D	E	F	G	H
3		GBP	EUR	JPY	CAD	CHF
4		0.66519	0.94522	122.93	1.33668	1.02979
5	USA $	UK £	Euros €	Japan ¥	Canada $	Switzerland fr.
6	1,700,000	1,130,823				

3 Consider what will happen if you AutoFill this formula.

AutoFill was covered in: *Lesson 2-15: Use AutoFill to adjust formulas.*

As the formula is AutoFilled downward, the number part of each formula is incremented like this:

	C	D
6	1700000	=C6*D4
7	330000	=C7*D5
8	493095	=C8*D6

The reference to cell C6 is being correctly adjusted to point to the price of each car in the list. There is a problem with the reference to cell D4 as it should not be adjusted.

You may be thinking that this problem is exactly the same as the one solved in: *Lesson 3-11: Understand absolute and relative cell references.*

Why not simply make D4 into an absolute reference? Like this:

	C	D
3		GBP
4		0.66519
5	USA $	UK £
6	1700000	=C6*$D$4

tip

A faster way to add dollar signs to create mixed references

1. Click on the formula bar so that the cursor is touching the cell reference you want to convert to mixed:

2. Press the **<Fn>+<F4>** keys repeatedly on the keyboard.

   Each time you press **<Fn>+<F4>**, Excel cycles through all possible absolute and mixed references:

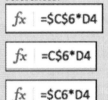

This will work just fine for the GBP prices, but think carefully about what will then happen when you AutoFill to the right.

AutoFill knows that when you fill right you *usually* want the letter part of each formula incremented like this:

	C	D	E
3		GBP	EUR
4		0.66519	0.94522
5	USA $	UK £	Euros €
6	1700000	=C6*$D$4	=D6*$D$4
7	330000	=C7*$D$4	
8	493095	=C8*$D$4	

This will not correctly calculate the Euro price. AutoFill has made two errors.

1. It is still using the GBP exchange rate for the EUR prices because you made D4 an absolute reference.

2. It is referencing the UK price of the Bugatti instead of the US dollar price because C6 is a relative reference.

It's best to tackle each problem one at a time

1. You want the GBP exchange rate to adjust to the EUR exchange rate as the formula is filled to the right. In this case the D part of D4 should be relative but the 4 part should be absolute. This can be denoted by D$4 instead of $D$4.

2. You want the US Dollar price to always be used against the US Dollar exchange rates in row 4. Therefore, you want the C part of C6 to be absolute. As AutoFill fills downward you need the price to be adjusted to the relevant car, so the 6 part of C6 needs to be relative. This can be denoted by $C6 instead of $C$6.

4   Correct the formula so that it will AutoFill correctly.

Enter the formula =**$C6*D$4** into cell D6.

This will AutoFill correctly like this:

	C	D	E	F
3		GBP	EUR	JPY
4		0.66519	0.94522	122.93
5	USA $	UK £	Euros €	Japan ¥
6	1700000	=$C6*D$4	=$C6*E$4	=$C6*F$4
7	330000	=$C7*D$4	=$C7*E$4	=$C7*F$4
8	493095	=$C8*D$4	=$C8*E$4	=$C8*F$4

5   AutoFill across to cell H6.

The correct Bugatti prices are shown in five currencies.

6   AutoFill down to cell H17.

The correct prices are shown for all cars and all currencies.

7   Make the columns wide enough to display the prices.

8   Save your work as *International Price List-1*.

Lesson 3-13: Understand templates

A template is simply a partially completed, normal workbook that contains the starting point for a task that you often need to do. You can put anything into a template that you can put into a regular workbook.

What are sample templates?

A sample template is a template that was created by Microsoft or another third-party. Sample templates aim to give you a starting point to solve common problems with Excel.

Several sample templates are shown on the *New* dialog (within the dialog that you see when you first start Excel), such as a *Daily Schedule* and *Annual Financial Report*.

There are many thousands more sample templates available online.

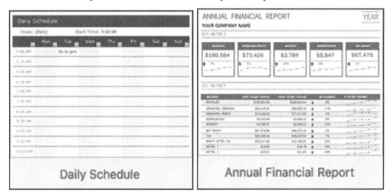

Daily Schedule | Annual Financial Report

It may seem, at first, as if sample templates are a replacement for having to learn Excel, but they are not quite as useful as they first promise to be.

There are three potential problems in using them:

1. Sample templates often appear to provide a solution that is *almost* what you need. You may find that the work involved in converting them to *exactly* what you need takes longer than starting from scratch.

2. Some templates include very advanced Excel features that non-expert users will find difficult to understand.

3. Some templates include VBA (Visual Basic for Applications) custom program code to extend Excel's normal features. It can be impossible to maintain or customize workbooks containing program code unless you have access to a competent VBA programmer (see sidebar).

What is a custom template?

A custom template is a template that you have created yourself. Because you completely understand how custom templates work, you may find them far more useful than sample templates.

You'll often find yourself making copies of older workbooks that are nearly the same as the one you need. You'll then delete the bits you don't need and add the bits that you do.

If you find this happening, it's time to make a custom template. You'll learn how to make your first custom template later, in: *Lesson 3-14: Create a template.*

note

This worksheet looks flashy!

If you are wondering how to make your own worksheets look as flashy as this one, you'll only need a little more patience.

You'll learn every skill you need to make your worksheets look as good, and even a lot better than this one in the next session: *Session Four: Making Your Worksheets Look Professional.*

Lesson 3-14: Create a template

1 Open *First Quarter Sales and Bonus* from your sample files folder.

	A	B	C	D	E
1	First quarter sales and bonus				
2					
3	Sales				
4					
5	First Name	Last Name	Sales	Target	Over Target Sales
6	Andrew	Fuller	7,639.30	5,000	2,639.30
7	Anne	Dodsworth	2,979.30	5,000	- 2,020.70
8	Janet	Leverling	29,658.60	5,000	24,658.60
9	Laura	Callahan	19,271.60	5,000	14,271.60
10	Margaret	Peacock	44,795.20	5,000	39,795.20
11	Michael	Suyama	4,109.80	5,000	- 890.20
12	Nancy	Davolio	15,330.10	5,000	10,330.10
13	Robert	King	21,461.60	5,000	16,461.60
14	Steven	Buchanan	2,634.40	5,000	- 2,365.60
15			Total:	147,879.90	
16					
17	Bonus				
18					
19	First Name	Last Name	Salary	Bonus	Total
20	Andrew	Fuller	2,500	131.97	2,631.97
21	Anne	Dodsworth	2,000	-	2,000.00
22	Janet	Leverling	2,600	1,232.93	3,832.93
23	Laura	Callahan	2,800	713.58	3,513.58
24	Margaret	Peacock	3,000	1,989.76	4,989.76
25	Michael	Suyama	1,800	-	1,800.00
26	Nancy	Davolio	4,500	516.51	5,016.51
27	Robert	King	2,000	823.08	2,823.08
28	Steven	Buchanan	3,000	-	3,000.00
29			Total:	24,200	5,407.82	29,607.82

This is exactly the type of workbook you'd probably want to convert into a template. Only the data in cells C6:D14 will change each quarter.

Every quarter you could simply open last quarter's workbook, save it with a new name and then delete the old values in cells C6:D14. But you'd have to do that every quarter and then, one day, you might forget the *save it with a new name* step and end up overwriting the old file.

A much more efficient solution would be to save a copy of the workbook, with blank values in cells C6:D14, as a template.

2 Delete the contents of cells *C6:D14.*

This is the data that changes every quarter. Deleting it provides an empty template, ready to be populated with each quarter's figures.

3 Replace the text in cell A1 with the words:
Bonus Calculator

This is a more generic title that can be used for any quarter.

4 Save your work as: *Bonus Calculator.*

5 Save the workbook again, this time as a template.

1. Click: ⌘→File→Save as Template.

2. Click the drop-down list arrow labeled *File Format* at the bottom of the dialog.

3. The best choice for this workbook is: *Excel Template.*

   If this template needed to be used by users with very old versions of Excel, you'd choose *Excel 97-2004 Template.*

   If the workbook contained macros you'd need to choose *Excel Macro-Enabled Template.* Working with macros is an Expert level skill covered fully in the *Expert Skills* book in this series.

4. Click the *Save* button to save the template to the default templates folder.

   The existing name: *Bonus Calculator* is fine.

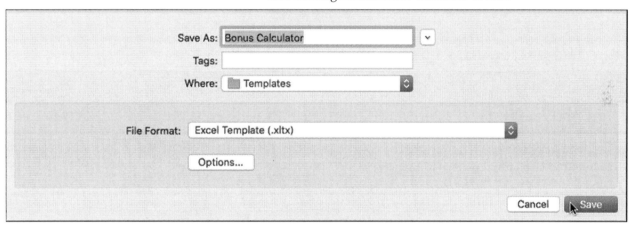

6   Close Excel.

Lesson 3-15: Use a template

1   Open Excel.

2   Display your own custom templates.

1.   Click the *New* tab if it isn't already selected.

2.   Click *Personal* at the top of the screen.

All of the templates that you have created yourself are displayed.

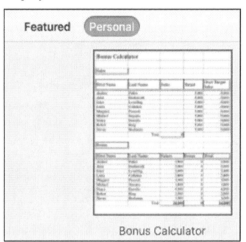

Bonus Calculator

You should see the *Bonus Calculator* template that you saved in: *Lesson 3-14: Create a template*.

3   Double click the *Bonus Calculator* template.

A new workbook is created from the template.

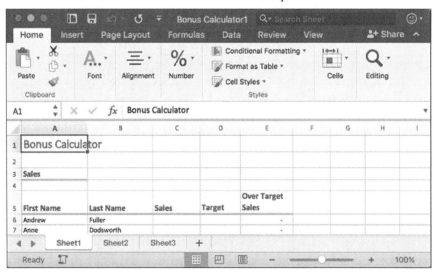

Notice that the workbook has been named *Bonus Calculator1*. You are not looking at the template but a new workbook created from the template.

4   Use a sample template.

A set of Microsoft sample templates are included with every copy of Excel.

1. Click: ⌘→File→New from Template.

    You are returned to the Excel startup screen.

2. Click *Featured* at the top of the screen if it isn't already selected.

    The sample templates included with Excel are displayed.

3. Double click one of Microsoft's sample templates.

    A workbook is created from the template.

    Some of Microsoft's sample templates may seem a little overwhelming at the moment, but they'll seem far less intimidating by the time you reach the end of this book.

5   Create a workbook from Microsoft's library of online templates.

You'll need to be connected to the Internet to use an online template.

Microsoft have a huge library containing thousands of templates that they add to all of the time and make available to you for free.

1. Click: ⌘→File→New from Template.

2. Type: **Calendar** in the *Search All Templates* box at the top right of the screen.

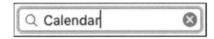

3. Press the <**Enter**> key.

    After a few moments a huge scrolling list of calendars appears on the screen.

4. Double click on any of the calendar templates.

    A workbook (containing a nicely formatted calendar) is created from the template.

note

Don't worry if you can't understand how some of the templates have been constructed

Don't worry if you can't understand how some of the calendar templates work yet.

Many have been constructed using very advanced techniques and some have even had features added using VBA (Visual Basic for Applications) programming code to extend Excel's normal feature set.

For the above reasons you may find that sample templates are not useful for real-world projects when you need to thoroughly understand how they have been constructed.

note

What are Office Add-Ins useful for?

Task Pane and Content Add-Ins are a relatively new feature (introduced in Excel 2013) and it is likely that thousands of new add-ins of this type will become available over the coming years.

Three add-in categories seem to be the most useful:

New Chart types

As you'll discover in: *Session Five: Charts and Graphics,* Excel already has a huge range of chart types. If the built-in chart types do not address a specific business need, it is now possible to pay a programmer to create any chart type that can be described as an *Excel Content Add-in.*

The *Gauge* content add-in shown in the lesson is a good example of this.

Interfacing with real-time data

Many users will need to interface with current real-time data (data that is constantly changing). Examples would include exchange rates or share and commodity prices.

There are many add-ins available to provide current currency exchange rates and stock prices.

Interfacing with databases

One of my favourite free content add-ins is the *Bing Maps content add-in.*

This allows you to reference place names (for example *London* or *New York*) and associated data (for example the population of each city) in a worksheet range.

The location is then found in the Bing maps database and displayed as a map embedded within the worksheet. Hotspots on the map can then be clicked to display the associated data.

Lesson 3-16: Understand Office Add-Ins

For many years Excel has supported add-ins. Add-ins allow programmers to create new components that you can add to a workbook. These components can add functionality that isn't present in the standard Excel product.

The traditional add-in was installed on your local hard drive and added new functionality to your copy of Excel. The *Expert Skills* book in this series comprehensively covers this type of add-in.

Office 2013 introduced two new types of add-in that were originally all called: *Excel Apps.* In the Excel 2019 release the two new add-in types are individually called *Task Pane Add-ins* and *Content Add-ins* and are collectively referred to as *Office Add-ins.*

Office Add-ins can only be accessed from the Microsoft Store (though many are free of charge).

Office Add-Ins do not require any installation as they are usually hosted on a remote web site (though it is also possible for an IT department to host them on a local network). This means that you normally require an Internet connection in order to use an Office Add-In. If you are disconnected from the Internet, the add-in may stop working.

Task Pane Add-Ins

A good example of a task pane add-in is the *Wikipedia* add-in (free at time of writing in September 2018). The Wikipedia add-in provides a task pane that can be used to research any subject via the Wikipedia application on the Internet and then to copy and paste data from any Wikipedia article into a worksheet.

In this example, I have used the Wikipedia add-in to research the average *GDP per hour worked* by country. I've then copied and pasted the table from the task pane onto my worksheet for further analysis:

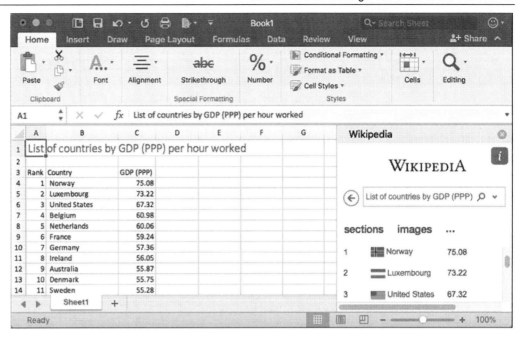

You'll learn how to add a *Task Pane Add-in* to a workbook later, in: *Lesson 3-17: Add an Office Add-In to a workbook.*

Content Add-Ins

Content add-ins float within the Excel grid (in a similar way to charts, which you will learn about later, in: *Session Five: Charts and Graphics*).

Content add-ins are useful for adding components to a worksheet. A good example of a content add-in is the *Gauge* add-in. This allows a value to be graphically represented on a dial gauge:

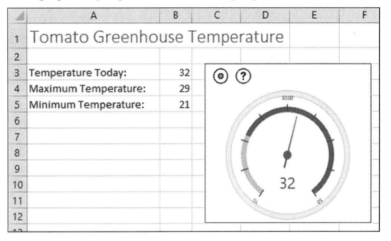

Excel does not support dial gauges by default. The above worksheet was created by adding a *Gauge* content add-in to a worksheet.

Lesson 3-17: Add an Office Add-In to a workbook

You will need to be connected to the Internet and logged in to a *Microsoft Account* in order to follow-through with this lesson (You'll learn more about Microsoft accounts in: *Session Eight: Cloud Computing*).

1 Open a new blank workbook.

2 Add the *Merriam Webster dictionary* add-in to the workbook.

   1. Click: Insert→Add-ins→Store.

     The *Office Add-ins* dialog appears.

     A dialog opens and displays a list of add-ins available at the Office Store.

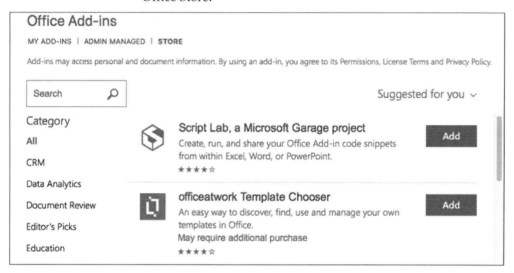

   2. Type: **Dictionary** into the search box and press the **<Enter>** key.

     Several dictionary add-ins are displayed:

     Note that, because this is an online facility, you'll probably see a different list on your screen (see sidebar).

important

The Internet is constantly changing

After you click:

Insert→Add-ins→Store

…you are viewing web pages delivered from Microsoft's web servers.

This allows Microsoft to change their content constantly if they wish to.

It is likely that Microsoft's web store pages will have changed since this book was written.

It is also possible that the *Merriam Webster dictionary* application will have ceased to exist, or will no longer be free, by the time you read this book.

In either case, this lesson should give you enough information to figure out how to navigate Microsoft's site and install a similar add-in.

3. Click the *Add* button next to the *Dictionary-Merriam-Webster* add-in (or another free dictionary add-in if this is no longer available).

   The *Merriam-Webster Dictionary* task pane appears on the right of your screen.

3 Use the Merriam-Webster Dictionary to research the meaning of the word: **Computer**.

1. Type the word: **Computer** into the search box.

2. Press the **<Enter>** key.

   The dictionary displays its definition:

Lesson 3-18: Freeze columns and rows

1   Open *Sales First Quarter 2016* from your sample files folder.

Notice that it is easy to see which data is in each column when you are at the top of the worksheet and can see the top row:

	A	B	C	D
1	Date	First Name	Last Name	Company Name
2	01-Jan-16	Nancy	Davolio	Eastern Connection
3	01-Jan-16	Nancy	Davolio	Eastern Connection
4	01-Jan-16	Nancy	Davolio	Eastern Connection

But things get confusing when you scroll further down the list:

	A	B	C	D
128	17-Feb-16	Margaret	Peacock	Rancho grande
129	17-Feb-16	Margaret	Peacock	Rancho grande
130	18-Feb-16	Janet	Leverling	Blondel père et fils

It is no longer clear what information is contained in each column because the top row has disappeared.

2   Press **<Ctrl>+<Home>** (↖) to quickly move to cell A1.

3   Click: View→Window→Freeze Top Row.

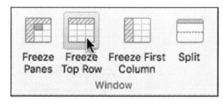

A small black line appears beneath the first row.

4   Scroll down the list.

Notice that as you scroll down, the top row now remains in place.

	A	B	C	D
1	Date	First Name	Last Name	Company Name
47	16-Jan-16	Margaret	Peacock	Simons bistro
48	16-Jan-16	Margaret	Peacock	Simons bistro
49	16-Jan-16	Margaret	Peacock	Simons bistro

5   Unfreeze the top row.

Click: View→Window→Unfreeze Panes.

The first choice has now changed to *Unfreeze Panes*. Click this menu item to put things back to normal.

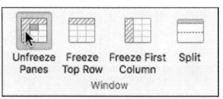

6   Freeze the first column.

note

Another way to freeze the top row would be to convert the range into a table.

Excel automatically freezes column headers in tables.

Working with tables is an Expert level skill covered fully in the *Expert Skills* book in this series.

Sales First Quarter 2016

Do exactly as you did before, but this time select *Freeze First Column* from the *View* tab.

Notice that the date column is now locked into place. As you scroll to the right, the date remains in the first column.

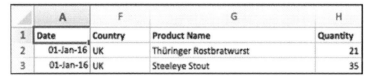

	A	F	G	H
1	Date	Country	Product Name	Quantity
2	01-Jan-16	UK	Thüringer Rostbratwurst	21
3	01-Jan-16	UK	Steeleye Stout	35

7   Unfreeze the panes.

8   Freeze the first two rows and the left most three columns.

While a simple freezing of the top row or first column may sometimes be what you need, you'll often want to freeze both columns *and* rows.

You'll sometimes also want to freeze more than one column and/or row.

1.   Click in cell D3 to make it the active cell.

This is your way of telling Excel that you want to freeze all cells above, and to the left of, cell D3.

2.   Click: View→Window→Freeze Panes.

3.   The first two rows and first three columns are frozen.

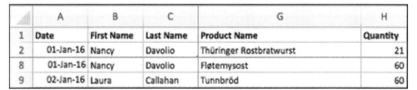

	A	B	C	G	H
1	Date	First Name	Last Name	Product Name	Quantity
2	01-Jan-16	Nancy	Davolio	Thüringer Rostbratwurst	21
8	01-Jan-16	Nancy	Davolio	Fløtemysost	60
9	02-Jan-16	Laura	Callahan	Tunnbröd	60

9   Unfreeze the panes.

Lesson 3-19: Split the window into multiple panes

1 Open *Sales First Quarter 2016* from your sample files folder (if it isn't already open).

2 Press **<Ctrl>+<End> (↘)** to quickly move to the end of the worksheet (cell J242).

This is quite a long list. Imagine that you need to compare sales for 3rd February 2016 to sales for 3rd March 2016.

This could involve a lot of scrolling unless you split the window into two panes.

3 Split the window into two horizontal panes.

1. Click in a cell in column A that is positioned around half way down the screen.

As you'll see later in this lesson, the active cell determines whether the window will be split horizontally, vertically, or both horizontally and vertically.

For a horizontal split, the active cell needs to be a cell within column A.

The position of the active cell also determines where the screen will be split. By positioning it half way down the screen you will split the screen into two equally-sized panes.

2. Click: View→Window→Split.

The screen is split into two independently scrolling horizontal panes.

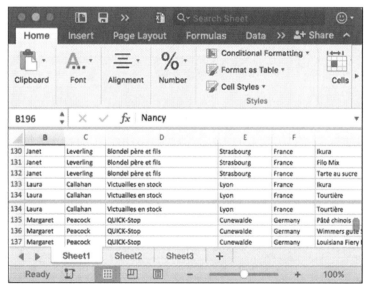

4 Scroll the lower pane so that the first sale on 3rd March 2016 is shown on the first line.

5 Scroll the upper pane so that the first sale on 3rd February 2016 is shown on the first line.

Sales First Quarter 2016

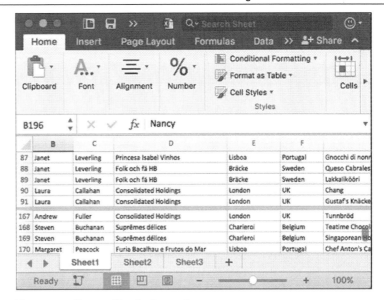

6   Remove the split window view.

Click: View→Window→Split.

OR

Double click the split bar with the mouse.

7   Split the window into two vertical panes.

1.   Click in cell D1.

      If the active cell is in row 1, the screen will be split into two vertical panes.

2.   Click: View→Window→Split.

      The window is split into two vertical panes

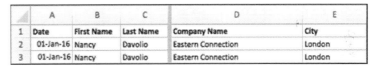

8   Move the split bar so that the left pane shows columns A to E.

Click and drag the split bar to its new location:

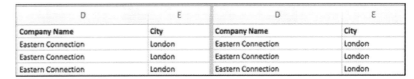

9   Remove the split window view.

10   Split the window into four panes.

If the active cell is not in row 1 or column A, the screen will split into four panes at the cursor position.

1.   Click in a cell towards the center of the screen

2.   Click: View→Window→Split.

      The screen is split into four windows.

11   Remove the split window view.

Lesson 3-20: Check spelling

Excel shares the same powerful spell checker that is included with Word and other Office applications.

Most European companies have a corporate standard for their spelling, often American English or British English. Excel also includes standard support for eighteen different dialects of English as well as other languages.

While most words are included in Excel's dictionary, you will sometimes be warned that a correct spelling is misspelled. When this is the case you can add the word to the dictionary so that Excel doesn't keep bothering you about it in the future.

1 Open *Empire Car Sales Stock List* from your sample files folder.

	F	G
5	Colour	Selling points
6	Black	Can accelarate faster than most sports cars.
7	Topaz Blue	One concientous owner from new.
8	Yellow	Acheives nearly 50 miles to the gallon.
9	Silver	Particulaly clean example of this executive coupe.
10	Blue	Reconised as one of the safest cars on the road.
11	Brown	A collector's car strictly for connisseurs.

You'll have to hope that Empire's cars are better than their spelling!

You may find it fun to try to identify their spelling errors before you set the Spell Checker loose on the job. The *Selling points* column contains many frequently incorrectly spelled words.

2 Check the spelling for the words in the range F5:G7.

If you select a range of cells before invoking the spell checker, only the selected range will be checked.

1. Select the range F5:G7.

2. Click: Review→Proofing→Spelling to start the spell checker.

   If all of the words are spelled correctly, the spell checker does not display. In this case there are errors, so the *Spelling* dialog is displayed.

In the example shown in the sidebar, note that the language was set to English (United States). The British spelling of the word *colour* does not appear in the American English dictionary because, in America, it is spelled: *color*.

If your Mac is configured to use the English (United Kingdom) language, you will not see this error because *colour* is the correct UK English spelling.

See the sidebar on the facing page if you want to change your dictionary to a different language.

3 Click *Change* to accept Excel's suggested correction.

Empire Car Sales Stock List

note

Setting the default language

By default, Excel uses the language settings defined by your computer.

If you want to configure your Mac to use a different language, you can do so by going to the *System Preferences* dialog and then clicking the *Language and Region* button.

You first saw how to access the *System Preferences* dialog in: *Lesson 1-1: Configure your mouse and understand right clicking.*

If you only want certain cells to use a different language, you can do this by selecting the required cells and clicking:

🍎→Tools→Language

note

Dictionaries for other languages

The English version of Excel includes support for English, French and Spanish.

Microsoft also offer language packs for 35 other languages ranging from Chinese to Ukrainian.

4   Click *Change* twice more to accept Excel's suggestions for *accelerate* and *conscientious*.

The spell checker exits and advises you that the spell check is complete.

5   Click the *OK* button to dismiss the dialog.

6   Spell check the single word *Particulaly* in cell G9.

Sometimes you'll type a single word and be unsure that it is correctly spelled. You will want to be able to quickly check the single word.

1. Click cell G9 and then select the word: *Particulaly* in the formula bar at the top of the window.

> *fx* | **Particulaly** clean example of this executive coupe.

2. Click: Review→Proofing→Spelling to start the spell checker.

3. Click the *Change* button to accept the correct spelling.

4. Click the *OK* button to dismiss the dialog.

7   Spell check the entire worksheet.

1. Click in any cell on the worksheet. When you don't select a range, or a single word, the spell checker checks the entire worksheet.

   If you don't click cell A1, cells to the right and beneath the selected cell are checked first and then Excel asks: *Do you want to continue checking at the beginning of the sheet?*

2. Click: Review→Proofing→Spelling to start the spell checker.

8   Click: *Change* to accept each change until you are prompted for CLK.

CLK is the correct model name for the Mercedes CLK, but it isn't in the Excel dictionary. Perhaps Empire sells a lot of CLKs and their employees don't want to be pulled up by the spell checker every time the word is used.

To prevent this from happening, click the *Add* button. This adds CLK to the dictionary so that Excel will recognize the word in the future.

9   Continue to click *Change* to accept each change until you are prompted for Alfasud.

Alfasud is another real word for a car (a model produced by Alfa Romeo between 1976 and 1989) that isn't in the Excel dictionary.

Once again, click the *Add* button to add Alfasud to the dictionary.

10   Click: *Change* to accept Excel's correction for connoisseurs.

When the spell check has ended, a dialog will display advising that the spell check is complete. Click the *OK* button to dismiss the dialog.

11   Save your work as *Empire Car Sales Stock List-1*.

Session 3: Exercise

1 Open *The Best Selling Albums of All Time* from your sample files folder.

2 Insert one row above row 7, type *AC/DC* for the Artist and *Back in Black* for the Album.

3 Use AutoComplete to put the text *Hard Rock* into cell C7 and type *50* for copies sold (millions).

4 Delete rows 11 and 12 to remove the *Eagles* and *Bee Gees* from the list.

5 Insert a formula in cell E6 to calculate how much revenue the album sales would have generated if sold at the *Average Album Price* shown in cell E3.

Don't forget that the reference to cell E3 will have to be an absolute reference.

6 AutoFill the formula to the end of the list to see the estimated revenue for the top five bestselling albums.

7 Use AutoSum to add values for total copies sold and total revenue to cells D11 and E11.

8 Remove the decimal places displayed in cells E6:E11 so that the revenue is rounded to the nearest million.

9 Add a comment to cell B6 saying *"Thriller was Michael Jackson's sixth studio album and was produced with a budget of $750,000."*

10 Save your work as *The Best Selling Albums of All Time-1*.

	A	B	C	D	E
1	Best Selling Albums of All Time				
2					US$
3				Average Album Price	14.99
4					
5	Artist	Album	Genre	Copies Sold (millions)	Revenue (Million USD)
6	Michael Jackson	Thriller	Pop/R&B	65	974
7	AC/DC	Back in Black	Hard Rock	50	750
8	Pink Floyd	Dark Side of the Moon	Rock	45	675
9	Whitney Houston	The Bodyguard	Pop/R&B	44	660
10	Meat Loaf	Bat Out of Hell	Hard Rock	43	645
11		Total:		247	3703
12					
13					
14					

Mike Smart:
Thriller was Michael Jackson's sixth studio album and was produced with a budget of $750,000.

The Best Selling Albums of All Time

If you need help slide the page to the left

Session 3 Exercise answers

These are the questions that students find the most difficult to answer:

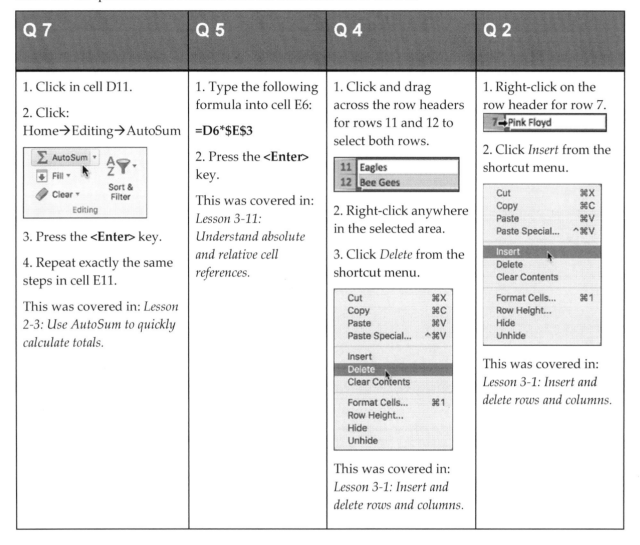

Q 7	Q 5	Q 4	Q 2
1. Click in cell D11. 2. Click: Home→Editing→AutoSum	1. Type the following formula into cell E6: **=D6*$E$3**	1. Click and drag across the row headers for rows 11 and 12 to select both rows.	1. Right-click on the row header for row 7.
3. Press the **<Enter>** key. 4. Repeat exactly the same steps in cell E11. This was covered in: *Lesson 2-3: Use AutoSum to quickly calculate totals.*	2. Press the **<Enter>** key. This was covered in: *Lesson 3-11: Understand absolute and relative cell references.*	2. Right-click anywhere in the selected area. 3. Click *Delete* from the shortcut menu. This was covered in: *Lesson 3-1: Insert and delete rows and columns.*	2. Click *Insert* from the shortcut menu. This was covered in: *Lesson 3-1: Insert and delete rows and columns.*

If you have difficulty with the other questions, here are the lessons that cover the relevant skill:

1   Refer to: Lesson 1-7: Download the sample files and open/navigate a workbook.

3   Refer to: Lesson 3-2: Use AutoComplete and fill data from adjacent cells.

6   Refer to: Lesson 2-15: Use AutoFill to adjust formulas.

8   Refer to: Lesson 3-5: Use Paste Values and increase/decrease decimal places displayed.

9   Refer to: Lesson 3-8: Insert cell comments.

10   Refer to: Lesson 1-8: Save a workbook.

Session Four: Making Your Worksheets Look Professional

> It is only shallow people who do not judge by appearances.
>
> *Oscar Wilde (1854 - 1900)*

Never under-estimate the importance of presentation. In many areas of life, it is valued more than content.

This session will enable you to make your worksheets get noticed.

By the end of this session everybody will be convinced that you are an Excel genius because your worksheets will be visually excellent.

Session Objectives

By the end of this session you will be able to:

- Format dates
- Understand date serial numbers
- Format numbers using built-in number formats
- Create custom number formats
- Horizontally and Vertically align the contents of cells
- Merge cells, wrap text and expand/collapse the formula bar
- Unmerge cells and Center Across Selection
- Understand themes
- Use cell styles and change themes
- Add borders and lines
- Create your own custom theme
- Create your own custom cell styles
- Use a master style book to merge styles
- Use simple conditional formatting
- Manage multiple conditional formats using the Rules Manager
- Bring data alive with visualizations
- Create a formula driven conditional format
- Insert a Sparkline into a range of cells
- Apply a common vertical axis and formatting to a Sparkline group
- Apply a date axis to a Sparkline group and format a single Sparkline
- Use the format painter
- Rotate text

Lesson 4-1: Format dates

You may notice that I've been very careful to use internationally safe date formats throughout this book.

A classic cause of errors when dealing with international worksheets is the use of a date such as the following:

10/03/2016

This means *10th March 2016* in some countries (such as the UK) and *3rd October 2016* in others (such as the USA).

If your work may be viewed by an international audience, it is far better to use a date format that cannot possibly cause confusion.

In this lesson you'll re-format a date into the compact and universally readable format of: *10-Mar-16*.

1   Open *Sales Week Ended 14th March 2016* from your sample files folder.

Notice the hashes in the date column. This tells you that the column isn't wide enough to display the date.

	A	B	C	D
1	Invoice No	Date	Customer	Country
2	10918	############	Bottom-Dolla	Canada
3	10917	############	Romero y ton	Spain
4	10926	############	Ana Trujillo Er	Mexico

If you're used to calling the hash (#) a **pound sign** or **number sign** see the sidebar in: *Lesson 2-9: Re-size rows and columns* for an explanation.

2   Auto-resize cells A1:G17 so that their contents are fully visible.

This was covered in: *Lesson 2-9: Re-size rows and columns.*

3   Format the dates in column B so that they display in the format: *10-Mar-16*

At present the dates are formatted with the month spelled out in full:

	A	B	C
1	Invoice No	Date	Customer
2	10918	Thursday, 10 March 2016	Bottom-Dollar Markets
3	10917	Thursday, 10 March 2016	Romero y tomillo
4	10926	Thursday, 10 March 2016	Ana Trujillo Emparedados y helados

You're going to re-format them to the shorter form: *10 Mar 16*.

1.   Select cells B2:B17.

2.   Right-click anywhere in the selected range and choose *Format Cells…* from the shortcut menu.

You can also do this with the Menu Bar or keyboard (see sidebar).

The *Format Cells* dialog appears.

note

Launching the Format Cells dialog using the Menu Bar or keyboard

To open the Format Cells dialog using the Menu Bar, click:

⌘→Format→Cells

To open Format Cells using the keyboard, press:

<Cmd>+<1>

Sales Week Ended 14th March 2016

3. Click the *Number* tab (if it isn't already selected) and then choose *Date* from the *Category* list box.

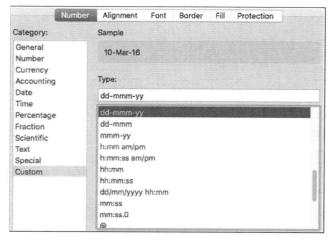

The dates you see may be different from those shown above (see sidebar).

You want the format *14-Mar-2016* but that isn't in the list. When you need a special format, it is worth checking the *Custom* category to see whether there is a pre-defined format available.

4. Click *Custom* in the category list box.

5. Click on one of the entries in the *Type* list box and then use the **<UpArrow>** and **<DownArrow>** keys to move through the list, keeping your eye on the preview in the *Sample* frame.

If you reach the format *dd-mmm-yy* you will see *10-Mar-16* in the sample box. If the format *dd-mmm-yy* isn't shown for your locale (see sidebar) you'll need to manually type it into the *Type* box.

note

Why do I see different date formats in the Format Cells dialog?

The date formats shown in the *Format Cells* dialog may change based upon your macOS (OS X) calendar settings.

Your default calendar is set in your macOS *Language & Region* settings. You can find these in the *System Preferences* dialog.

6. Click the *OK* button.

4   Save your work as *Sales Week Ended 14ᵗʰ March 2016-1*.

Lesson 4-2: Understand date serial numbers

Excel stores dates in a very clever way. Understanding Excel's date storage system empowers you to use date arithmetic. You can use date arithmetic to compute the difference between two dates (in days) or to shift date ranges by a given time interval.

How Excel stores dates

Dates are stored as simple numbers called *date serial numbers*. The serial number contains the number of days that have elapsed since 1st January 1900 (where 1st January 1900 is 1).

The world began in 1900

An interesting shortcoming of Excel is its inability to easily work with dates before 1900. Excel simply doesn't acknowledge that there were any dates before this time. If you work with older dates, you will have to work-around this limitation.

In Excel every time is a date, and every date is a time

This one is an eye opener! You've already realized that 5th January 1900 is stored as the number 5. What would the number 5.5 mean? It would mean midday on 5th January 1900.

It is possible to format a date to show only the date, only the time, or both a time and a date.

When you enter a time into a cell without a date, the time is stored as a number less than one. Excel regards this as having the non-existent date of 00 January 1900!

When you enter a date into a cell without a time, the time is stored as midnight at the beginning of that day.

1   Create a new blank workbook and put the numbers 1 to 5 in cells A1:A5.

2   Type the formula **=A1** into cell B1 followed by the **<Enter>** key, and then AutoFill the formula to the end of the list.

   AutoFill was covered in: *Lesson 2-14: Use AutoFill for text and numeric series.*

	A	B
1	1	1
2	2	2
3	3	3
4	4	4
5	5	5

trivia

The peculiar case of the Excel date bug and Lotus 1-2-3

Here's the Gregorian leap year rule © 1582 Pope Gregory XIII:

Every year that is exactly divisible by four is a leap year, except for years that are exactly divisible by 100; the centurial years that are exactly divisible by 400 are still leap years.

This means that the year 1900 wasn't a leap year but 2000 was (causing many millennium software bugs).

Lotus 1-2-3 was a spreadsheet product that was the market leader until Excel overtook it in the early 1990's.

The designers of Lotus 1-2-3 weren't paying enough attention to Pope Gregory's rules. Their DATE() function thought that 1900 was a leap year and thus recognised the non-existent date: February 29th 1900.

Because Excel needed to be compatible with Lotus 1-2-3, Microsoft had to replicate the Lotus bug when they designed Excel.

Try entering 29th Feb 1900 into a worksheet and Excel will gladly accept it.

This bug has the effect of introducing a one-day error into any date arithmetic you may do that spans 29th February 1900.

3 Apply a date format to column A that will show a four-digit year.

This was covered in: *Lesson 4-1: Format dates.*

	A	B
1	01 January 1900	1
2	02 January 1900	2

This reveals that the numbers 1 to 5 represent the dates 1-Jan-1900 to 05-Jan-1900.

4 Change the date format in column A so that it shows both dates and times.

Setting a custom format was covered in: *Lesson 4-1: Format dates.*

Choose the custom format: **dd mmm yyyy hh:mm** (if it isn't shown in the list you will need to type it into the *Type* box).

Notice that when you enter a date without a time, the time is set to midnight at the beginning of that day.

	A	B
1	01 January 1900 00:00	1
2	02 January 1900 00:00	2

5 Change the time in cell A2 to 12:00.

Notice that the number in cell B2 has changed to 2.5, showing that times are stored by Excel as the decimal part of a number.

	A	B
1	01 January 1900 00:00	1
2	02 January 1900 12:00	2.5

6 Compute the number of days that occurred between 01/01/1900 and 01/01/2000.

Now that you have a good grasp of Excel's serial numbers, this task is easy.

1. Enter the two dates in cells D1 and D2, one beneath the other.

2. Click in cell D3 to make it the active cell.

3. Click: Home→Number→Comma Style. [›]

   You'll be learning more about the comma style in: *Lesson 4-3: Format numbers using built-in number formats.*

4. Subtract one date from the other by entering the formula: **=D2-D1** into cell D3.

	D
1	01/01/1900
2	01/01/2000
3	36,525.00

You now know that 36,525 days occurred during the twentieth century (actually 36,524 due to the Lotus 1-2-3 bug – see sidebar).

7 Close the workbook without saving.

Lesson 4-3: Format numbers using built-in number formats

Formatting fundamentals

When you format a number you never change its value. For example, if you format the number:

483.45495

... so that it only displays two decimal places, the number displays like this:

483.45

It is important to realize that the actual value in the cell remains at the old value of 483.45495. All you have done is to change the way in which the value is presented to the user.

1   Open *Sales Week Ended 14ᵗʰ March 2016-1* from your sample files folder.

2   Apply the comma style to column E.

There is an extremely useful quick format button called the *comma style*. This is perfect for formatting monetary values with a single click. The comma style places a comma after thousands and displays exactly two decimal places.

1.   Select all of column E.

2.   Click: Home→Number→Comma Style.

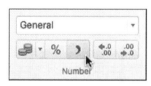

3.   Widen column E if necessary so that it is wide enough to display its contents.

All of the values in column E now display correctly.

	D	E	F	G
1	Country	Amount	Tax	Total
2	Canada	1,447.50	0.175	1700.8125
3	Spain	365.89	0.175	429.92075

Note that you can also use the *Accounting Number Format* style.

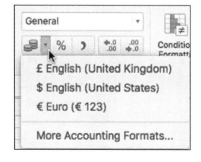

note

The Comma[0] and Currency[0] styles

With pre-2007 versions of Excel, I was forever applying the comma style and then removing the decimal places as a quick way to add the thousand separators to whole numbers. This used to take three clicks (comma style|decrease decimal|decrease decimal).

Excel 2019 saves a click with the Comma[0] and Currency[0] styles.

To apply these styles, you'll need to display the *Cell Styles Gallery*.

Look in the Home→Styles group. If you hover the mouse cursor over the *Cell Styles Gallery*, an arrow appears below it:

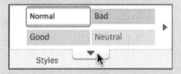

When you click the arrow you'll see the *Comma[0]* and *Currency[0]* styles at the bottom of the pane:

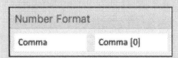

You'll be learning a lot more about cell styles later in this session.

Sales Week Ended
14ᵗʰ March 2016-1

note

Solutions to the "penny rounding" problem

Formatting a floating point number to two decimal places often results in the *penny rounding problem* when you sum a column of numbers.

There are two solutions to the problem. One is a very good solution, the other can cause problems.

Best practice

The best solution to the problem is to address it when the column is first calculated.

In this lesson's example worksheet, the formula used to calculate the value in cell G2 is:

=E2*(F2+1)

Excel has a ROUND() function that can be used to round the result to two decimal places at the point of calculation.

The new formula would become:

=ROUND(E2*(F2+1),2)

Changing precision

1. Click: ⌘→Excel→Preferences.

2. Click *Calculation*.

3. In the *When Calculating Workbooks* group, click the *Set precision as displayed* check box.

This alters the default behaviour of Excel so that each value in the worksheet is regarded as being precisely the same as its display value when performing calculations.

Using this option can cause data to become inaccurate as it is a global setting, affecting the entire worksheet (and any other worksheets you may open before turning it off).

Use this feature with extreme caution, or better still, don't use it at all!

This is very similar to the comma style but adds a leading currency symbol and an appropriate number of decimal places. The *More Accounting Formats…* option supports a vast number of international currency styles.

Try the *Accounting Number Format* style out to see how it works. I've found that the comma style is more appropriate for most of my work, as I'm usually working in one country and one currency, making the currency type obvious.

3 Apply the comma style to column G.

Column G has many decimal places in some cases, as the sales tax calculation results in as many as six decimal places.

Apply the comma style to column G and notice how all of the values are displayed rounded to the nearest two decimal places.

It is a key concept (as discussed in the introduction to this lesson) to realize that the values in the cells have not changed. For example, if you add two cells containing the value 1.4, the result will be 1.4+1.4=2.8. If you then format the cells as whole numbers, you'll see that 1+1=3 as each number is rounded up or down.

See the sidebar for potential solutions to this problem.

4 Apply the percentage style to column F.

The example sales tax rate is 17.5%. When working with percentages, it is useful to enter them so that you can calculate a percentage simply by multiplying by the cell.

Instead of 17.5 (more readable) the values are entered as 0.175 (easier to use in formulas). In order to make percentages both readable and easy to use, Microsoft has created the percentage style. If you type 17.5% into a cell, the actual value within the cell will be 0.175.

1. Select column F.

2. Click: Home→Number→Percent Style.

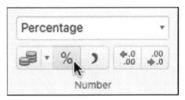

3. Click: Home→Number→Increase Decimal ⬆.0/.00 once, to make the values in column F display one decimal place.

	D	E	F	G
1	Country	Amount	Tax	Total
2	Canada	1,447.50	17.5%	1,700.81
3	Spain	365.89	17.5%	429.92

5 Save your work as *Sales Week Ended 14ᵗʰ March 2016-2*.

Lesson 4-4: Create custom number formats

The built-in number formats are very quick and convenient but are also quite limited. For example, there was a credit note on 11-Mar-16 for 637.49 plus tax. You could easily miss the little minus sign to the left of the amount.

	D	E	F	G
6	Germany	500.00	17.5%	587.50
7	Italy	637.49	17.5%	749.05
8	Italy	- 637.49	17.5% -	749.05

Old-school accountants like to show brackets around negative values. You just can't miss those brackets! Here's what you want to see:

	D	E	F	G
6	Germany	500.00	17.5%	587.50
7	Italy	637.49	17.5%	749.05
8	Italy	(637.49)	0.18	(749.05)

There's one little problem with this requirement. For many locales, Excel 2019 doesn't have this style in any of the built-in or pre-defined custom formats. Fortunately, it is possible to create your own custom format when none of the built-in styles fit your requirements.

Overview of custom formats

There's plenty of documentation in the help system and on the Internet about the rather cryptic formatting codes provided with Excel 2019. Just about everything is possible once you've got to grips with the basic concepts.

To communicate the custom format to Excel, you must construct a custom format string.

Zeros mean "Display significant zeros". You tell Excel how many you want within the format string. For example, 0.00 means *display at least one leading zero and two decimal places*. The following examples should make things clear:

Custom Format String	Value	Display
0	1234.56	1235
0.0	1234.56	1234.6
	1234.5	1234.5
	.5	0.5
0.00	1234.56	1234.56
	1234.5	1234.50
	.5	0.50
00.000	4.56	04.560
0.000	1234.56	1234.560

note

Use the ? custom format string symbol to make number values line up

The question mark inserts a space (when needed) in order to make sure that values that do not display a fixed number of decimal places line up properly.

I must admit that I've never had to use it in a real-world worksheet as I much prefer to pad numbers with trailing zeros.

For example, here's two numbers formatted with the default *General* format:

15.5
17.775

The decimal points don't line up because both numbers are, by default, right aligned.

The custom format:

0.??

Will cause the numbers to round to two places and display as follows:

15.5
17.78

Sales Week Ended
14th March 2016-2

note

More about custom number formats

It is only possible to give you a broad overview of custom number formats in a single lesson. This should be all that you need to discover more using Excel's help system or the Internet.

Here are a couple of other insights that may help if you want to explore them further:

- You can embed colors into number formats. For example, to make every negative value red you could use:

  0.00;[Red]0.00

- There are four possible parts to a number format:

  Positive format; Negative format; Zero format; Text format. Applying the custom format string:

  0.00;-0.00;"Zero";[Blue]

  To these cells:

  | Mike | 0 | 120.119 | -345.5744 |

  Would result in:

  | Mike | Zero | 120.12 | -345.57 |

(Text in first cell is colored blue).

note

Hiding values with the three semicolon trick

You will often want to hide the values in specific cells, even though you want other values in the same column to display.

A common way of doing this is to format the cell with a white foreground color upon a white background.

A better solution is to create a custom format consisting of three semicolons:

;;;

The hash symbol (#) is mainly used to add comma separators to thousands and millions.

Custom Format String	Value	Display
#	123.4500	123
#.##	123.45	123.45
	123.50	123.5
#,#	1234.56	1,236
#,#.##	1234.56	1,234.56
	1234.50	1,234.5
	12341234.56	12,341,234.56

Because the hash symbol can be used in conjunction with zeroes it is also possible to indicate that you want both thousand separators *and* a specific number of leading or trailing zeroes.

Custom Format String	Value	Display
#,#0.00	12341234.5	12,341,234.50

You can also specify two different format strings separated by a semi colon. The first provides formatting for positive values and the second for negative values. This information enables you to construct the custom format string required.

Custom format string	Value	Display
#,#0.00;(#,#0.00)	12341234.5	12,341,234.50
	-12341234.5	(12,341,234.50)

1 Open *Sales Week Ended 14th March 2016-2* from your sample files folder (if it isn't already open).

2 Select columns E and G (but not column F).

   This was covered in: *Lesson 2-6: Select adjacent and non-adjacent rows and columns.*

3 Right-click anywhere in column E or G and then select *Format Cells…* from the shortcut menu.

4 Select *Custom* from the *Category* list on the left of the dialog.

5 Type the custom format: **#,##0.00;(#,##0.00)** into the box labeled *Type* and click the *OK* button.

   To type a # symbol on a standard Apple keyboard, press **<Alt>+<3>**.

   Type:

   #,##0.00;(#,##0.00)

   The negative values are now surrounded by brackets.

   | Italy | 637.49 | 17.5% | 749.05 |
   | Italy | (637.49) | 17.5% | (749.05) |

6 Save your work as *Sales Week Ended 14th March 2016-3.*

Lesson 4-5: Horizontally align the contents of cells

Icon	Description	What it does	Example
General ▾	General (the default)	Aligns numbers and dates to the right and text to the left.	Canada 1,447.50 / Spain 365.89
(align left icon)	Align Left	Aligns cell contents left. If the cell contains text and the adjacent cell is empty, text spills to the right. If the cell contains text and the adjacent text isn't empty, text is truncated.	Bottom-Dollar Markets Bottom-Dollar Markets Bottom-Dollar M Canada
(align center icon)	Align Center	Aligns cell contents to the center. If the cell contains text and the adjacent cells are empty, text spills to the left and right. If the cell contains text and the adjacent cells are not empty, text is truncated.	Bottom-Dollar Markets Bottom-Dollar Markets 10-Mar-08 om-Dollar Mar Canada
(align right icon)	Align Right	Aligns cell contents to the right. If the cell contains text and the adjacent cell is empty, text spills to the left. If the cell contains text and the adjacent cell isn't empty, text is truncated.	Bottom-Dollar Markets Bottom-Dollar Markets 10-Mar-08 om-Dollar Markets C
No icon	Justify	Text lines up to the left and right of the cell (like a newspaper)	to be or not to be, that is the question.
No icon	Distributed	Words are distributed evenly across the cell.	City of London
No icon	Center Across Selection	Words are centered across several selected cells.	Bottom Dollar Markets

Sales Week Ended
14th March 2016-3

note

How to access the Justify, Distributed, Fill and Center Across Selection options

There are several alignment options that aren't available via the Ribbon, as most users wouldn't ever find a use for them.

These options can be accessed from the *Format Cells* dialog.

To access the *Format Cells* dialog, right-click any cell and choose *Format Cells...* from the shortcut menu.

You'll then find a *Horizontal alignment* drop-down list on the *Alignment* tab, containing every possible horizontal alignment option. This list includes the *Fill* option mentioned below.

note

The Fill format

Fill repeats text until the cell is filled.

For example, if a cell contained the word *Cat*, here's how it would look after the *Fill* format was applied:

CatCatCatCatCatCat

I have seen the Fill format used in very old Excel versions to create separator lines by adding a row of characters (such as a dash) to a cell:

Because Excel 2019 has very sophisticated underline and drawing features, it is unlikely that you will ever find a use for the Fill format.

The table on the facing page summarizes Excel's different horizontal alignment options.

1 Open *Sales Week Ended 14th March 2016-3* from your sample files folder (if it isn't already open).

2 Notice that the text in row 1 doesn't align with the column contents.

Numerical and date values are, by default, right aligned.

Columns E, F and G contain numerical data but the text headings of their columns are left aligned.

You can see the problem more clearly if the columns are widened:

E	F	G
Amount	Tax	Total
1,447.50	17.5%	1,700.81
365.89	17.5%	429.92

3 Right-align the column headers for columns E, F and G.

1. Select cells E1:G1.

2. Click: Home→Alignment→Align Right

The column headers now look much better.

E	F	G
Amount	Tax	Total
1,447.50	17.5%	1,700.81
365.89	17.5%	429.92

4 Right-align cell B1.

Column B also has a problem as the dates and column header do not align.

1. Select cell B1.

2. Click: Home→Alignment→Align Right.

	B	C
1	Date	Customer
2	10-Mar-16	Bottom-Dollar Markets
3	10-Mar-16	Romero y tomillo

You will normally align column headers to the right for numeric/date columns, and to the left for text columns.

5 Bold-face row 1.

1. Select row 1.

2. Click: Home→Font→Bold.

	A	B	C
1	Invoice No	Date	Customer
2	10918	10-Mar-16	Bottom-Dollar Markets

6 Save your work as *Sales Week Ended 14th March 2016-4.*

note

The Merge Cells feature taught in this lesson should generally be avoided

Excel has a newer feature called: *Center Across Selection* that does almost the same thing as *Merge Cells*.

You'll learn about the *Center Across Selection* feature later, in: *Lesson 4-7: Unmerge cells and Center Across Selection.*

For new work, it is usually better to use the newer *Center Across Selection* feature in place of *Merge Cells*.

You still need to know how to use *Merge Cells* as you'll find that a huge number of existing workbooks use the *Merge Cells* feature extensively.

Lesson 4-6: Merge cells, wrap text and expand/collapse the formula bar

1   Open *Sales Week Ended 14th March 2016-4* from your sample files folder (if it isn't already open).

2   Insert three blank rows above row 1.

This was covered in: *Lesson 3-1: Insert and delete rows and columns.*

3   In cell A1, type: **Sales Week Ended 14th March 2016**

4   Center the title across columns A to G.

The title cell (A1) doesn't look bad, but wouldn't it be nice to center it above the transactions listed beneath? You could simply copy and paste the title text into cell D1, but that wouldn't be perfectly central.

The solution is to merge cells A1:G1 so that they turn into one big cell. It will then be possible to center the text inside the merged cell. Excel provides a handy *Merge and Center* button to do this in one click.

1.   Select cells A1:G1.

2.   Click: Home→Alignment→Merge & Center.

The title appears at the center of the merged cell.

5   View the text in cell A22.

There is a long description in cell A22. You probably can't see all of it on your screen.

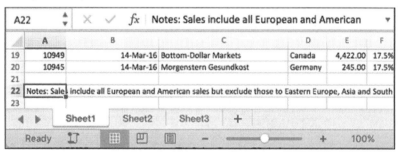

Re-sizing the formula bar allows all of the text to be read.

Click cell A22 and then click the *Expand Formula Bar* button.

The text becomes visible in the enlarged formula bar:

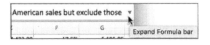

6   Resize the formula bar.

Sometimes there isn't enough space in the expanded formula bar to view all of the text.

If this is the case, hover the mouse over the bottom border of the formula bar until you see the double-headed arrow cursor shape.

When the double-headed arrow is visible, click and drag downward or upward to resize the formula bar as required.

7   Collapse the formula bar.

After you have read the text there is no need to keep the formula bar expanded. Click the same button used to expand the formula bar and the bar will collapse.

8   Merge cells A22:G22.

Expanding the formula bar isn't a great solution. Instead, you will create a box at the bottom of the report to display all of the text.

1.   Select cells A22:G22.

2.   Click: Home→Alignment→Merge & Center (drop-down).

A drop-down menu is displayed.

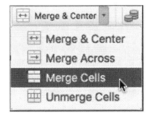

3.   Click *Merge Cells* to make all of the selected cells into one large cell. (This is just like *Merge & Center* but without centering).

9   Make row 22 deep enough to display all of the text.

This was covered in: *Lesson 2-9: Re-size rows and columns.*

The cell is now deep enough to display the text, but you can still only see one line. This is because the text isn't *wrapping*.

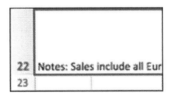

10   Wrap the text within the merged cells.

Click: Home→Alignment→Wrap Text.

The text now displays well, except that it appears at the bottom of the cell. You'll discover how to fix this later, in: *Lesson 4-8: Vertically align the contents of cells.*

> Notes: Sales include all European and American sales but exclude those to Eastern Europe, Asia and South Africa. Salesmen reported that clients are not ordering as much stock as usual because we are nearing the end of the first quarter.

11   Save your work as *Sales Week Ended 14ᵗʰ March 2016-5.*

note

Problems caused by merged cells

1. If you apply a format to a single column it will not be applied to a merged cell that spans the column.

2. You cannot AutoFill across a merged cell.

3. You cannot select a range within a single column if it contains a merged cell. This is the problem that you encounter at the beginning of this lesson.

4. When working with values it can be unclear which cell a merged value belongs to. This can cause errors when the values in a column that contain a merged cell are totalled.

	A	B
1	Joe	Bill
2		5
3	10	10
4	15	10

In the example above cells A2:B2 are merged and the merged cell has been right-aligned. The value of 5 is actually in column A, causing the totals in row 4 to seem incorrect.

5. If you copy and paste a merged cell, the destination cells will also merge.

6. When you merge cells, only the data in the left-most cell remains. Values in all other cells are discarded.

7. You cannot *Fill Down* a cell if it is part of a merged set of cells.

8. If you progress to the *Expert Skills* book in this series you will learn how to sort data. Any merged cells in a data set will interfere with sort results.

Lesson 4-7: Unmerge cells and Center Across Selection

In: *Lesson 4-6: Merge cells, wrap text and expand/collapse the formula bar,* you learned how to merge cells.

The *Merge Cells* feature is a widely used Excel feature. You'll often encounter merged cells in workbooks that were created by other Excel users. Perhaps after reading this lesson you will decide not to use the *Merge Cells* feature in your own worksheets.

Unfortunately, the *Merge Cells* feature can cause a number of problems (see sidebar). For this reason, many Excel professionals advise against ever using the *Merge Cells* feature. That's because there is a very similar Excel feature called *Center Across Selection* that doesn't cause any of the problems associated with *Merge Cells*.

Some Excel professionals even advise that existing workbooks containing merged cells should be converted to use *Center Across Selection* instead.

In this lesson, you will take a workbook that has many merged cells and then unmerge them before achieving the same effect using *Center Across Selection.*

1   Open *Cash and Credit Sales Analysis* from your sample files folder.

	A	B	C	D
1				
2			Total	
3		Analysis Type	Cash	Credit
4		London		
5		Beverages	22,998	30,319
6		Meat/Poultry	63,452	55,030
7		Vegetables	33,351	42,196
8		Paris		
9		Oct	42,972	55,220
10		Nov	34,472	42,216
11		Dec	42,357	51,150
12		New York		
13		UK	53,847	48,230
14		USA	40,040	51,196
15		Canada	25,914	32,215

This workbook has been formatted using Excel's *Merge Cells* feature. You learned how to merge cells in: *Lesson 4-6: Merge cells, wrap text and expand/collapse the formula bar.*

To make the merged cells easier to identify they have been shaded.

You can see that this worksheet has had border lines added to enhance appearance. You'll learn to use border lines to create a very similar worksheet later, in: *Lesson 4-11: Add borders and lines.*

2   Appreciate some of the problems caused by merged cells

In: *Lesson 2-7: Select non-contiguous cell ranges and view summary information,* you learned that it is simple and convenient to view the total value of several cells by selecting them with the mouse.

note

The Center Across Selection feature cannot be easily added to the Quick Access Toolbar

In: *Lesson 1-14: Customize the Quick Access Toolbar and preview the printout,* you learned that just about every Excel feature can be quickly and easily added to *the Quick AccessToolbar.*

Unfortunately, *Center Across Selection* is one of the very few Excel features that cannot be easily added to the *Quick Access Toolbar* in the normal way.

The *Expert Skills* book in this series provides a full understanding of Excel's *macro* feature and also teaches how to customize the Ribbon. With this knowledge, it is possible to work-around Excel's usual limitations and add a button to the *Ribbon* or *Quick Access Toolbar* using a different (macro based) technique.

The total value of the selected cells is then shown on the status bar at the bottom-right of the screen.

Try to select cells C5:C15 to report the combined cash sales for London, Paris and New York. You will find this impossible to do because of the merged cells in rows 8 and 12.

3   Remove merged cells.

1.   Select cell C2. This selects the merged cell range C2:D2.

2.   Click Home→Alignment→Merge & Center.

The *Merge & Center* button is no longer highlighted and cells C2 and D2 are unmerged.

3.   Do the same thing to unmerge cells B4, B8 and B12.

All worksheet cells are now unmerged. You will now find no difficulty in selecting cells C5:C15.

4   Use Center Across Selection to merge cells C2:D2.

1.   Select cells C2:D2.

2.   Right-click anywhere in the selected range and choose *Format Cells…* from the shortcut menu.

The *Format Cells* dialog appears.

3.   Click the *Alignment* tab.

4.   Click the drop-down arrow on the side of the *Horizontal alignment* box.

5.   Click: *Center Across Selection* from the drop-down list.

6.   Click the OK button to dismiss the dialog.

The text in cells C2:D2 now looks the same as when the two cells were merged. The key difference is that you are now able to individually select cell C2 or D2.

This may only seem like a small difference but it avoids all of the problems listed in the facing-page sidebar.

5   Use Center Across Selection to merge cells B4:D4, B8:D8 and B12:D12.

The worksheet now looks exactly as it did at the beginning of this lesson. The worksheet also no longer contains any merged cells.

6   Select cells C5:C15 to report the combined cash sales of the London, Paris and New York branches.

This time there is no difficulty selecting the cells and you can read the combined cash sales figure from the status bar (359,403).

Average: 39,934   Count: 9   Min: 22,998   Max: 63,452   Sum: 359,403

7   Save your work as *Cash and Credit Sales Analysis-1.*

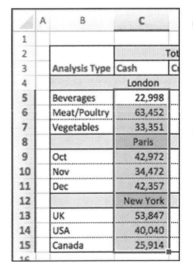

Lesson 4-8: Vertically align the contents of cells

This table summarizes Excel's different vertical alignment options.

Icon	Description	What it does	Example
General ▾	General (the default)	Aligns cell contents to the bottom of the cell.	Bottom-Dollar Markets
=	Top Align	Aligns cell contents to the top of the cell.	Bottom-Dollar Markets
=	Middle Align	Aligns cell contents to the middle of the cell.	Bottom-Dollar Markets
=	Bottom Align	Aligns cell contents to the bottom of the cell.	Bottom-Dollar Markets
No icon	Justify	Lines of text are spread out so that the space between each is equal, the first line is at the top and the last line is at the bottom.	to be or not to be, that is the question.
No icon	Distributed	The same as Justify!	to be or not to be, that is the question.

1 Open *Sales Week Ended 14th March 2016-5* from your sample files folder (if it isn't already open).

2 Top align the contents of cell A22.

The contents of cell A22 are currently bottom aligned (the default).

22	Notes: Sales include all European and American sales but exclude those to Eastern Europe, Asia and South Africa. Salesmen reported that clients are not ordering as much stock as usual because we are nearing the end of the first quarter.

When you place a block of text into a cell in this way, you will typically want it to be top-aligned.

1. Select cell A22.

Sales Week Ended
14th March 2016-5

2.   Click: Home→Alignment→Top Align 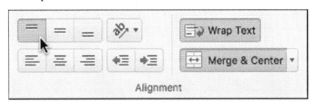 to align the text to the top of the cell.

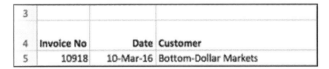

3   **Increase the height of row 4 so that it is about twice its present height.**

This was covered in: *Lesson 2-9: Re-size rows and columns.*

3			
4	**Invoice No**	**Date**	**Customer**
5	10918	10-Mar-16	Bottom-Dollar Markets

You can see why the default vertical alignment is *bottom align*. This alignment works really well for title rows.

4   **Wrap the text in cell A4.**

This was covered in*: Lesson 4-6: Merge cells, wrap text and expand/collapse the formula bar.*

5   **Split the words *Invoice* and *No* so that they appear on separate lines.**

1.   Double-click cell A4 to enter Edit mode and then position the cursor to the left of the word *No*.

2.   Press **<Alt>+<Enter>**.

3.   Press the **<Enter>** key again to exit Edit mode.

The two words now appear on separate lines.

6   **Horizontally right-align the text in cell A4.**

This was covered in: *Lesson 4-5: Horizontally align the contents of cells.*

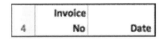

7   **Automatically resize columns A to G so that each column is just wide enough for the cell contents.**

This was covered in: *Lesson 2-9: Re-size rows and columns.*

8   **Save your work as *Sales Week Ended 14ᵗʰ March 2016-6*.**

note

What are serifs?

Serifs are the little lines at the edges of text that allow the eye to more easily scan words.

Serifs

Sans Serif

note

Can I change the default theme?

The default theme is simply the theme applied to the *Blank Workbook* template.

If you want to use a different default theme (or change any of the standard Excel options) you will need to create an empty workbook, apply the new theme to it, and then save it as a template (for example: *My Blank Workbook*). You learned how to do this in: *Lesson 3-13: Understand templates.*

It will then appear in the list of templates when you open Excel.

When you create new blank workbooks in future, you can then use your own customized *My Blank Workbook* custom template in place of Microsoft's *Blank Workbook* template.

Lesson 4-9: Understand themes

A theme is simply a set of fonts and colors that go very nicely together.

Font sets

A font set consists of two complementary fonts that work well as a pair.

A golden rule of typesetting is to never have more than two fonts in a document. Old school typesetters would always use a serif font for the body text (also called the *Normal* text) and a sans-serif font for the titles (just as this book does). See sidebar for the difference between serif and sans-serif fonts.

There's a modern school of thought that suggests that breaking this rule is cool and Microsoft have done just that with their default set for Excel 2019 (called the *Office* set) by choosing a sans-serif font (Calibri Light) for titles and also a sans-serif font (Calibri) for normal text.

You can see all 25 pre-defined font sets by clicking:

Page Layout→Themes→Fonts

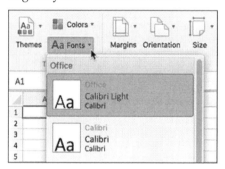

Color sets

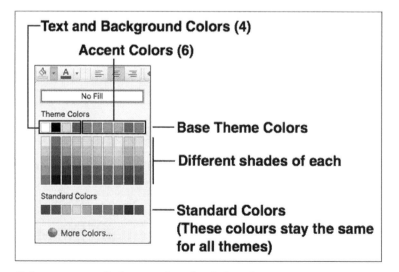

Color sets are a little more involved than font sets

trivia

Times New Roman is probably the most widely used and successful serif typeface in the world.

This font was commissioned by the British Times newspaper in 1931 and was used to print the Times until 1982 when it was replaced due to incompatibility with faster printing presses. It is still widely used in book publishing.

Times New Roman was the default font in Word for all versions right up to 2007.

Helvetica is probably the most widely used and successful sans-serif font. It was designed in Switzerland in 1957. Windows doesn't include Helvetica but uses *Arial*, a very similar font that most non-experts cannot distinguish from Helvetica.

I used to advise my students that if they stuck to the "killer combination" of Arial/Times New Roman they would never go far wrong, because readers are very used to them and thus find them extremely easy to read.

Microsoft has now changed all of the rules by introducing the Cambria and Calibri fonts.

Just as the Times newspaper designed their font to optimize reading at small type sizes in newspapers, Cambria and Calibri were designed specifically to be easy to read on computer screens using Microsoft's *Clear Type* rendering technology.

Clear Type works particularly well on LCD flat-panel displays.

Clear Type has saved me reams of paper because now, for the first time, I am able to proofread my books on-screen without causing eye strain. This has saved the life of several trees.

The ten colors along the top row are the *Theme colors*. The leftmost four are used for *Text and Background colors* and the other six are *Accent colors*. This set of colors has been selected by design professionals to work well together. There are actually twelve theme colors but you can only see ten of them. The two hidden theme colors are used for hyperlinks.

The *Standard colors* are best avoided. They are colors that will remain the same no matter which theme is in use. If you use standard colors (or the *More Colors…* option) the worksheet may look odd if the theme needs to be changed in the future. You can see all 23 pre-defined color sets by clicking:

Page Layout→Themes→Colors

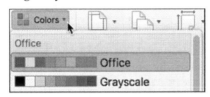

Themes

Themes are simply a group of one *color* set and one *font* set.

Because Microsoft have consistently named their Colors, Fonts and Themes, the *Office* theme consists of the *Office* color set and the *Office* font set.

Themes aren't just for Excel

The Themes feature is also included in Word, PowerPoint and Outlook.

Choosing the same theme for your documents, spreadsheets, presentations and Emails can give all of your communications a consistent and professional appearance.

Lesson 4-10: Use cell styles and change themes

note

Cell Styles will appear as a gallery if your screen is wide enough

If you have a wide enough screen, the *Cell Styles* button will appear as a gallery instead, allowing you to access the styles more quickly.

If this is happening on your computer, you will need to click the arrow below the gallery to access the full list of styles.

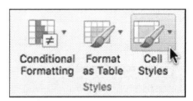

note

Removing a style from a cell

All cells have the *Normal* style by default. Select a cell or range of cells and click:

Home→Styles→
Cell Styles→Normal

You will then remove the cell style, and all other cell formatting such as bold face or underline, from the cell or range.

Sales Week Ended 14ᵗʰ March 2016-6

In order for themes to work their magic, you must get into the habit of using cell styles to format cells based only upon the options available in the current theme.

For many years, expert Word users have used styles to quickly produce professional documents. Their mortal sin would be to apply a font size or color directly to a document.

Now that Excel also supports styles (they were introduced in Excel 2007), professional Excel users should adopt the same discipline.

1 Open *Sales Week Ended 14ᵗʰ March 2016-6* from your sample files folder (if it isn't already open).

2 Apply the *Title* style to cell A1.

Even though cell A1 now encompasses cells A1:G1 it retains the cell reference A1.

A novice user might apply a font and color directly to cell A1 but you're going to do things the professional way and use the *Title* style.

1. Select cell A1.

2. Click: Home→Styles→Cell Styles.

The styles gallery appears.

3. Click *Title* to apply the Title style to cell A1.

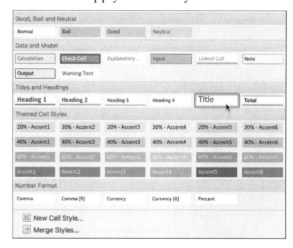

Cell A1 is formatted with the *Title* style.

3 Apply the *Heading 3* style to cells A4:G4.

1. Select cells A4:G4.

2. Click: Home→Styles→Cell Styles→Heading 3.

4 Apply the *Note* style to cell A22.

1. Select cell A22.

2. Click: Home→Styles→Cell Styles→Note.

5 Apply the *20% - Accent 1* style to cells A5:D20.

    1. Select cells A5:D20.

    2. Click: Home→Styles→Cell Styles→20% - Accent 1.

6 Apply the *20% - Accent 2* style to cells E5:G20.

    1. Select cells E5:G20.

    2. Click: Home→Styles→Cell Styles→ 20% - Accent 2.

The worksheet now looks very different:

	A	B	C	D	E	F	G
1			Sales Week Ended 14th March 2016				
2							
3							
4	Invoice No	Date	Customer	Country	Amount	Tax	Total
5	10918	10-Mar-16	Bottom-Dollar Markets	Canada	1,447.50	17.5%	1,700.81
6	10917	10-Mar-16	Romero y tomillo	Spain	365.89	17.5%	429.92
7	10926	10-Mar-16	Ana Trujillo Emparedados y helad	Mexico	514.40	17.5%	604.42
8	10929	11-Mar-16	Frankenversand	Germany	1,174.75	17.5%	1,380.33
9	10934	11-Mar-16	Lehmanns Marktstand	Germany	500.00	17.5%	587.50
10	10939	11-Mar-16	Magazzini Alimentari Riuniti	Italy	637.49	17.5%	749.05
11	10939	11-Mar-16	Magazzini Alimentari Riuniti	Italy	(637.49)	17.5%	(749.05)
12	10925	12-Mar-16	Hanari Carnes	Brazil	475.14	17.5%	558.29
13	10944	12-Mar-16	Bottom-Dollar Markets	Canada	1,025.32	17.5%	1,204.75
14	10923	12-Mar-16	La maison d'Asie	France	748.79	17.5%	879.83
15	10937	13-Mar-16	Cactus Comidas para llevar	Argentina	644.80	17.5%	757.64
16	10947	13-Mar-16	B's Beverages	UK	220.00	17.5%	258.50
17	10933	13-Mar-16	Island Trading	UK	920.60	17.5%	1,081.71
18	10938	14-Mar-16	QUICK-Stop	Germany	2,731.87	17.5%	3,209.95
19	10949	14-Mar-16	Bottom-Dollar Markets	Canada	4,422.00	17.5%	5,195.85
20	10945	14-Mar-16	Morgenstern Gesundkost	Germany	245.00	17.5%	287.88
21							
22	Notes: Sales include all European and American sales but exclude those to Eastern Europe, Asia and South Africa. Salesmen reported that clients are not ordering as much stock as usual because we are nearing the end of the first quarter.						

7 Insert a row above row 21.

This was covered in: *Lesson 3-1: Insert and delete rows and columns.*

8 Use AutoSum to place a total in cell G21.

This was covered in: *Lesson 2-3: Use AutoSum to quickly calculate totals.*

9 Apply the *Total* style to cell G21.

    1. Select cell G21.

    2. Click: Home→Styles→Cell Styles→Total.

Argentina	644.80	17.5%	757.64
UK	220.00	17.5%	258.50
UK	920.60	17.5%	1,081.71
Germany	2,731.87	17.5%	3,209.95
Canada	4,422.00	17.5%	5,195.85
Germany	245.00	17.5%	287.88
			18,137.37

10 Re-size all columns if necessary so that they are wide enough to display the total.

The total cell is neatly formatted.

11 Preview your finished work under different themes.

Because you did things the professional way, using styles instead of directly formatting cells, it is now possible to cycle through the themes. You may find one of the other themes more attractive.

    1. Click: Page Layout→Themes→Themes.

    2. Try clicking on different themes. You'll be amazed at how your work completely changes as each theme's style set is applied.

    3. After you've finished trying different themes, click the *Office* theme to return to the default fonts and colors.

12 Save your work as *Sales Week Ended 14th March 2016-7.*

Lesson 4-11: Add borders and lines

1   Open *Sales Analysis* from your sample files folder.

You're going to use the powerful *borders and lines* feature to make this worksheet more readable.

Before

	A	B	C	D	E
1					
2			Total		
3		Analysis Type	Cash	Percent	
4		By Category			
5		Beverages	25,326	20%	
6		Meat/Poultry	65,780	52%	
7		Vegetables	35,679	28%	
8		Total	126,785		
9		By Month			
10		Oct	45,300	36%	
11		Nov	36,800	29%	
12		Dec	44,685	35%	
13		Total	126,785		
14		By Country			
15		UK	56,175	44%	
16		USA	42,368	33%	
17		Canada	28,242	22%	
18		Total	126,785		
19					

After

	A	B	C	D	E
1					
2			Total		
3		Analysis Type	Cash	Percent	
4		By Category			
5		Beverages	25,326	20%	
6		Meat/Poultry	65,780	52%	
7		Vegetables	35,679	28%	
8		Total	126,785		
9		By Month			
10		Oct	45,300	36%	
11		Nov	36,800	29%	
12		Dec	44,685	35%	
13		Total	126,785		
14		By Country			
15		UK	56,175	44%	
16		USA	42,368	33%	
17		Canada	28,242	22%	
18		Total	126,785		
19					

2   Add cell styles to rows 2,3,4,9 and 14.

1.   Select cells B2:D3.

2.   Click: Home→Styles→Cell Styles→40% Accent 6.

3.   Select cells B4:D4, B9:D9 and B14:D14.

This was covered in: *Lesson 2-7: Select non-contiguous cell ranges and view summary information.*

4.   Click: Home→Styles→Cell Styles→20% Accent 6.

5.   Select cells B2:D3.

6.   Click: Home→Styles→Cell Styles→Heading 4.

3   Switch off the worksheet gridlines.

When you are working with borders, it is always a good idea to switch off the gridlines so that you can have a better idea of how the worksheet will print.

This feature appears in two different places on the Ribbon. Uncheck either of the following check boxes:

View→Show→Gridlines

OR

Page Layout→Sheet Options→Gridlines→View

4   Add a solid border around the entire range.

1.   Select cells B2:D18.

Sales Analysis

2. Click:
   Home→Font→Borders drop-down→Outside Borders.

5   Add solid borders inside cells C2:D3.

   1. Select cells C2:D3.

   2. Click: Home→Font→Borders drop-down→All Borders.

tip

Use the draw border tool to quickly add complex borders

The fastest way to quickly add borders is to simply draw them into place using the *Draw Border* tool.

Click:

Home→Font→
Borders drop-down→
Draw Border

You can then simply draw borders straight onto the grid. There's also an *Erase Border* tool available from the same menu.

note

Changing the border line style or color from the drop-down menu

The ability to change line style and color from the menu means you'll rarely have to resort to using the *Format Cells* dialog for borders.

To change line style or color from the *Borders* drop-down menu, select *Line Color or Line Style.*

The selected color and/or style will remain active until you close Excel. Next time you open Excel it will have returned to the default.

6   Add top and bottom borders to *By Category, By Month* and *By Country.*

   1. Select cells B4:D4, B9:D9 and B14:D14.

   2. Click: Home→Font→Borders drop-down→
      Top and Bottom Border.

7   Add dotted outlines to the borders of cells B5:D8, B10:D13 and B15:D18.

   1. Select cells B5:D8, B10:D13 and B15:D18.

   2. Right-click any of the selected cells and click *Format Cells…* from the shortcut menu.

      The *Format Cells* dialog appears.

   3. Click the *Border* tab of the *Format Cells* dialog.

   4. Click the *Dotted Line* style.

   5. Click the *Inside* button.

   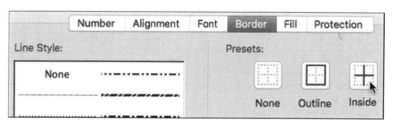

   6. Click the *OK* button.

      The dotted lines are displayed within the cells.

8   Add left and right borders to cells C5:C8, C10:C13 and C15:C18.

   1. Select cells C5:C8, C10:C13 and C15:C18.

   2. Click: Home→Font→Borders→Left Border.

   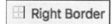

   3. Click: Home→Font→Borders→Right Border.

   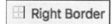

9   Save your work as *Sales Analysis-1.*

Lesson 4-12: Create your own custom theme

If none of the 35 built-in themes suffice, you can create your own from any combination of the built-in color and font sets.

This allows you to define your own custom theme that can be applied to any document in any Office application.

1 Open *Sales Week Ended 14th March 2016-7* from your sample files folder (if it isn't already open).

2 Select a different set of theme colors.

1. Click: Page Layout→Themes→Colors.

   All of the pre-defined sets of colors are displayed (see sidebar). Try clicking on them one at a time, to see how your worksheet looks with different colors.

2. Choose a different set that you think looks attractive.

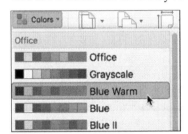

3 Select a different set of fonts.

As discussed in: *Lesson 4-9: Understand themes,* a theme consists of a color set and a font set.

A font set consists of two fonts: a heading font and a body font.

1. Click: Page Layout→Themes→Fonts.

   All of the pre-defined sets of fonts are displayed. Try clicking different font sets to see how your worksheet looks with a different set of fonts.

2. Choose a different set that you think looks attractive.

4 Save the custom theme.

1. Click: Page Layout→Themes→Themes→Save Current Theme.

2. Enter the name: **TSM Corporate** in the *File Name* text box.

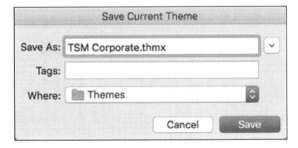

3. Click the *Save* button.

5 Revert to the standard *Office* theme.

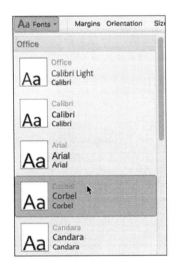

Sales Week Ended 14th March 2016-7

1. Click: Page Layout→Themes→Themes.

Notice that your custom theme is listed at the top in the *Custom* group.

2. Click the *Office* theme to put things back the way they were.

6 Close the workbook without saving.

Lesson 4-13: Create your own custom cell styles

Excel 2019 has a large number of pre-defined cell styles grouped into:

- Good, Bad and Neutral – to mark particularly good or bad results.

- Data and Model – usually used in a worksheet containing formulas to mark cells that require user input or contain formula results.

- Titles and Headings – for section titles and column headers.

- Themed Cell Styles – to color cells based upon the theme colors.

- Number Format – to quickly apply number formats.

Custom styles are only available in the workbook in which they were originally created. In order to use them in another workbook, you need to use Excel's *merge styles* feature. The *merge styles* feature will be covered later, in: *Lesson 4-14: Use a master style book to merge styles.*

1 Open *Sales Week Ended 14th March 2016-7* from your sample files folder (if it isn't already open).

2 Modify an existing cell style.

Click cell A23 to make it the active cell. This is the cell containing the *Note* text.

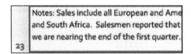

1. Click: Home→Styles→Cell Styles.

2. Right-click the *Note* style and click *Modify* from the shortcut menu.

The *Modify Cell Style* dialog appears.

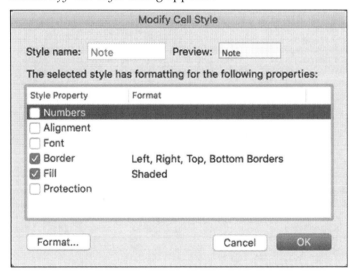

3. Click the *Format…* button. The *Format Cells* dialog appears.

4. Click the *Fill* tab and select a light green background color.

5. Click the *OK* button and then the *OK* button once more.

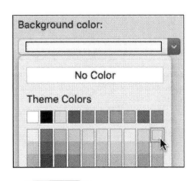

Sales Week Ended 14th March 2016-7

6. If cell A23 isn't green, click: Home→Styles→Cell Styles and click once on the *Note* style.

Notice that the background color of cell A23 (which has the *Note* style applied to it) has now turned light green.

You haven't permanently changed the *Office* theme's *Note* style. You've simply changed it for this workbook only. When you open another workbook that uses the *Office* theme, the *Note* style will be light yellow once again.

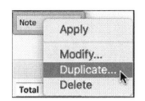

3   Duplicate the *Note* built-in cell style.

1. Click: Home→Styles→Cell Styles to display the *Cell Styles* gallery.

2. Right-click the *Note* cell style and then click *Duplicate* from the shortcut menu.

The *Modify Cell Style* dialog appears, suggesting the name *Note 2* for your new cell style.

3. Change the *Style name* to **Blue Note** (you're going to change the color in a moment) and click the *OK* button.

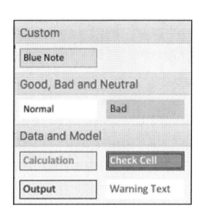

4. Click: Home→Styles→Cell Styles to display the *Cell Styles* gallery once more. Notice that the *Blue Note* style is at the top of the gallery in the *Custom* section.

5. Change the background color of the new *Blue Note* style to light blue using the technique learned in: *Step 2 - Modify an existing cell style*.

4   Create a custom cell style *By Example*.

This is the easiest way to create custom cell styles.

1. Select cell A23.

2. Click: Home→Font→Fill Color Drop-down and choose the *Gold, Accent 4, Lighter 80%* theme color.

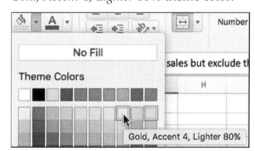

3. Click: Home→Styles→Cell Styles→New Cell Style.

The style automatically copies all of the formatting information from cell A23.

4. Change the style name to **Gold Note** and click the *OK* button.

5   Save your work as *Sales Week Ended 14ᵗʰ March 2016-8*.

Lesson 4-14: Use a master style book to merge styles

When you create custom styles, they are only available within the workbook in which they were created. Sometimes it is useful to have the same set of custom styles available across multiple workbooks.

In this lesson you'll cater for the following scenario at Empire Car Sales:

Syd Slater, the owner of Empire Car Sales, knows that you have to keep your stock turning over.

His salesmen are allowed to discount 10% of the sticker price on all cars.

If the car has been on the forecourt for more than two weeks they are allowed to discount 15%, after three weeks 20%, and after four weeks the car goes back to auction.

Syd's salesmen need to know the maximum discount they can offer, but Syd doesn't want the customers to find this out, so they use a cunning system of color coding on the stock list:

10% Max Discount: Blue

15% Max Discount: Green

20% Max Discount: Orange

The stock list is produced each week in Excel with three custom cell styles, one for each discount.

To avoid having to constantly re-create custom cell styles, they are stored in a master style book called *Empire Styles,* which Syd merges with his worksheets so that the three styles are always available.

1   Open a new blank workbook.

2   Create a custom style called *10% Max Discount* with a background color of *Light Blue*.

> This was covered in: *Lesson 4-13: Create your own custom cell styles.*

3   Create a custom style called *15% Max* Discount with a background color of *Light Green*.

4   Create a custom style called *20% Max* Discount with a background color of *Light Orange*.

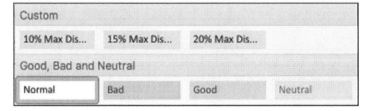

Because you have used theme colors for the custom styles, their color will change if the theme is changed.

For example, if you change the theme to *Slate,* the *10% Max Discount* becomes red, *15%* becomes brown and *20%* becomes tan.

**Empire Car Sales
Stock List-1**

For this reason, you could argue that it would be better to set the colors using the *More Colors* option so that the colors remained the same even if the theme is changed.

For the purposes of this lesson you will assume that Syd will not change from the *Office* theme and will follow the normal rule of restricting color choice to theme colors (see: *Lesson 4-9: Understand themes*, for an explanation of why this is best practice).

5   Save the workbook as *Empire Styles* but don't close it.

6   Open *Empire Car Sales Stock List-1* from your sample files folder.

7   Merge the styles from the *Empire Styles* master style book.

  1.   Click: Home→Styles→Cell Styles→Merge Styles…

  2.   The *Import Cell Styles* dialog appears.

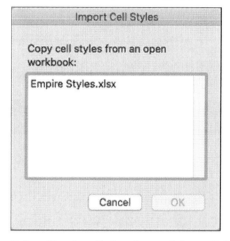

  3.   Select *Empires Styles.xlsx* and then click the *OK* button.

  4.   If prompted to replace existing styles, click *Skip*.

  The three custom styles are now available within the current workbook.

8   Apply the 20% style to the Volkswagen and Mercedes.

9   Apply the 15% style to the BMW and Alfa Romeo.

10   Apply the 10% style to the Volvo and Ford.

  Syd's salesmen are now ready to start selling!

	A	B	C	D	E	F	G
1	Empire Car Sales						
2							
3	Current stock list						
4							
5	Make	Model	Year	Mileage	Price	Color	Selling points
6	Volkswagen	Golf GT	2013	26000	18000	Black	Can accelerate faster than most sports cars.
7	BMW	320i	2011	44000	3190	Topaz Blue	One conscientious owner from new.
8	Ford	Fiesta	2012	16000	3750	Yellow	Achieves nearly 50 miles to the gallon.
9	Mercedes	CLK	2009	78000	8000	Silver	Particularly clean example of this executive coupe.
10	Volvo	V70 Estate	2006	73000	4500	Blue	Recognized as one of the safest cars on the road.
11	Alfa Romeo	Alfasud	1989	92000	750	Brown	A collector's car strictly for connoisseurs.

11   Save your work as *Empire Car Sales Stock List-2*.

Lesson 4-15: Use simple conditional formatting

Simple conditional formatting applies a format to a cell based upon the value of the cell. In this lesson you'll change the cell background color to red if the cell has a value of less than 5,000 and to green if the value is over 30,000.

The same technique learned in this lesson can be used to apply conditional formats based upon text that begins with, ends with, or contains specific characters.

You can also apply conditional formats to cells containing dates. For example, you can highlight dates such as *today, tomorrow, in the last seven days, last week* and *this week.* Conditional formatting will then cause the worksheet to change every time that you open it based upon the current date.

1   Open *Sales Report* from your sample files folder.

2   AutoFit cells A4:A26.

     1.   Select cells A4:A26.

     2.   Click: Home→Cells→Format→AutoFit Column Width.

     This was covered in: *Lesson 2-9: Re-size rows and columns.*

3   AutoFit cells D4:D13.

4   Apply the *Comma* style to columns B and E.

     This was covered in: *Lesson 4-3: Format numbers using built-in number formats.*

5   Merge cells A3:B3, D3:E3 and D18:E18.

     This was covered in: *Lesson 4-6: Merge cells, wrap text and expand/collapse the formula bar.*

6   Apply the *Title* style to cell A1.

     This was covered in: *Lesson 4-10: Use cell styles.*

7   Apply the *Heading 2* style to cells A3, D3 and D18.

8   Apply the *Heading 3* style to cells A4:B4, D4:E4 and D19:E19.

9   Apply the *Total* style to cells A26:B26, D13:E13 and D26:E26.

     The worksheet is now well formatted and has a professional appearance:

	A	B	C	D	E
1	Sales Report - 6 Months ended March 2016				
2					
3	Sales By Country			Sales by Category	
4	Country	Total Sales		Category	Total Sales
5	Argentina	762.60		Beverages	70,168.10
6	Austria	33,462.58		Condiments	24,938.06

Sales Report

note

You can have as many conditional formats as you need

Excel versions prior to Excel 2007 were limited to three conditional formats per cell.

In Excel 2019 you can define an unlimited number of conditional formats.

3	Sales By Country	
4	Country	Total Sales
5	Argentina	762.60
6	Austria	33,462.58
7	Belgium	6,109.48
8	Brazil	20,524.42
9	Canada	21,306.29
10	Denmark	16,658.80
11	Finland	5,525.00
12	France	26,155.54
13	Germany	28,361.38
14	Ireland	6,157.76
15	Italy	2,585.69
16	Mexico	3,524.30
17	Norway	1,058.40
18	Poland	459.00
19	Portugal	5,584.13

3	Sales By Country	
4	Country	Total Sales
5	Argentina	762.60
6	Austria	33,462.58
7	Belgium	6,109.48
8	Brazil	20,524.42
9	Canada	21,306.29
10	Denmark	16,658.80
11	Finland	5,525.00
12	France	26,155.54
13	Germany	28,361.38
14	Ireland	6,157.76
15	Italy	2,585.69

10 Select cells B5:B25.

11 Conditionally format the selected range so that any country with sales below 5,000 has a light red fill with dark red text.

1. Click: Home→Styles→Conditional Formatting→ Highlight Cells Rules→Less Than…

    The *New Formatting Rule* dialog appears.

2. Type **5,000** in the right-hand text box and choose *Light Red Fill with Dark Red Text* from the *Format with* menu.

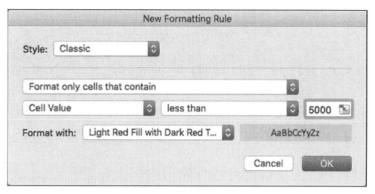

    Note also that there's a *custom format...* option (in the *Format with* drop-down list) which enables you to choose effects such as underlines as well as any color.

3. Click the *OK* button.

    Cells that have a value of less than 5,000 are now highlighted in red (see sidebar).

12 Add another conditional format to the same range, so that any country with sales above 30,000 has a green fill with dark green text.

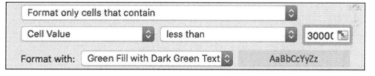

Both conditional formats now display, with the two sales values over 30,000 displayed in green (see sidebar).

13 Remove both conditional formats.

1. Select cells B5:B25.

2. Click: Home→Styles→Conditional Formatting→ Clear Rules→Clear Rules from Selected Cells.

    The conditional formats are removed.

14 Save your work as *Sales Report-1.*

Lesson 4-16: Manage multiple conditional formats using the Rules Manager

The conditional formats applied in the previous lesson depended upon the value of a single cell.

Often you will want a cell to be formatted based upon its relationship to other cells in a range.

In this lesson you'll color the top 25% of sales green, the middle 50% yellow and the bottom 25% red.

This lesson also introduces the *Rules Manager,* which allows you to edit conditional format rules and to specify the order in which conditional formats are applied.

1   Open *Sales Report-1* from your sample files folder (if it isn't already open).

2   Select cells B5:B25.

3   Conditionally format the selected range so that any country whose sales are in the top 25% has a green fill with dark green text.

    1.   Click: Home→Styles→Conditional Formatting→ Top/Bottom Rules→Top 10%.

        The *New Formatting Rule* dialog appears.

    2.   Change the value to 25% and choose *Green Fill with Dark Green Text* for the fill.

    3.   Click the *OK* button.

3	Sales By Country	
4	Country	Total Sales
5	Argentina	762.60
6	Austria	33,462.58
7	Belgium	6,109.48
8	Brazil	20,524.42
9	Canada	21,306.29
10	Denmark	16,658.80
11	Finland	5,525.00
12	France	26,155.54
13	Germany	28,361.38
14	Ireland	6,157.76
15	Italy	2,585.69

Sales Report-1

4   Conditionally format the selected range so that any country whose sales are in the bottom 25% has a light red fill with dark red text.

The top and bottom 25% of sales are now highlighted as specified in the two conditional formats (see sidebar).

5   Add another conditional format so that any country with sales greater than zero has a yellow fill with dark yellow text.

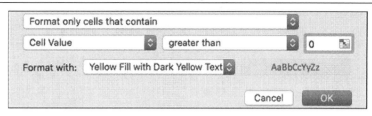

Remember that the specification was to color the middle 50% of sales yellow.

Unfortunately, all sales are now yellow because the yellow cells are over-writing the red and green cells.

6 Use the *Rules Manager* to control the order in which conditional formats are applied.

1. Select cells B5:B25.

2. Click:
    Home→Styles→Conditional Formatting→Manage Rules.

    The *Manage Rules* dialog is displayed.

3. Click the first rule (the *Cell Value > 0* rule).

4. Use the *Move Down* button ⬇ to move the *Cell Value > 0* rule to the bottom of the list (if you don't see the *Move Down* button it is because you haven't selected the rule).

5. Click the *OK* button.

    The red, green and yellow formatting rules are now applied as required. This works because of the conflict resolution rules (see sidebar).

7 Use the *Rules Manager* to edit the rules so that the top and bottom 30% values are now highlighted.

1. Select cells B5:B25.

2. Click:
    Home→Styles→Conditional Formatting→Manage Rules.

3. Select the *Bottom 25%* rule.

4. Click the *Edit Rule...* button **Edit Rule...** and change the criteria to: *30%*.

5. Edit the *Top 25%* rule in the same way so that it will show the top 30% values.

8 Remove all three conditional formats.

    This was covered in: *Lesson 4-15: Use simple conditional formatting.*

9 Close the workbook without saving.

© 2018 The Smart Method® Ltd

---

note

Conflict resolution rules

In this lesson you applied three different conditional formats to the selected range.

Sometimes there will be a conflict between different conditional formatting rules.

Consider this specification:

- Format every value over 50 as blue, underlined and bold.

- Format every value over 75 as red and italic.

The rules manager has a dilemma with a value of 80. Should it be blue or red, bold, italic, underlined or all three?

To resolve the conflict, rules are applied in the order listed in the *Rules Manager*. Attributes are applied only if an earlier conditional format has not set a conflicting condition.

1. The value is over 50 so apply blue, underlined, bold-face.

2. The value is over 75. Can't format red because the earlier condition has made the cell blue.

3. The value is over 75. Apply italics.

Lesson 4-17: Bring data alive with visualizations

	A	B
3	**Sales By Country**	
4	Country	Total Sales
5	Argentina	762.60
6	Austria	33,462.58
7	Belgium	6,109.48
8	Brazil	20,524.42
9	Canada	21,306.29
10	Denmark	16,658.80
11	Finland	5,525.00
12	France	26,155.54
13	Germany	28,361.38
14	Ireland	6,157.76

	D	E
3	**Sales by Category**	
4	Category	Total Sales
5	Beverages	70,168.10
6	Condiments	24,938.06
7	Confections	31,883.54
8	Dairy Products	49,902.95
9	Grains/Cereals	19,570.36

	D	E
18	**Sales by Month**	
19	Date	Total Sales
20	Oct	37,515.73
21	Nov	45,600.05
22	Dec	45,239.63
23	Jan	61,258.07
24	Feb	38,483.64
25	Mar	38,547.22
26	**Grand Total**	**266,644.33**

Visualizations are a half-way house between raw data and charts. With a few clicks of the mouse they allow you to express numbers in a visual manner.

1   Open *Sales Report-1* from your sample files folder (if it isn't already open).

2   Add a data bar visualization to the *Sales by Country* figures.

1.   Select cells B5:B25.

2.   Click: Home→Styles→Conditional Formatting→ Data Bars→Gradient Fill→Red Data Bar.

The visualization is applied (see sidebar).

3   Add a color scale visualization to the *Sales by Category* figures.

1.   Select cells E5:E12.

2.   Click: Home→Styles→Conditional Formatting→ Color Scales→Green - Yellow Color Scale.

The visualization is applied (see sidebar).

4   Add an icon set visualization to the *Sales by Month* figures.

1.   Select cells E20:E25.

2.   Click: Home→Styles→Conditional Formatting→Icon Sets→ Indicators→3 Flags.

3.   If necessary, re-size column E so that it is wide enough to display the values.

The visualization is applied (see sidebar).

When the icon set contains three icons, Excel assigns the relative icons to the top third, middle third, and bottom third of the value range.

You will often need to change these arbitrary values.

5   Use the *Rules Manager* to modify the *Sales by Month* visualization so that three green flags are shown.

The *Sales by Month* visualization may discourage your salesmen because only one month is flagged as green, with four months flagged red. You will now adjust the criteria for flag allocation so that three months are shown as green.

1.   Select cells E20:E25.

2.   Click: Home→Styles→Conditional Formatting→ Manage Rules…

The *Manage Rules* dialog is displayed.

3.   Click the *Edit Rule* button. Edit Rule...

Sales Report-1

4. Change the criteria in the dialog so that values over 45,000 are green, values over 38,000 are yellow and values under 38,000 are red.

You'll need to set the criteria as follows:

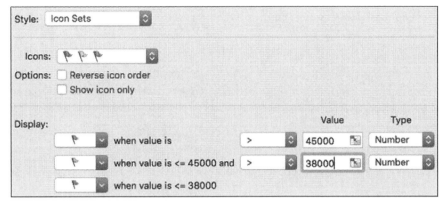

5. Click *OK* and *OK* again.

The flags are displayed as required, with three green flags (see sidebar).

6 Use the *Rules Manager* to show the visualizations for *Sales by Country* without the underlying data.

1. Select cells B5:B25.

2. Click:
Home→Styles→Conditional Formatting→Manage Rules.

The *Manage Rules* dialog is displayed.

3. Click the *Edit Rule* button. **Edit Rule...**

4. Check the *Show data bar only* check box.

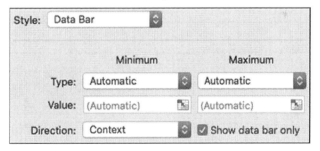

5. Click the *OK* button on each dialog to close them.

The bars are shown without the values (see sidebar).

7 Use the *Rules Manager* to bring back the values for *Sales by Country*.

Follow the same procedure as in the previous step to uncheck the *Show data bar only* check box.

8 Save your work as *Sales Report-2*.

	D	E
18	**Sales by Month**	
19	Date	Total Sales
20	Oct	37,515.73
21	Nov	45,600.05
22	Dec	45,239.63
23	Jan	61,258.07
24	Feb	38,483.64
25	Mar	38,547.22
26	**Grand Total**	**266,644.33**

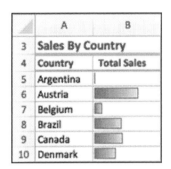

	A	B
3	**Sales By Country**	
4	Country	Total Sales
5	Argentina	
6	Austria	
7	Belgium	
8	Brazil	
9	Canada	
10	Denmark	

tip

Use the Show data bar only feature to create quick charts

To create a "quick chart" for cells E5:E12:

1. Type the formula =E5 into cell F5.

2. AutoFill cell F5 down to F12.

3. Create a data bar visualization for cells F5:F12 with the *Show data bar only* option checked.

4. Widen column F to display a "quick chart".

Total Sales	
70,168.10	
24,938.06	
31,883.54	
49,902.95	

note

A more expert solution using mixed cell references

In my classroom courses I always teach this lesson as presented here.

I like to keep things simple by solving the problem using a simple formula.

The reason I do this is that many students find mixed cell references challenging (the subject of: *Lesson 3-12: Understand mixed cell references*).

If you completely understood *Lesson 3-12: Understand mixed cell references* you might find it interesting to solve this problem in a more efficient way.

You can apply a single mixed cell reference to all four columns in a single operation:

1. Select columns A to D.

2. Click: Home→Styles→ Conditional Formatting→ New Rule...

3. Select: *Use a formula to determine which cells to format.*

4. Type this formula (note the use of a mixed cell reference) into the text box:

   =$C1="USA"

5. Click the *Format...* button.

6. Click the *Fill* tab and select a light orange color for the conditional fill.

7. Click *OK* and *OK* again.

Lesson 4-18: Create a formula driven conditional format

While the built-in conditional format options are very powerful, you will occasionally have a conditional format requirement that is not catered for.

For example, I've lost count of the number of times I have been asked if it is possible to highlight an entire row, rather than a single cell within a row, based upon the value in one of the row's cells.

This lesson will show you how to achieve this using a formula-driven conditional format.

1 Open *Sales Summary First Quarter 2016* from your sample files folder.

   Your challenge will be to highlight the entire row when the *Country* column contains the value: *USA*.

2 Apply a conditional format to column C to change the background color to light orange when the cell contains the text: USA.

   1. Select column C and apply a *Text that Contains...* conditional formatting rule, selecting *Custom Format* as the fill color:

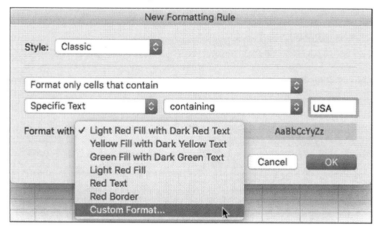

   This was covered in: *Lesson 4-15: Use simple conditional formatting.*

   2. Click the *Fill* tab and select a light orange color for the conditional fill.

   3. Click the *OK* button once, and then again, to close both dialogs.

   Every cell in column C that contains the text *USA* is now shaded light orange.

Sales Summary First Quarter 2016

	B	C	D
40	Familia Arquibaldo	Brazil	100.00
41	Hungry Coyote Import Store	USA	62.40
42	Hungry Coyote Import Store	USA	40.00
43	Wartian Herkku	Finland	146.00

3   Apply a formula-driven conditional format to column B so that the same rows are highlighted.

This is a lot more difficult than the simple conditional format applied to column C.

1. Select column B.

2. Click: Home→Styles→Conditional Formatting→New Rule…

   The *New Formatting Rule* dialog appears.

3. Select *Classic* from the *Style* drop-down menu.

4. Select *Use a formula to determine which cells to format* from the second drop-down menu.

5. Type the formula **=C1="USA"** into the formula text box.

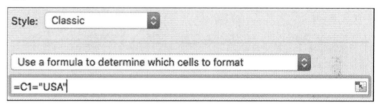

See sidebar for a discussion of this formula.

6. Click *Custom Format* from the *Format with* menu, then the *Fill* tab and apply the same light orange fill color.

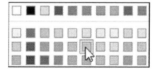

7. Click the *OK* button once, and then again, to close both dialogs.

   Both columns now have a light orange fill when the country is USA.

	A	B	C	D
40	14-Jan-16	Familia Arquibaldo	Brazil	100.00
41	15-Jan-16	Hungry Coyote Import Store	USA	62.40
42	15-Jan-16	Hungry Coyote Import Store	USA	40.00
43	16-Jan-16	Wartian Herkku	Finland	146.00

4   Apply the same formula-driven conditional format to columns A and D so that the whole row is highlighted.

	A	B	C	D
40	14-Jan-16	Familia Arquibaldo	Brazil	100.00
41	15-Jan-16	Hungry Coyote Import Store	USA	62.40
42	15-Jan-16	Hungry Coyote Import Store	USA	40.00
43	16-Jan-16	Wartian Herkku	Finland	146.00

5   Save your work as *Sales Summary First Quarter 2016-1*.

note

Why does the formula relate to cell C1?

At first it seems rather odd that you refer to cell C1 in the conditional formatting formula.

C1 is in the title row so how can this be right?

The answer is to be found in Excel's treatment of absolute and relative cell references (originally explained in: *Lesson 3-11: Understand absolute and relative cell references*).

Excel regards the cell reference to be relative to the first row in the selected range.

Since you selected an entire column, row 1 is the reference row used to adjust the formula for every other row within the column.

In other words, Excel will look at cell C2 when applying conditional formatting to row 2, C3 when applying to row 3... and so on.

This is exactly what you want to happen.

Lesson 4-19: Insert a Sparkline into a range of cells

Sparklines were introduced for the first time in Excel 2010. They solve a very common worksheet problem.

In *Lesson 4-17: Bring data alive with visualizations,* you discovered how visualizations can illustrate the differences between values in a single column of data (see example in sidebar).

In: *Session Five: Charts and Graphics,* you will discover Excel's ability to create fantastic charts of all descriptions. These are especially useful when your data has two dimensions (several columns per row). You'll create this chart:

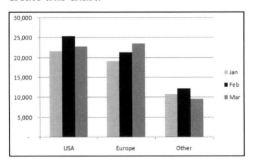

But imagine you had a large number of rows of two-dimensional data to compare. This is the case in the sample worksheet for this lesson, where there are 36 rows (one for each branch), each having six values (Jan-Jun):

	A	B	C	D	E	F	G	H
4	Country	Branch	Jan	Feb	Mar	Apr	May	Jun
5	USA	Chicago	671,185	359,811	745,471	685,637	- 16,562	711,009
6	USA	Dallas	708,157	276,972	227,227	482,136	377,175	198,273

The worksheet contains data for 36 branches and would produce a very confusing chart (with 36 data series, one for each branch):

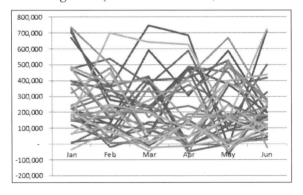

A *Sparkline* is a chart that can be inserted into a single cell, typically charting the values on its left-hand side.

Sparklines provide an elegant way to present users with a visual depiction of large two-dimensional data sets, even when they contain thousands of rows.

	A	B	C	D	E	F	G	H	I
4	Country	Branch	Jan	Feb	M			un	
5	USA	Chicago	671,185	359,811		**Sparklines**		711,009	
6	USA	Dallas	708,157	276,972				198,273	

First Half-Year Profit Report

1 Open *First Half-Year Profit Report* from your sample files folder.

2 Create a *Line Sparkline* in cell I5 that charts the data in cells C5:H5.

1. Click in cell I5.

2. Click: Insert→Sparklines→Sparklines→Line.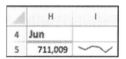

The *Insert Sparklines* dialog appears.

3. Click in the *Select a data range for the sparklines* box and then select cells C5:H5

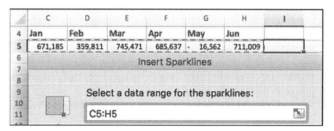

4. Click the *OK* button.

A Sparkline appears in cell I5:

	H	I
4	Jun	
5	711,009	⌇

3 AutoFill the Sparkline to cells I6:I40.

You learned how to do this in: *Lesson 2-14: Use AutoFill for text and numeric series.*

You can now see how Sparklines visualize each branch's performance in a way that is beyond the scope of Visualizations and Charts.

	A	B	C	D	E	F	G	H	I
4	Country	Branch	Jan	Feb	Mar	Apr	May	Jun	
5	USA	Chicago	671,185	359,811	745,471	685,637 -	16,562	711,009	⌇
6	USA	Dallas	708,157	276,972	227,227	482,136	377,175	198,273	⌇
7	USA	Houston	468,592	358,841	426,955 -	2,625	86,518	96,686	⌇

4 Use the same technique to place a *Column Sparkline* in cells J5:J40 that charts the same data range (C5:H5).

5 Use the same technique to place a *Win/Loss Sparkline* in cells K5:K40 that charts the same data range (C5:H5).

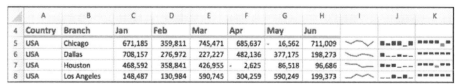

	A	B	C	D	E	F	G	H	I	J	K
4	Country	Branch	Jan	Feb	Mar	Apr	May	Jun			
5	USA	Chicago	671,185	359,811	745,471	685,637 -	16,562	711,009	⌇	▪▄▪▪_▪	▪▪▪▪▪_▪
6	USA	Dallas	708,157	276,972	227,227	482,136	377,175	198,273	⌇	▪_▄▄_	▪▪▪▪▪▪▪
7	USA	Houston	468,592	358,841	426,955 -	2,625	86,518	96,686	⌇	▪▄▪_ _	▪▪▪_▪▪
8	USA	Los Angeles	148,487	130,984	590,745	304,259	590,249	199,373	⌇	_ _▪_▪	▪▪▪▪▪▪

The *Column Sparkline* is very similar to the *Line Sparkline* but represents data as a bar chart.

Notice how the *Win/Loss Sparkline* enables you to see at a glance that Chicago and Houston had one loss-making month while Dallas and Los Angeles made a profit every month.

6 Save your work as *First Half Year Profit Report-1*.

Lesson 4-20: Apply a common vertical axis and formatting to a Sparkline group

Consider the following column Sparklines:

	A	B	C	D	E	F	G	H	J
4	Country	Branch	Jan	Feb	Mar	Apr	May	Jun	
5	USA	Chicago	671,185	359,811	745,471	685,637 -	16,562	711,009	▐▄▐▐_▐
28	UK	Manchester	180,988	209,763	203,761	2,201	165,328	124,392	▐▐▐_▐▄

If you only looked at the sparklines (and not the values) you'd guess that Manchester made more profit in the first three months than Chicago.

A glance at the actual profit values shows that Chicago actually made about three times more profit than Manchester.

The *Column* Sparklines are misleading because, by default, Excel only considers each row's values when setting the *Maximum* and *Minimum* values for the bars (also called the *Vertical Axis* values).

In this lesson you'll change this behavior so that the size of the bars gives a true indication of each branch's profit relative to the other branches in the list.

1 Open *First Half-Year Profit Report-1* from your sample files folder (if it isn't already open).

2 Delete columns I and K so that only the Column Sparklines remain.

> You learned how to do this in: *Lesson 3-1: Insert and delete rows and columns*. Removing the two other Sparklines will help to focus upon the *Column Sparkline*.

3 Set a common Maximum and Minimum value for all Sparklines.

1. Click on any of the Sparklines in column I.

   Notice that a thin blue line has appeared around all of the Sparklines in column I. This happens because Excel views all of the Sparklines as a *Sparkline Group*. This means that, when you use any of the *Sparkline Design* tools on the Ribbon, the settings will apply to all Sparklines in the group.

2. Click: Sparkline→Group→Axis.

   The *Axes* dialog appears.

3. Click the *Vertical* tab.

4. Click *Same for all sparklines* under *Minimum value*.

5. Click *Same for all sparklines* under *Maximum value*.

6. Click the *OK* button.

7. Notice the change in the Chicago and Manchester Sparklines:

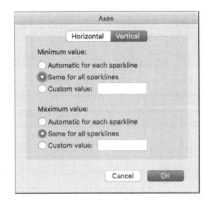

First Half-Year Profit
Report-1

---

note

You can change the size of a Sparkline by re-sizing the cell that contains it

In the lessons in this session, the Sparkline cells have been left at their default size for neatness and to keep the worksheet compact.

If you resize a cell that contains a Sparkline it will automatically resize to fill the cell:

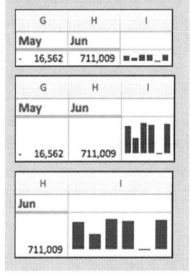

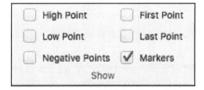

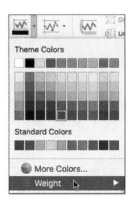

	F	G	H	I
4	Apr	May	Jun	
5	685,637 -	16,562	711,009	▮▬▮▮_▮
28	2,201	165,328	124,392	▬▬▬__▬▬

It is now clear, from looking at the bars alone, that in every month (except May) Manchester produced far less profit than Chicago.

4   Explore Sparkline formatting options.

The *Sparkline Design* tab on the Ribbon provides many ways in which you can change the appearance of a group of Sparklines. Try experimenting with them.

1. Use the *Show* and *Marker Color* options.

    The *Show* check boxes allow you to apply a chosen color to any of the following points on a Sparkline.

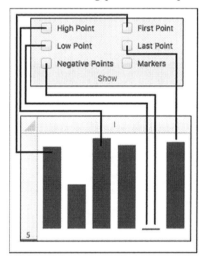

    You can choose a color for each of the options you check from the Sparkline→Style→Marker Color drop down.

2. Choose a new *Sparkline Style* from the *Style* gallery.

    Styles allow you to change the color scheme for your Sparkline. Note that the styles use theme colors and will change if you change the current theme. (You learned about themes in: *Lesson 4-9: Understand themes*).

3. Change the *Sparkline Type* to *Line* by clicking: Sparkline→Type→Line.

4. Add *Markers*.

    Click: Sparkline→Show→Markers.

    When the *Sparkline Type* is *Line*, you are able to select the *Markers* option in the *Show* group. Each data point on the Sparkline is then marked with a dot.

5. Click: Sparkline Design→Style→Sparkline Color.

6. Change the line color.

7. Change the line thickness by clicking *Weight*.

5   Close *First Year Profit Report-1* without saving.

Lesson 4-21: Apply a date axis to a Sparkline group and format a single Sparkline

Sometimes you will encounter data that is attached to dates with uneven time intervals. Here's some of the sample data for this lesson:

	A	B	C	D	E	F	G	H
1	Number of Rings to Answer Phone Survey							
2								
3	Country	Branch	01-Mar-16	03-Mar-16	04-Mar-16	07-Mar-16	08-Mar-16	09-Mar-16
4	USA	Chicago	3	1	1	2	3	2
5	USA	Dallas	2	3	1	3	2	1
6	USA	Houston	10	8	11	7	11	5
7	USA	Los Angeles	1	3	2	3	3	1

This company has a policy that the telephone should be answered within three rings. To make sure the staff are hitting this target, head office phones each branch occasionally and records the number of rings taken to answer. You can see that Chicago, Dallas and Los Angeles are doing well, but Houston is performing well below standard.

Head office don't phone every day – only when they have time to do so. This means that they didn't phone at all on 2nd, 5th and 6th March.

By default, a Sparkline will assume that the data is at equal intervals and chart like this:

	C	D	E	F	G	H	I
3	01-Mar-16	03-Mar-16	04-Mar-16	07-Mar-16	08-Mar-16	09-Mar-16	
4	3	1	1	2	3	2	▪_ _ _ ▪▪ ▪ _
5	2	3	1	3	2	1	_ ▪ ▪ _ ▪ ▪ _ _
6	10	8	11	7	11	5	▪ _ ▪ _ ▪ _ ▪ _
7	1	3	2	3	3	1	_ ▪ _ ▪ ▪▪ _

… but you'd like the Sparklines to have a common vertical axis and show a gap for the missing dates like this:

	E	F	G	H	I
3	04-Mar-16	07-Mar-16	08-Mar-16	09-Mar-16	
4	1	2	3	2	▪ _ _ _ ▪▪▪
5	1	3	2	1	_ ▪ ▪ _ ▪▪ _
6	11	7	11	5	▪ _ ▪▪ _ ▪ _
7	2	3	3	1	_ ▪ ▪ _ ▪▪ _

1 Open *Phone Survey* from your sample files folder.

2 Insert a Column Sparkline in cell I4 to chart data in cells C4:H4 and AutoFill it to the end of the range.

   You learned how to do this in: *Lesson 4-19: Insert a Sparkline into a range of cells.*

3 Set the *Vertical Axis Minimum Value* and *Vertical Axis Maximum Value* to be the same for all Sparklines.

   You learned how to do this in: *Lesson 4-20: Apply a common vertical axis and formatting to a Sparkline group.*

   Your worksheet should now look like this:

Phone Survey

	D	E	F	G	H	I
3	03-Mar-16	04-Mar-16	07-Mar-16	08-Mar-16	09-Mar-16	
4	1	1	2	3	2	_ _ _ _ _
5	3	1	3	2	1	_ _ _ _ _
6	8	11	7	11	5	▮▬▮▬▮▬
7	3	2	3	3	1	_ _ _ _ _

note

Options for worksheets that contain Hidden and Empty cells

In:

Lesson 5-14: Chart non-contiguous source data by hiding rows and columns

And:

Lesson 5-16: Deal with empty data points

… you will learn the concept of hidden rows and columns, and also learn how to use Excel's *Hidden and Empty Cells* dialog.

You'll then also be able to use these options when you add a Sparkline to worksheets that contain empty cells or hidden rows and columns.

4   Set the *Sparkline Date Range* to C3:H3.

1. Click any Sparkline in column I to select the Sparkline group.

2. Click:

   Sparkline→Group→Axis.

   The *Axes* dialog appears.

3. Click *Date axis* and click in the *Select the date range for the sparkline* box.

4. Select cells C3:H3 with the mouse.

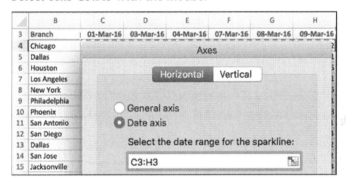

5. Click the *OK* button.

   The Sparklines are now shown with gaps for the missing dates:

	E	F	G	H	I
3	04-Mar-16	07-Mar-16	08-Mar-16	09-Mar-16	
4	1	2	3	2	▮ _ _ ▬▮▬
5	1	3	2	1	_ ▮_ ▮▬_
6	11	7	11	5	▮ ▬▮ _▮_
7	2	3	3	1	_ ▮▬ ▮▮_

5   Format the *Houston* Sparkline (in cell I6) so that all bars are orange.

To format a single Sparkline it is necessary to *Ungroup* the Sparklines. When Sparklines are ungrouped it is possible to format them individually.

1. Click in cell I6.

2. Click: Sparkline→Group→Ungroup.

3. Click:

   Sparkline→Style→Sparkline Color→
   Orange Accent 2

   The *Houston* Sparkline is now colored orange, while all other Sparklines remain blue.

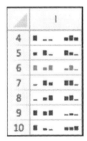

6   Save your work as *Phone Survey-1*.

Lesson 4-22: Use the format painter

The format painter is one of the most useful tools in Microsoft Office.

You can use the format painter in PowerPoint, Word and all other Office applications.

I find that at least half of the experienced Excel users who attend my classroom courses have never discovered the format painter. I love it when they gasp in amazement at the enormous amount of time and effort they will save in future when using this tool.

In this lesson you're going to take a worksheet that is partially formatted and use the format painter to quickly copy formatting information (as opposed to values) from one cell to another.

1 Open *Sales Report-FP* from your sample files folder.

This worksheet has been partially formatted.

	A	B	C	D	E
1	Sales Report - 6 Months ended March 2016				
2					
3	Sales By Country			Sales by Category	
4	Country	Total Sales		Category	Total Sales
5	Argentina	762.6		Beverages	70168.1
6	Austria	33462.58		Condiments	24938.055
7	Belgium	6109.48		Confections	31883.54
8	Brazil	20524.42		Dairy Products	49902.95
9	Canada	21306.29		Grains/Cereals	19570.36
10	Denmark	16658.8		Meat/Poultry	35767.63
11	Finland	5525		Produce	17109.18
12	France	26155.54		Seafood	17304.51
13	Germany	28361.38		Grand Total	266644.325
14	Ireland	6157.755			

2 Apply the comma style to all of the values in column B.

This was covered in: *Lesson 4-3: Format numbers using built-in number formats.*

Values are now formatted with two decimal places and a thousand comma separator.

	A	B
9	Canada	21,306.29
10	Denmark	16,658.80
11	Finland	5,525.00

3 Use the format painter to copy formatting from the values in column B to the ranges E5:E13 and E20:E26.

1. Click any value in column B.

2. Click: Home→Clipboard→Format.

The cursor shape changes to a paint brush.

Sales Report-FP

note

AutoFill and Paste are also able to match formatting in the same way as the format painter

The format painter is the fastest and most convenient way to match formatting when you only have to deal with a small range of cells.

Sometimes you'll need to match formatting in very large ranges containing thousands of cells. This would take a long time using the format painter but can be quickly achieved by using *AutoFill,* or by using *Paste* along with the skills you learned in: *Lesson 2-8: AutoSelect a range of cells.*

AutoFill

AutoFill options were covered in depth in: *Lesson 2-16: Use AutoFill options.*

When you AutoFill using a right-click and drag (or AutoFill and then look at the Smart tag options) you'll notice that there's a *Fill Formatting Only* option.

Paste

Copy and Paste were covered in depth in: *Lesson 3-3: Cut, copy and paste.*

When you paste there's also a *Formatting* option in the *Paste Options.*

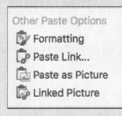

3. Click and drag across cells E5:E13.

   The format of cells E5:E13 changes to match those of the values in column B.

	D	E
4	Category	Total Sales
5	Beverages	70,168.10
6	Condiments	24,938.06

4. Click on any value in column B.

5. Click: Home→Clipboard→Format.

6. Drag across cells E20:E26.

   All values in this worksheet are now formatted with the comma style.

4 Use the format painter to copy formatting from cell A3 to cells D3 and D18.

This time you will use the format painter in a slightly different way.

If you double-click the format painter icon a *sticky format painter* appears. This will stay switched on until you click the format painter icon again to switch it off.

1. Click on cell A3 to make it the active (source) cell.

2. Double-click: Home→Clipboard→Format.

   | Format |

   The cursor shape changes to a paint brush.

3. Click cell D3. The format now matches cell A3, but the cursor remains the same.

4. Click cell D18. The format now matches cell A3, but the cursor remains the same.

5. Click: Home→Clipboard→Format to switch off the format painter. The cursor reverts to the normal shape.

5 Copy formatting from cell A4 to cells D4:E4 and D19:E19 using the format painter.

6 Apply the *Total* style to cell B26.

This was covered in: *Lesson 4-10: Use cell styles and change themes.*

7 Copy the total style from cell B26 to cells E13 and E26 using the format painter.

8 Save your work as *Sales Report-FP-1.*

Lesson 4-23: Rotate text

1   Open *Top 20 Films* from your sample files folder.

2   Insert a new column to the left of column A.

This was covered in: *Lesson 3-1: Insert and delete rows and columns.*

3   Cut and paste the contents of cell B1 to cell A1.

This was covered in: *Lesson 3-3: Cut, copy and paste.*

4   Apply the *Title* style to cell A1, the *Heading 2* style to cells A3:E3 and the *Heading 4* style to cell D25.

This was covered in: *Lesson 4-10: Use cell styles and change themes.*

5   Type: **Over 1,500M** into cell A4, **Over 1,100M** into cell A9 and **Over 1,000M** into cell A18.

6   Make column A slightly wider so that all text in the column is visible.

This was covered in: *Lesson 2-9: Re-size rows and columns.*

7   Select cells A4:A8.

	A	B	C
3		Title	Year
4	Over 1,500M	Avatar	2009
5		Titanic	1997
6		Jurassic World	2015
7		The Avengers	2012
8		Furious 7	2015
9	Over 1,100M	Avengers: Age of Ultron	2015

8   Merge the selected cells.

This was covered in: *Lesson 4-6: Merge cells, wrap text and expand/collapse the formula bar.*

9   Rotate the text through ninety degrees.

1.   Click: Home→Alignment→Orientation.

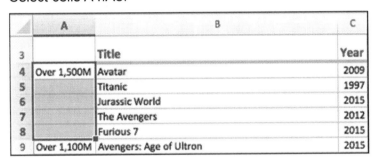

2.   Select *Rotate Text Up* from the drop-down list.

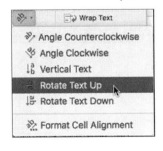

---

note

Other ways to rotate text

You can also rotate text using the *Format Cells* dialog, though you'll nearly always find the Ribbon method faster and more convenient.

The *Format Cells* dialog is slightly more powerful as it allows you to rotate text by any angle.

1.   Right-click a cell or range and click *Format Cells* from the shortcut menu.

2.   Click the *Alignment* tab.

3.   In the *Orientation* pane either type in the number of degrees of rotation or click and drag the red diamond to set it visually.

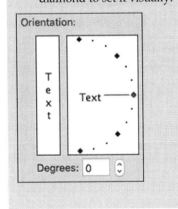

Top 20 Films

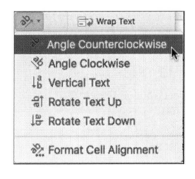

	A
3	**Title**
4	Avatar
5	Titanic
6	Jurassic World
7	The Avengers
8	Furious 7
9	Avengers: Age of
10	Harry Potter and
11	Frozen
12	Iron Man 3
13	Minions
14	Transformers: Da
15	The Lord of the R
16	Skyfall
17	Transformers: Ag
18	The Dark Knight F
19	Pirates of the Car
20	Toy Story 3
21	Pirates of the Car
22	Jurassic Park
23	Star Wars Episode

(sidebar labels: Over 1,500M, Over 1,100M, Over 1,000M)

10 Merge and rotate the text in cells A9:A17 and A18:A23.

Your worksheet should now look like the sidebar.

11 Select cells A4:A18 and set the horizontal alignment to *center* and the vertical alignment to *middle.*

This was covered in: *Lesson 4-5: Horizontally align the contents of cells* and *Lesson 4-8: Vertically align the contents of cells.*

12 Apply the *Heading 4* style to cells A4:A18.

13 AutoFit cells A4:A18 so that they are just wide enough for the text.

This was covered in: *Lesson 2-9: Re-size rows and columns.*

14 Apply the *40% Accent 3* style to cell A4.

This was covered in: *Lesson 4-10: Use cell styles and change themes.*

Note that the cell reference for the old range A4:A8 is now the single cell reference A4.

15 Apply the *40% Accent 6* style to cell A9.

16 Apply the *40% Accent 2* style to cell A18.

17 Re-size row 3 so that it is about three times the normal height.

18 Rotate the text in row 3 through 45 degrees.

1. Select row 3.

2. Click: Home→Alignment→Orientation [icon] → Angle Counterclockwise.

19 Make columns C and E a little wider.

	A	B	C	D	E
1		Top 20 Films By USA Box Office Takings			
2					
3		*Title*	*Year*	*Studio*	*Gross**
4		Avatar	2009	20th Century Fox	2,788
5		Titanic	1997	20th Century Fox/Paramount	2,187
6		Jurassic World	2015	Universal	1,669
7		The Avengers	2012	Walt Disney	1,520
8		Furious 7	2015	Universal	1,515
9		Avengers: Age of Ultron	2015	Walt Disney	1,405
10		Harry Potter and the Deathly Hallows – Part 2	2011	Warner Bros.	1,342
11		Frozen	2013	Walt Disney	1,280
12		Iron Man 3	2013	Walt Disney	1,215
13		Minions	2015	Universal	1,157
14		Transformers: Dark of the Moon	2011	Paramount Pictures	1,124
15		The Lord of the Rings: The Return of the King	2003	New Line Cinema	1,120
16		Skyfall	2012	MGM/Columbia	1,109
17		Transformers: Age of Extinction	2014	Paramount	1,104
18		The Dark Knight Rises	2012	Warner Bros.	1,085
19		Pirates of the Caribbean: Dead Man's Chest	2006	Buena Vista Pictures	1,066
20		Toy Story 3	2010	Walt Disney	1,063
21		Pirates of the Caribbean: On Stranger Tides	2011	Walt Disney	1,046
22		Jurassic Park	1993	Universal	1,030
23		Star Wars Episode I: The Phantom Menace	1999	20th Century Fox	1,027
24					
25				*USA Box office takings in millions of dollars	

(sidebar labels within table: Over 1,500M, Over 1,100M, Over 1,000M)

20 Save your work as *Top 20 Films-1.*

Session 4: Exercise

1   Open *House Mortgage* from your sample files folder.

2   Merge and center cells B3:J3.

3   Apply the *Title* style to cell A1, the *Heading 1* style to cell B3, and the *Heading 3* style to cells A4:J4 and A10:C10.

4   Apply the *Heading 4* style to cells A5:A8 and cells A11:A16.

5   Apply the *Percentage* style to cells B4:J4.

6   Apply the *Comma* style to cells B5:J8.

7   Apply the *Percentage* style to cells B11:C16 and then increase decimals to one place.

8   Type the word *Average* into cell A17 and use the *Format Painter* to match the formatting to that of the cell above (A16).

9   Horizontally right-align the text in cell A17.

10   Use *AutoSum* to place an *Average* function into cells B17 and C17.

11   Place a thin black border beneath cells A16:C16.

12   Apply a *20% Accent 1* cell style to cells B4:J4 and B10:C10.

13   Change the theme to *Celestial*.

14   Save your work as *House Mortgage-1*.

	A	B	C	D	E	F	G	H	I	J
1	House Mortgage Monthly Payments - 25 year term									
2										
3						Interest rate				
4	House Value	2%	3%	4%	5%	6%	7%	8%	9%	10%
5	50000	211.93	237.11	263.92	292.30	322.15	353.39	385.91	419.60	454.35
6	100000	423.85	474.21	527.84	584.59	644.30	706.78	771.82	839.20	908.70
7	150000	635.78	711.32	791.76	876.89	966.45	1,060.17	1,157.72	1,258.79	1,363.05
8	200000	847.71	948.42	1,055.67	1,169.18	1,288.60	1,413.56	1,543.63	1,678.39	1,817.40
9										
10	Historical Base/Fed. Fund Rates	UK	USA							
11	1990	14.8%	0.07							
12	1995	6.7%	0.0583							
13	2000	6.0%	0.0624							
14	2005	4.7%	0.0322							
15	2010	0.5%	0.0018							
16	2014	0.5%	0.009							
17	Average	5.5%	3.9%							

House Mortgage

If you need help slide the page to the left

Session 4: Exercise answers

These are the questions that students find the most difficult to answer:

Q 13	Q 11	Q 10	Q 8
1. Click Page Layout→Themes→Themes→Celestial. This was covered in: *Lesson 4-10: Use cell styles and change themes.*	1. Select cells A16:C16. 2. Click: Home→Font→Borders→ Bottom Border. This was covered in: *Lesson 4-11: Add borders and lines.*	1. Select cells B17:C17. 2. Click: Home→Editing→ AutoSum→Average 3. Press the **<Enter>** key. This was covered in: *Lesson 2-11: Use AutoSum to quickly calculate averages.*	1. Click in cell A16. 2. Click: Home→Clipboard→ Format 3. Click in cell A17. This was covered in: *Lesson 4-22: Use the format painter.*

If you have difficulty with the other questions, here are the lessons that cover the relevant skills:

1   Refer to: Lesson 1-7: Download the sample files and open/navigate a workbook.

2   Refer to: Lesson 4-6: Merge cells, wrap text and expand/collapse the formula bar.

3   Refer to: Lesson 4-10: Use cell styles and change themes.

4   Refer to: Lesson 4-10: Use cell styles and change themes.

5,6,7 Refer to: Lesson 4-3: Format numbers using built-in number formats.

9   Refer to: Lesson 4-5: Horizontally align the contents of cells.

11   Refer to: Lesson 4-3: Format numbers using built-in number formats.

12   Refer to: Lesson 4-10: Use cell styles and change themes.

14   Refer to: Lesson 1-8: Save a workbook to a local file.

5

Session Five: Charts and Graphics

> A picture is worth a thousand words.
>
> *Frederick R. Barnard in "Printers' Ink", 8th Dec 1921.*

In this session you'll learn to present your data in a chart. You'll also learn some valuable "tricks of the trade" to present your data in the most effective way.

Session Objectives

By the end of this session you will be able to:

- Understand chart types, layouts and styles
- Create a simple chart with two clicks
- Move, re-size, copy and delete a chart
- Create a chart using the Recommended Charts feature
- Add and remove chart elements using Quick Layout
- Apply a pre-defined chart style and color set
- Manually format a chart element
- Format 3-D elements and add drop shadows
- Move, re-size, add, position and delete chart elements
- Change a chart's source data
- Assign non-contiguous source data to a chart
- Understand Data Series and Categories
- Change source data using the Select Data Source dialog tools
- Chart non-contiguous source data by hiding rows and columns
- Create a chart with numerical axes
- Deal with empty data points
- Add data labels to a chart
- Highlight specific data points with color and annotations
- Add gridlines and scale axes
- Emphasize data by manipulating pie charts
- Create a chart with two vertical axes
- Create a combination chart containing different chart types
- Add a trend line
- Add a gradient fill to a chart background
- Create your own chart templates

Lesson 5-1: Understand chart types, layouts and styles

The Excel designers noted that there are three things that control the design of a chart:

Chart Type

There are many different *types* of chart. The most common are: *Column Charts*, *Line Charts* and *Pie Charts*.

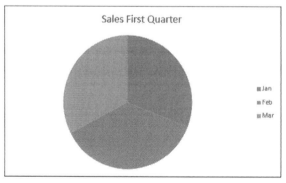

You'll discover how to choose a suitable *Chart Type* in: *Lesson 5-2: Create a simple chart with two clicks.*

Chart Layout

The layout of a chart can be thought of as a list of the *elements* that a chart contains.

Elements are artifacts such as a *Title, Axis Titles* or *Legend*.

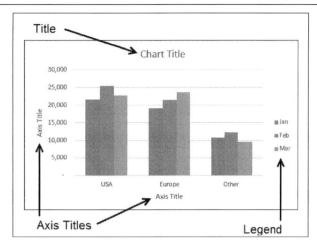

In: *Lesson 5-5: Add and remove chart elements using Quick Layout,* you'll discover how to quickly select a group of common elements for a chart.

Chart Style

The *Chart Style* determines the font, color and positioning of each chart element. Here are two charts that have an identical *Type* and *Layout* but have different styles:

You can see that both charts are of the same type (*Clustered Column*), and that both have the same elements (that include the *Axis Titles, Chart Title* and *Legend* elements).

The differences in appearance (colors, shading of bars, fonts used and position of legend) are collectively referred to as the chart's *Style.*

You'll learn how to change a chart's style in: *Lesson 5-6: Apply a pre-defined chart style and color set.*

tip

You can create a chart without selecting any data

When your data and labels form a complete range (as is the case in this lesson) you don't need to select the data.

If you simply click anywhere within the range and then click:

Insert→Charts→...

Excel will assume that you want to chart the entire range and select it for you.

note

The keyboard shortcut to create a chart

Excel uses the keyboard shortcut <Fn>+<F11> as the shortcut to create a chart, but it's unlikely that it will work if you try it.

The reason this doesn't work is that it conflicts with one of the default keyboard shortcuts in macOS (OS X).

The only way to enable this to work is to disable the F11 keyboard shortcut within your Mac's System Preferences.

important

Charts are dynamic

If the values underpinning a chart change, the chart will instantly change to represent the new values.

World Sales

Lesson 5-2: Create a simple chart with two clicks

1 Open *World Sales* from your sample files folder.

This is a very simple worksheet containing January, February and March sales data for three regions.

	A	B	C	D
1	Month	USA	Europe	Other
2	Jan	21,600	19,200	10,800
3	Feb	25,400	21,400	12,200
4	Mar	22,800	23,600	9,600

2 Select all of the values and all of the labels (cells A1:D4).

When Excel creates a chart, it needs both values and labels. For this reason, you must always select the labels *as well as* the values before you create your chart.

Missing the labels is one of the most common errors in my classroom courses.

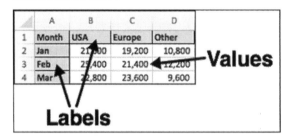

3 Click: Insert→Charts→Insert Column or Bar Chart and examine the charts in the gallery.

The graphics in the gallery give you an idea of how each chart will look when it is displayed on the worksheet.

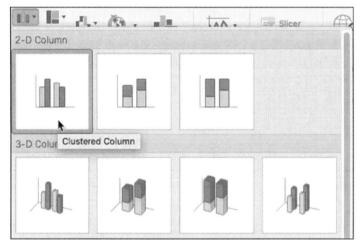

4 Click the left-most 2-D Column chart (the *Clustered Column* chart).

In just two clicks you have created a very presentable chart.

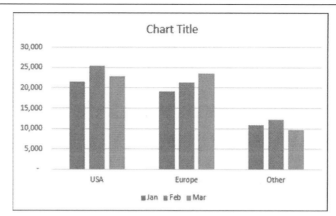

note

Changing the chart type of an existing chart

You may create a chart but later decide that you really need a different chart type.

For example, you might create a *column chart*, but later decide you would have preferred a *pie chart* or *line chart*.

To change the type of an existing chart:

1. Right-click on the chart.

2. Click: *Change Chart Type* from the shortcut menu.

Because you have only specified the chart *Type*, Excel has chosen a default *Layout* and *Style* for you. You'll learn how to change these default choices later in this session.

5   Understand chart activation.

In this example the worksheet only contains one chart.

It is possible that a worksheet will contain more than once chart.

For this reason, you need to indicate to Excel which chart you want to work on. To do this the chart needs to be *activated.*

To activate a chart, you simply click anywhere inside the chart.

When the chart is activated two things happen:

1. The *Chart Design* and *Format* tabs appear on the Ribbon:

2. A frame (with sizing handles) appears around the chart:

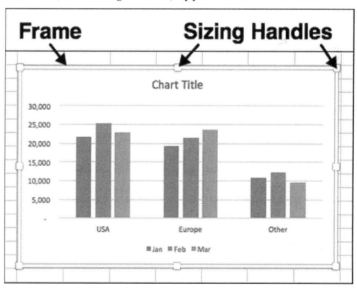

6   Save your work as *World Sales-1.*

Lesson 5-3: Move, re-size, copy and delete a chart

1   Open *World Sales-1* from your sample files folder (if it isn't already open).

2   Move the chart to a different position on screen.

    1.   Click just inside the border of the chart to activate it.

        When the chart is activated you will see a frame and corner handles around it.

        Excel also displays the *Chart Design* and *Format* tabs.

    2.   Hover with the mouse cursor just inside the border of the selected chart until you see the four-headed arrow cursor shape.

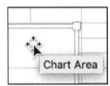

    3.   Click and drag the chart to the required position.

3   Re-size the chart.

    1.   Click just inside the border of the chart to activate it.

    2.   Hover over one of the corner or side sizing handles on the edges of the chart until you see the two-headed arrow cursor shape.

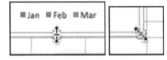

    3.   When you see the two-headed arrow cursor shape, click and drag to re-size the chart.

        If you hold down the **<Shift>** key as you click-and drag one of the corners of the chart, the perspective will remain constant (i.e. the chart will get proportionately wider as it gets taller).

4   Create a duplicate chart using copy and paste.

    1.   Click just inside the border of the chart to activate it.

    2.   Right-click on the border of the activated chart (just inside the border works too) and click *Copy* from the shortcut menu.

    3.   Right-click anywhere on the worksheet and click *Paste* from the shortcut menu to create the duplicate chart.

---

tip

The Selection Pane makes it easy to find charts

You can easily switch between charts by using the *Selection Pane*.

To make this task pane appear, first activate a chart and then click:

Format→Arrange→ Selection Pane

The Selection Pane shows all of the charts in your workbook and allows you to switch between them by simply clicking on the chart's name.

The Selection Pane also allows you to give your charts more meaningful names than the default *Chart 1, Chart 2* etc.

To rename a chart, double click its current name within the *Selection Pane.*

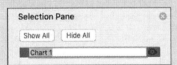

Meaningful names make it easier to find the chart that you are looking for.

It is also possible to show or hide charts by clicking the eyeball symbol to the right of the relevant chart.

World Sales-1

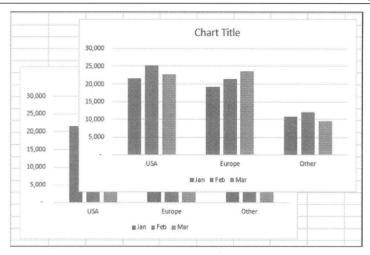

Note that even though the new chart is a duplicate, it is not linked to the original chart in any way. You can freely change any part of either chart and it will never affect the other.

5 Delete one of the charts.

1. Click just inside the border of either of the charts to activate it.

2. Press the **<Delete>** key on the keyboard.

6 Move the chart to its own chart worksheet.

Sometimes it is better to keep charts and data separate by placing a chart in its own *chart worksheet*. A chart worksheet is a special worksheet without any cells that can only contain a single chart.

1. Right-click just inside the border of the chart to activate it and then click *Move Chart...* from the shortcut menu.

2. Click the *New sheet* option button, name the new sheet **Sales Summary Chart** and click the *OK* button.

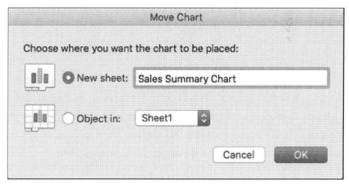

The chart is now displayed within its own dedicated chart worksheet.

7 Move the chart back to its original location.

1. Right-click just inside the border of the chart and click *Move Chart...* from the shortcut menu.

2. Click the *Object in* option button, choose *Sheet1* from the drop-down list and click the *OK* button.

8 Save your work as *World Sales-2*.

Lesson 5-4: Create a chart using the Recommended Charts feature

Excel is able to intelligently analyze your data and then try to guess which chart type will do the best job of representing it visually.

1 Open *Hawaii Temperature-1* from your sample files folder.

This worksheet contains temperature data for Honolulu, Hawaii (one of the nicest year-round climates in the world).

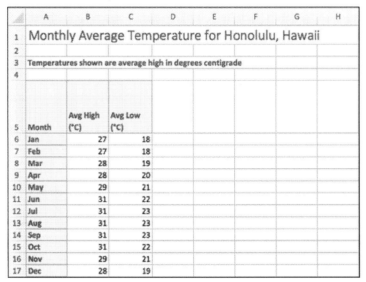

	Month	Avg High (°C)	Avg Low (°C)
1	Monthly Average Temperature for Honolulu, Hawaii		
2			
3	Temperatures shown are average high in degrees centigrade		
4			
5	Month	Avg High (°C)	Avg Low (°C)
6	Jan	27	18
7	Feb	27	18
8	Mar	28	19
9	Apr	28	20
10	May	29	21
11	Jun	31	22
12	Jul	31	23
13	Aug	31	23
14	Sep	31	23
15	Oct	31	22
16	Nov	29	21
17	Dec	28	19

2 Use *Recommended Charts* to select a suitable chart type.

1. Click anywhere inside the data (in a cell somewhere in the range A5:C17).

   You could also select the range A5:C17, but when you want to chart an entire range it is only necessary to select a single cell within the range.

2. Click: Insert→Charts→Recommended Charts.

   A gallery of recommended charts is displayed.

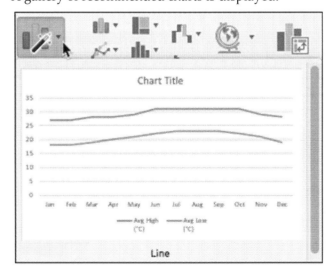

Hawaii Temperature-1

Notice that Excel's first choice for an appropriate chart type is a line chart.

This isn't a bad choice but perhaps Excel's second choice, the *Clustered Column* chart, will work better with this data.

3. Click the recommended *Clustered Column* chart.

A new *Clustered Column* chart appears.

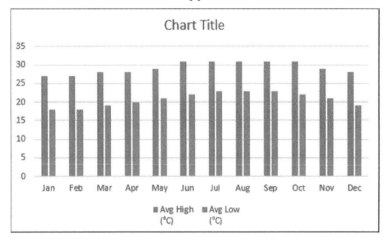

This chart does a very good job of visually showing the temperature range each month in Hawaii.

In: *Lesson 5-5: Add and remove chart elements using Quick Layout,* you'll learn how to change the *Chart Title* element to display appropriate text.

3   Save your work as *Hawaii Temperature-2.*

Lesson 5-5: Add and remove chart elements using Quick Layout

note

More about the horizontal and vertical axes

A chart normally shows category (non-numerical) data along the horizontal axis. The horizontal axis is also sometimes called the X axis.

The vertical axis normally contains numerical data. The vertical axis is also sometimes called the Y axis.

The chart used in this lesson has the non-numerical region categories (USA, Europe and Other) along the horizontal (or X) axis and numerical sales data along the vertical (or Y) axis.

The term *Layout* can be confusing. It is used to describe the *Elements* that a chart contains. For example, here is a simple chart containing only two elements:

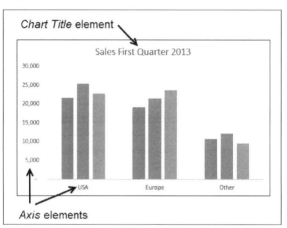

And here's a chart that contains four elements:

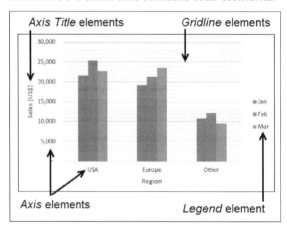

Some layouts also include a *Data Table* showing the source data for the chart:

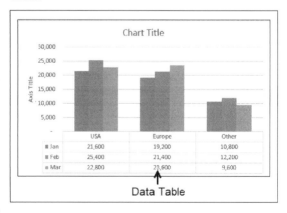

tip

Worksheet cells are more versatile than data tables

If you need to show data alongside an embedded chart, a data table isn't the best choice.

Placing an embedded chart adjacent to worksheet cells gives you far more formatting power.

Data tables can be useful when a chart is placed on its own chart sheet and you also need to show values.

World Sales-2

Don't confuse the *layout* (the elements that a chart contains) with the chart *style* (the colors and appearance of the chart elements).

In this lesson you will use Excel's *Quick Layout* feature to choose from nine common layouts with a single click.

1 Open *World Sales-2* from your sample files folder (if it isn't already open).

2 Change the *Chart Layout* to: *Layout 9*.

    1. Click just inside the border of the chart to activate it.

    2. Click: Chart Design→Chart Layouts→Quick Layout.

This gallery contains eleven pre-defined chart layouts. Each layout contains a group of elements.

Try clicking each layout to see how they affect your chart.

    3. Click: *Layout 9*.

This layout includes a *Chart Title* element, a *Legend* element, two *Axis* elements, two *Axis Title* elements and a *Gridlines* element.

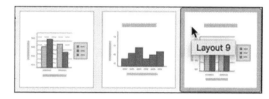

In: *Lesson 5-9: Move, re-size, add, position and delete chart elements*, you'll learn how to add elements one by one. You'll then appreciate how much faster it is to select all five elements with a single click instead of individually adding each one.

3 Click the *Chart Title* element and type: **Sales First Quarter**

If necessary, press the **<Delete>** key several times to remove the old chart title.

4 Click the *Vertical Axis Title* element and type: **Sales**

5 Click the *Horizontal Axis Title* element and type: **Region**

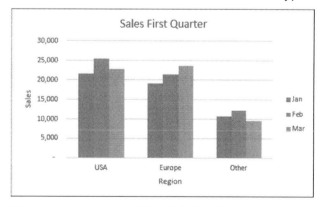

6 Save your work as: *World Sales-3.*

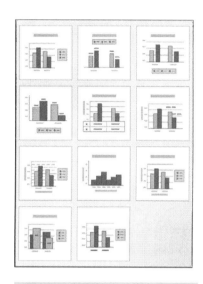

note

Use chart tips to discover chart element names

When you hover the mouse cursor over a chart element, the name of the element is displayed in a chart tip.

If this doesn't work on your machine, somebody has switched off the chart tips.

Here's how to switch them back on:

1. Click:

    →Excel→Preferences

2. Click *Chart*.

3. Make sure that *Show names of chart elements on rollover* is checked.

Lesson 5-6: Apply a pre-defined chart style and color set

1   Open *World Sales-3* from your sample files folder (if it isn't already open).

2   Change the chart style.

   1.   Click just inside the border of the chart to activate it.

   2.   Click: Chart Design→Chart Styles→
        Chart Styles Gallery.

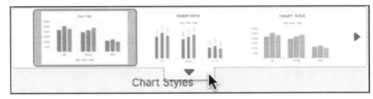

When you click the *Gallery* button 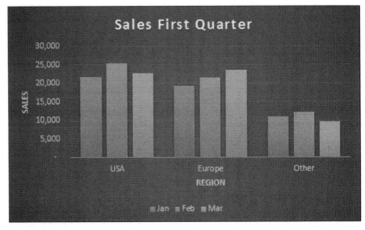 you are able to choose a new chart style from 14 pre-defined options. Each chart style uses theme colors, so the chart's appearance will change if you later change the workbook's theme (you learned about themes in: *Lesson 4-9: Understand themes*).

Try clicking the different styles to see how the appearance of your chart is affected.

   3.   Click a new chart style to change the appearance of your chart.

        In the example below, I have chosen *Style 8*.

![Sales First Quarter column chart showing Jan, Feb, Mar sales for USA, Europe, and Other regions]

3   Change the chart's color set.

In: *Lesson 4-9: Understand themes,* you learned that every theme has a related color set and that it is good practice to restrict colors to theme colors.

Excel provides a quick and convenient way to choose a new set of colors (from the current theme's color set) for your chart.

   1.   Click just inside the border of the chart to activate it.

   2.   Click: Chart Design→Chart Styles→Change Colors.

World Sales-3

A set of color palettes (each consisting of six colors) are displayed. All colors belong to the current theme (in this example, the default *Office* theme).

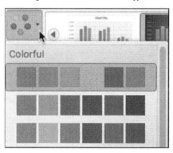

3. Click any of the color sets to select one. The new color set is applied to the chart.

4   Close the workbook without saving.

You want to stay with the original default style, so close this workbook without saving. The chart will then retain the default style.

note

Chart titles can display the contents of a specific worksheet cell

Normally you will simply type the text that you need directly into the *Chart Title* element.

It is also possible to link the *Chart Title* to a worksheet cell so that it displays whatever text is in the specified cell.

Here's how it is done:

1. Click the *Chart Title* element.

2. Click inside the formula bar.

3. Type: = to start the formula.

4. Click on cell A1 (or the worksheet cell containing the value that you want to be displayed).

5. Press the **<Enter>** key.

This will add a fully qualified cell reference such as:

=Sheet1!$A$1

This is required when you reference a cell from a *Chart Title* element. A simple reference such as:

=A1

…will not work.

You'll learn more about fully qualified cell references later, in: *Lesson 6-5: Create cross worksheet formulas.*

The contents of cell A1 are then displayed in the *Chart Title* element and will change whenever the text in cell A1 changes.

Lesson 5-7: Manually format a chart element

Up until now you've selected a pre-defined chart style and color set from a gallery.

Sometimes you may have a requirement that is not catered for within the selection of pre-defined styles offered by the *Chart Styles* gallery.

In this case you will need to manually format one or more chart elements.

Once you have the hang of how to format one element it becomes easy to work with any other element, because the options are broadly the same.

In this lesson you'll manually format the *Chart Title* element.

1   Open *World Sales-3* from your sample files folder (if it isn't already open).

2   Click the *Chart Title* element to select it.

A frame appears:

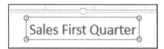

3   Right-click the *Chart Title* element and click *Format Chart Title…* from the shortcut menu.

The *Format Chart Title* task pane appears.

4   Apply a *Blue Accent 1* fill (background color) to the *Chart Title* element.

1. Click the *Fill & Line* icon in the *Format Chart Title* task pane.

2. Click the *Fill* option to display the fly-out menu.

3. Click the *Solid fill* option button.

4. Click the *Fill Color* icon.

5. Click the *Blue, Accent 1* fill color.

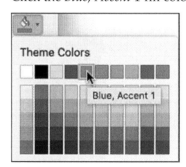

6. Drag the *Transparency* slider to the right to set the transparency to about 80%.

World Sales-3

Notice that the background color of the *Chart Title* element becomes lighter as you drag to the right, and darker as you drag to the left.

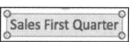

5   Apply a 1pt solid black border to the *Chart Title* element.

1.   Click the *Fill & Line* 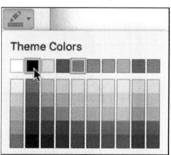 icon in the *Format Chart Title* task pane.

2.   Click the *Border* option to display the fly-out menu.

3.   In the *Border* section, click the *Solid Line* option button.

4.   Click the *Color* drop-down arrow and select a solid black color.

5.   In the *Border* section, set the *Width* to: **1 pt**

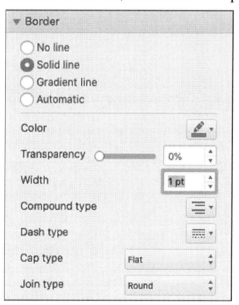

Notice that a solid black border has now been applied to the *Chart Title* element.

6   Close the *Format Chart Title* task pane.

7   Save your work as *World Sales-4.*

Lesson 5-8: Format 3-D elements and add drop shadows

The use of subtle shadows and 3-D formats will add a professional sheen to your work.

1   Open *World Sales-4* from your sample files folder (if it isn't already open) and click just inside the border of the chart to activate it.

2   Select the *Chart Title* element using the Ribbon.

Click: Format→Current Selection→
Chart Elements drop-down→Chart Title.

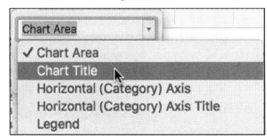

This is an alternative way to select chart elements. The drop-down shows every element in the currently selected chart.

Directly clicking on an element is usually faster, but there are some chart elements (such as gridlines) that can sometimes be difficult to select with the mouse.

Here are the elements available in the *Chart Elements* drop-down list for this chart:

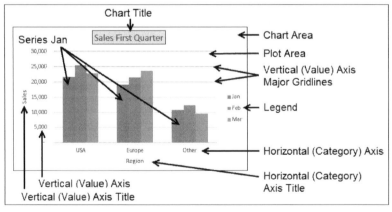

3   Display the *Format Chart Title* task pane.

Click: Format→Format→Format Pane.

This is an alternative way to bring up the *Format Chart Title* task pane.

4   Apply an *Offset Diagonal Bottom Right* shadow to the *Chart Title* element.

1.   Click the *Effects* ▣ icon in the *Format Chart Title* task pane.

note

More about data series

A data series is a group of data that is associated with a specific category.

For example, the *Series Jan* data series is a group of values, one for each of the categories *USA*, *Europe* and *Other*.

In this example there are three data series containing numerical data for each category.

Format Pane

Format

World Sales-4

2. Select *Shadow* from the four effects options.

3. Click the *Presets* icon.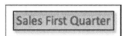

    While you can create your own shadows using the *Transparency, Size, Blur, Angle* and *Distance* sliders, you'll probably find that the presets will suffice. Presets will also maintain uniformity between different chart elements.

4. Click the *Offset Bottom Right* item in the shadow gallery.

    The effect is applied to the *Chart Title* element.

5   Apply a *Circle top bevel* 3D effect to the *Chart Title* element

Bevel effects make an element look like a button.

1. Click the *Effects* [icon] icon in the *Format Chart Title* task pane.

2. Select *3-D Format* from the four effects options.

3. Click the *Top Bevel* preset button to display the Top Bevel gallery and choose a *Circle* top bevel.

    Just like shadows, you'll probably find what you need in the 3-D presets rather than creating your own custom 3-D effects.

6   Use *Reset to Match Style* to restore the *Chart Title* element to its default state.

You've added a lot of fancy formatting to the *Chart Title* element but haven't really improved the appearance of the element.

Excel provides the *Reset to Match Style* feature to enable you to restore elements back to their original state.

1. Click on the *Chart Title* element to select it.

2. Click: Format→Current Selection→Reset to Match Style.

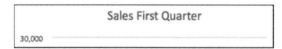

The *Chart Title* element is restored to its default state.

Sales First Quarter
30,000

7   Close the *Format Chart Title* task pane.

8   Save your work as *World Sales-5.*

Lesson 5-9: Move, re-size, add, position and delete chart elements

Several elements such as the *Chart Title*, *Legend* and *Horizontal/Vertical Axis Titles* can be moved by dragging and dropping.

In this lesson you'll see how to manually move these elements, and how to automatically restore them to their pixel-perfect locations if you change your mind.

You'll also manually add and remove single chart elements. Once you've got the hang of this you'll be able to custom design charts for any specific requirement.

1   Open *World Sales-5* from your sample files folder (if it isn't already open).

2   Click and drag the *Chart Title* element to the left-hand side of the chart.

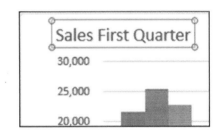

   1.   Click the *Chart Title* element to select it.

   2.   Hover the mouse cursor over the border of the *Chart Title* element until you see a four-headed arrow.

   3.   When you see the four-headed arrow, click and drag to move the element to the top left corner of the chart.

3   Move the *Chart Title* element back so that it is above the center of the chart.

You couldn't position this perfectly using the mouse.

   1.   Click on the *Chart Title* element to select it.

   2.   Click: Chart Design→Chart Layouts→
        Add Chart Element→Chart Title→Above Chart.

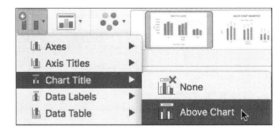

   The *Chart Title* element is restored to the center.

4   Delete the legend.

   1.   Click the *Legend* element to select it:

World Sales-5

2. Press the **<Delete>** key.

5   Display the legend at the top of the screen.

1. Select the chart.

2. Click: Chart Design→Chart Layouts→
    Add Chart Element→Legend→Top.

    The legend appears at the top of the chart.

6   Add a thin black border to the *Legend* element.

This was covered in: *Lesson 5-7: Manually format a chart element.*

7   Resize the *Legend* element so that it spans the entire width of the plot area.

1. Click the *Legend* element to select it. Notice the sizing handles on each corner and edge.

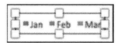

2. Hover over the sizing handle on the right-hand edge of the element. Notice that the cursor shape changes to a two-headed arrow.

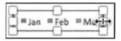

3. When you see the two-headed arrow, click and drag to re-size the legend so that it is the same width as the plot area. (You'll have to first re-size the right side and then the left).

8   Increase the size of the font within the *Legend* element.

1. Click the *Legend* element to select it.

2. Click: Home→Font→Font Size Drop-down.

3. Select *14 points* as the new text size.

    You'll often want to increase text sizes when you create charts for PowerPoint slides.

9   Save your work as *World Sales-6*.

Lesson 5-10: Change a chart's source data

You'll often want to chart a small number of columns from a much larger range (that may contain hundreds, or even thousands of columns).

You can do this by changing the chart's source data.

1   Open *World Sales-6* from your sample files folder (if it isn't already open).

2   Display the *Select Data Source* dialog.

note

Another way to display the Select Data Source dialog

You can also bring up the *Select Data Source* dialog from the Ribbon by clicking:

Chart Design→Data→ Select Data

1.   Right-click anywhere in the chart and click *Select Data...* from the shortcut menu.

The *Select Data Source* dialog appears.

Notice the *Chart data range* shown at the top of the dialog. For the moment this is all that I want you to concentrate upon.

The range is shown as: *Sheet1!$A$1:$D$4*.

This means the absolute range A1:D4 on the *Sheet1* worksheet.

(Absolute cell references were covered in*: Lesson 3-11: Understand absolute and relative cell references*).

3   Change the *Chart data range* so that only USA sales are charted.

The current range is A1:D4.

	A	B	C	D
1	Month	USA	Europe	Other
2	Jan	21,600	19,200	10,800
3	Feb	25,400	21,400	12,200
4	Mar	22,800	23,600	9,600

World Sales-6

If you change the range to A1:B4, the *Europe* and *Other* regions will be removed.

You could simply type the new reference into the *Chart data range* text box, but it is less error prone if you visually select the data with the mouse.

1. Delete the current contents of the *Chart data range* text box.

2. With the cursor still inside the empty *Chart data range* text box, click and drag with the mouse across cells A1:B4.

    The data range displays in both the *Chart data range* text box and as a marquee on the worksheet.

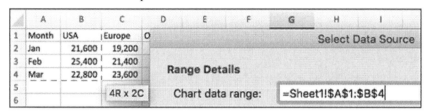

    It is very easy to mess up the data range in the text box. If you get an obscure error message, simply delete all of the contents of the *Chart data range* text box and re-select.

4   Click the *OK* button to view the new chart.

The chart changes to reflect the new data range.

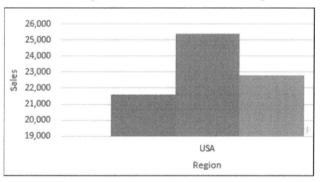

5   Change the *Chart data range* to A1:C4 to chart sales for the USA and Europe.

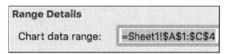

6   Click the *OK* button to view the new chart.

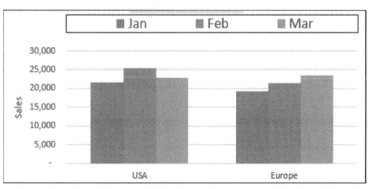

7   Save your work as *World Sales-7.*

Lesson 5-11: Assign non-contiguous source data to a chart

In the previous lesson it was easy to select the source data because it comprised of a single block (the word: *contiguous* is used for this type of range).

In this lesson you'll take things a little further by selecting data that isn't in a single block (i.e. non-contiguous data) to show sales for the *USA* and *Other* categories.

1 Open *World Sales-7* from your sample files folder (if it isn't already open).

2 Chart sales for all months in the *USA* and *Other* categories by changing the source data.

   1. Right-click in the plot area of the chart and click *Select Data* from the shortcut menu.

     The *Select Data Source* dialog appears.

   2. Delete the current contents of the *Chart data range* text box.

   3. With the cursor still inside the empty *Chart data range* text box, click and drag with the mouse across cells A1:B4.

   4. Release the mouse button.

   5. Hold down the **<Cmd>** key.

   6. Select the range D1:D4.

   7. Click the *OK* button.

     Selecting non-contiguous ranges was covered extensively in: *Lesson 2-7: Select non-contiguous cell ranges and view summary information.*

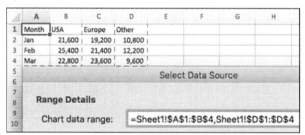

World Sales-7

3 Display the total sales for each month in column E.

Type the word: **Total** into cell E1 and then use AutoSum to place the totals for all regions into cells E2:E4.

AutoSum was covered in: *Lesson 2-3: Use AutoSum to quickly calculate totals.*

4   Change the source data so that only the *Total* category is charted.

1.   Right-click in the plot area of the chart.

2.   Click *Select Data* from the shortcut menu.

3.   Delete the current contents of the *Chart data range* text box.

4.   With the mouse cursor still inside the empty *Chart data range* text box, click and drag with the mouse across cells A1:A4.

5.   Hold down the **<Cmd>** key.

6.   Select cells E1:E4.

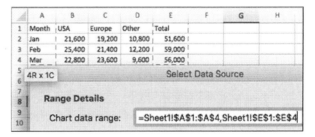

7.   Click the *OK* button to close the *Select Data Source* dialog.

5   Change the source data so that sales for *USA*, *Europe* and *Other* regions are shown (but not the total).

1.   Right-click in the plot area of the chart and click *Select Data* from the shortcut menu.

2.   Select cells A1:D4.

3.   Click the *OK* button to close the *Select Data Source* dialog.

6   Save your work as *World Sales-8*.

Lesson 5-12: Understand Data Series and Categories

In order to use the *Select Data Source* dialog in a more advanced way, you will need to understand how Excel automatically divides a range of data into *data series* and *categories*.

Data series and categories

Here is the data that you have been working with for most of this session:

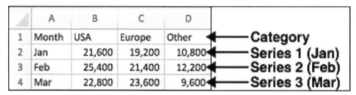

Excel interprets this data as having three data series (Jan, Feb and Mar).

In this example, each data series has three values. For example, the *Jan* data series has the three values 21,600, 19,200 and 10,800.

The values are plotted along the left-hand vertical axis (sometimes referred to as the Y axis).

Each of the values in a data series is associated with a *Category*. This is simply a label that identifies each value in the series. For example, the *Jan* series value of 19,200 belongs to the *Europe* category.

The category is shown along the bottom horizontal axis (sometimes referred to as the X axis).

Showing this on the chart makes things clearer:

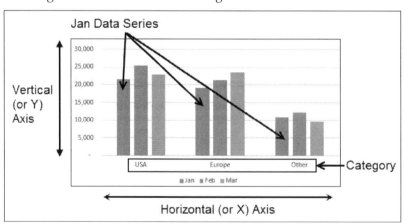

Swapping the Rows and Columns

It is also possible to take a different view of the same data.

The old data series become categories, and the old categories become data series.

World Sales-8

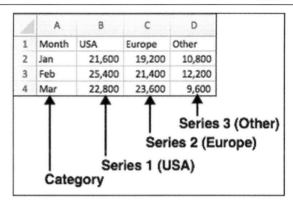

When the data is viewed in this way a different chart will result.

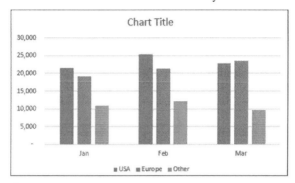

1   Open *World Sales-8* from your sample files folder (if it isn't already open).

At present, Excel regards months as data series and regions as categories:

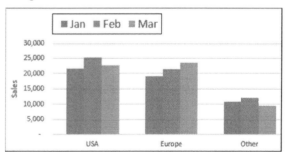

2   Switch the rows and columns so that the X axis shows months instead of regions.

1. Click just inside the border of the chart to select it.

2. Click: Chart Design→Data→Switch Row/Column.

Excel now regards the regions as data series, and the months as categories.

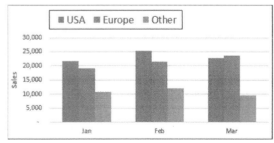

3   Save your work as *World Sales-9.*

Lesson 5-13: Change source data using the Select Data Source dialog tools

1 Open *World Sales-9* from your sample files folder (if it isn't already open).

2 Display the *Select Data Source* dialog.

1. Right-click anywhere in the chart and click *Select Data...* from the shortcut menu.

    The *Select Data Source* dialog appears.

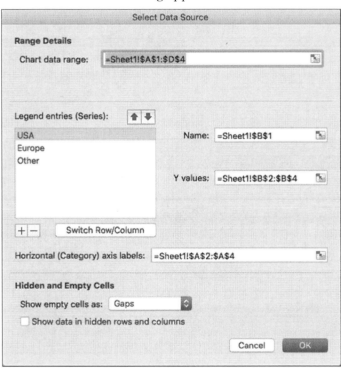

3 Add a *Total* data series.

Click the *Add* button ⊞ below the *Legend Entries (Series)* pane.

1. In the *Name* box, type: **Total**

2. Delete any text currently appearing in the *Y values* text box.

3. Select the range E2:E4 for the *Y values*.

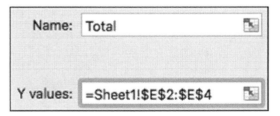

4. Click the *OK* button.

    The new series appears in the chart.

World Sales-9

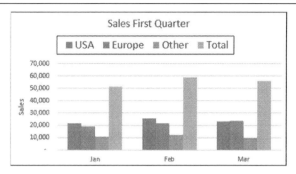

4   Delete the *Total* data series.

1.   Display the *Select Data Source* dialog.

2.   Click the *Total* data series in the *Legend entries (Series)* list to select it.

3.   Click the Remove button.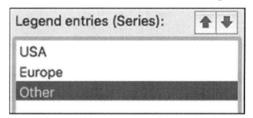

The series is removed from the dialog.

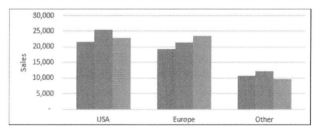

5   Switch the rows and columns so that the X axis shows regions instead of months.

You learned how to do this using the Ribbon in: *Lesson 5-12: Understand Data Series and Categories.*

You can do the same thing by clicking the *Switch Row/Column* button on the *Select Data Source* dialog.

6   Click the *OK* button to close the *Select Data Source* dialog.

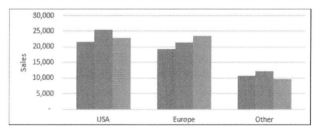

7   Save your work as *World Sales-10.*

Lesson 5-14: Chart non-contiguous source data by hiding rows and columns

In this lesson you'll look at an alternative method of charting a non-contiguous range simply by hiding the data elements that you don't want to chart.

Excel allows you to hide rows and columns in a worksheet by effectively setting their width to zero. The default behavior of charts is to ignore these hidden rows and columns.

It is also possible to override this default behavior and instruct Excel to chart hidden rows and columns.

1   Open *World Sales-10* from your sample files folder (if it isn't already open).

2   Remove the *Europe* series from the chart by hiding column C.

1.   Right-click on the column header button at the top of column C.

2.   Click *Hide* from the shortcut menu.

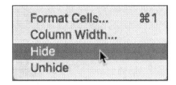

The *Europe* sales data is no longer shown on the chart.

3   Remove the *February* data from the chart by hiding row 3.

1.   Right-click on the row header button to the left of row 3.

2.   Click *Hide* from the shortcut menu.

February data is no longer shown on the chart.

4   Display the hidden data in the chart.

Excel allows you to chart hidden data if you want to.

note

The Hidden and Empty Cells options can also be used with Sparklines

If you select a Sparkline group and click:

Sparkline Tools→Design→
Sparkline→Edit Data→
Hidden & Empty Cells

… you will see the same options that are used in this lesson to deal with hidden rows and columns in charts.

You can use these in exactly the same way to deal with hidden rows and columns in Sparklines.

You learned how to create Sparkline groups in: *Lesson 4-19: Insert a Sparkline into a range of cells.*

1. Right-click anywhere in the chart and click *Select Data…* from the shortcut menu.

   The *Select Data Source* dialog appears.

2. In the *Hidden and Empty Cells* section, check the *Show data in hidden rows and columns* check box.

   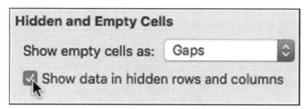

3. Click the *OK* button to dismiss the dialog.

   The previously hidden chart data re-appears.

   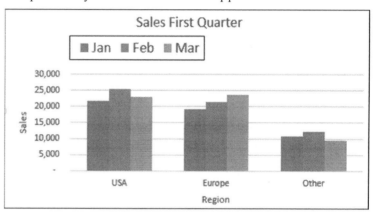

5 Unhide the hidden rows and columns.

1. Click any cell in the worksheet to de-activate the chart.

2. Click the *Select All* button at the top left corner of the worksheet to select every cell.

	A	B
1	Month	USA
2	Jan	21,600

3. Click: Home→Cells→Format→Hide & Unhide→Unhide Rows.

4. Click: Home→Cells→Format→Hide & Unhide→Unhide Columns.

6 Save your work as *World Sales-11.*

note

Unhiding rows and columns using the Menu Bar

As well as using the Ribbon, you can also unhide rows and columns using the following commands on the Menu Bar:

→Format→Row→Unhide

→Format→Column→Unhide

Lesson 5-15: Create a chart with numerical axes

Sometimes Excel gets a little confused when it attempts to automatically generate a chart.

Problems usually occur when you need to plot numerical information along the horizontal axis. Excel sees the numerical labels and assumes that they are a series.

In this lesson you'll use such a worksheet to confuse Excel and then fix things up manually using the *Select Data Source* dialog.

1   Open *Annual Sales Summary* from your sample files folder.

2   Display the range as a clustered column chart.

   1.   Click on any single cell inside the range.

        Note that it isn't necessary to select the range when you want to chart all of it.

        If you simply click any cell inside the range, Excel will automatically select the entire range for the chart's source data.

   2.   Click: Insert→Charts→Column→Clustered Column.

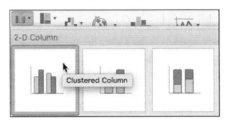

        The range is displayed as a chart, but there's a problem. Excel has assumed that the numbers in the *Year* column are a data series.

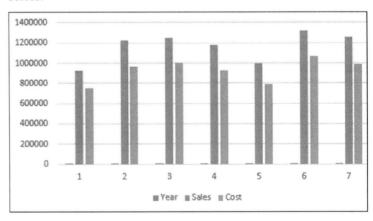

        Note that the numbers for the *Year* data are so small in relation to the *Sales* and *Cost* data that you can hardly see their bars in the bar chart. The bars are there, but they are so short that they are almost invisible.

3   Right-click anywhere in the chart and click *Select Data…* from the shortcut menu.

   The *Select Data Source* dialog is displayed.

Annual Sales Summary

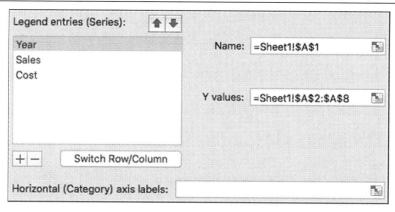

The problem is immediately apparent. Excel has wrongly identified the year as series data rather than as category axis labels.

4   Remove the *Year* data series and add the *Year* data as *Horizontal (Category) axis labels*.

1. Click *Year* in the left-hand pane of the dialog and then click the Remove button.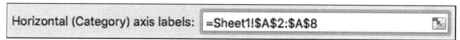

2. Click in the *Horizontal (Category) axis labels* box.

3. Select cells A2:A8 for the *Horizonal (Category) axis labels* (the year data but not the column header).

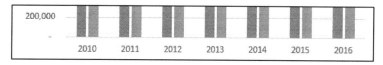

4. Click the *OK* button to close the dialog.

The chart now displays correctly.

200,000

2010   2011   2012   2013   2014   2015   2016

5   Save your work as *Annual Sales Summary-1*.

Lesson 5-16: Deal with empty data points

Sometimes you'll only have partial data for a series.

In the worksheet used for this lesson I'll share a secret with you. I weigh myself every day and keep a chart on my bathroom wall to make sure that I'm staying at a healthy weight.

Sometimes I'm away travelling and can't weigh in as usual. When I get back I need to fill in the gaps.

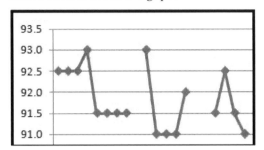

I use a line chart for my weight, so the best solution is to simply draw a line connecting the last data point recorded before I went away with the first recorded upon my return.

For a column chart, the best solution would be to show no columns for the missing days. In other words, there would be gaps for each date when there was a missing bar.

1   Open *Weight 2015* from your sample files folder.

This is a simple worksheet showing my weight in kilograms for each date in July 2015. Notice that there are missing days when I was away from home.

2   Display the range as a *Line with Markers* chart.

1.   Click on any of the date values within the range.

2.   Click: Insert→Charts→Line→Line with Markers.

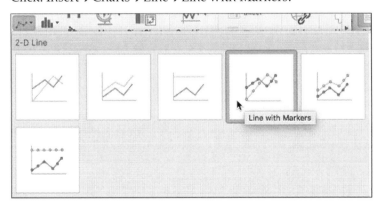

The chart displays, but there are gaps for the missing entries.

Weight 2015

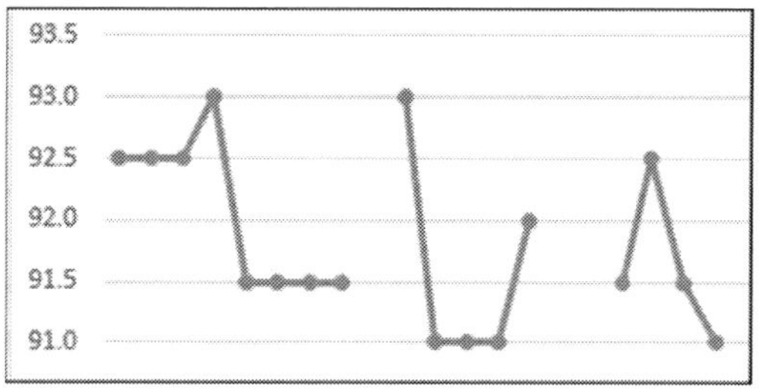

3 Tell Excel to connect the gaps in the chart with a line.

1. Right-click anywhere in the chart and click *Select Data* from the shortcut menu.

   The *Select Data Source* dialog is displayed.

2. Click the *Show empty cells as* drop-down menu at the bottom of the dialog.

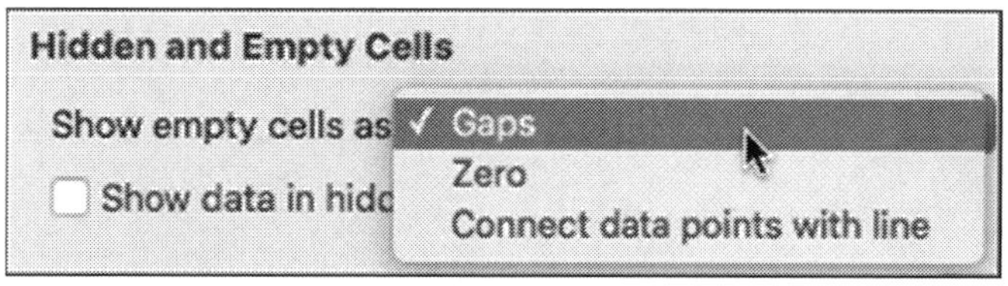

3. Click the *Connect data points with line* option.

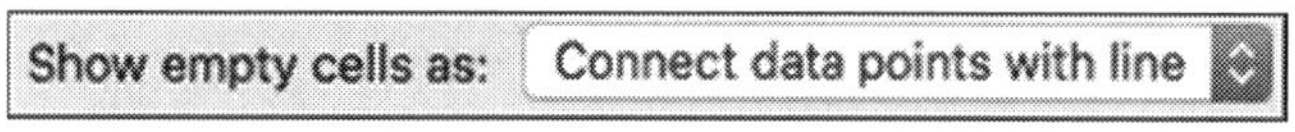

4. Click the *OK* button to dismiss the dialog.

   All data points are now connected with a line.

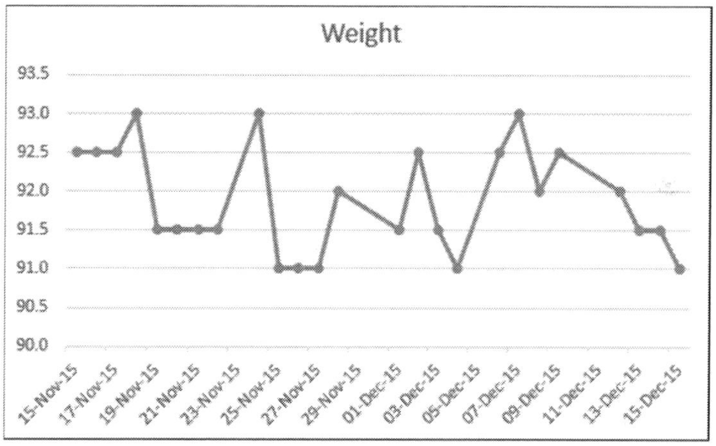

4 Save your work as *Weight 2015-1.*

note

The Hidden and Empty Cells settings can also be used with Sparklines

If you select a Sparkline group and click:

Sparkline Design→ Sparkline→Edit Data→ Hidden & Empty Cells

... you will see the same options that are used in this lesson to deal with empty data points in charts.

You can use these options in exactly the same way to deal with empty data points in Sparklines.

You learned how to create Sparkline groups in: *Lesson 4-19: Insert a Sparkline into a range of cells.*

Lesson 5-17: Add data labels to a chart

It is possible to approximate the values that are displayed in a chart by looking at the vertical axis.

Sometimes you will need to convey the precise values that are being charted. There are three ways of doing this:

- Embed the chart in the worksheet containing the source data so that the user can see both the chart and data.

- Add data labels to each point on the chart.

- Add a *Data Table* chart element to the bottom of the chart.

1   Open *Annual Sales Summary-1* from your sample files folder.

2   Change the chart's source data so that only sales (not costs) for 2013 to 2016 are charted.

This will allow you to test your understanding of the skills learned in: *Lesson 5-11: Assign non-contiguous source data to a chart, Lesson 5-13: Change source data using the Select Data Source dialog tools,* and *Lesson 5-15: Create a chart with numerical axes.*

1. In the *Select Data Source* dialog, select this (non-contiguous) range for the *Chart data range*:

	A	B	C	D	E	F
1	Year	Sales	Cost			
2	4R x 2C	923,859	755,087			
3		1,222,054	961,643			
4	2012	1,250,365	1,008,292			
5	2013	1,176,787	925,430			
6	2014	995,720	788,576			
7	2015	1,324,534	1,067,627			
8	2016	1,260,340	992,272			
9					Select Data Source	
10						
11		**Range Details**				
12						
13		Chart data range:	=Sheet1!$A$1:$B$1,Sheet1!$A$5:$B$8		
14						

2. In the *Select Data Source* dialog, select this data range for the *Horizontal (Category) axis labels.*

Horizontal (Category) axis labels: =Sheet1!$A$5:$A$8

You learned how to do this in: *Lesson 5-15: Create a chart with numerical axes.*

3. Remove the *Year* item from the *Legend Entries (Series).*

The *Select Data Source* dialog should now look like this:

Annual Sales Summary-1

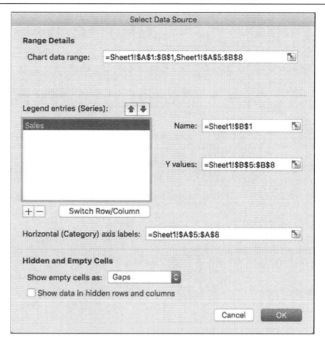

4. Click the *OK* button to close the dialog.

    This chart appears:

    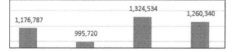

3   **Add data label elements outside the end of each bar.**

    1. Activate the chart by clicking just inside the chart's border.

    2. Click: Chart Design→Chart Layouts→Add Chart Element→
        Data Labels→Outside End.

        Data labels are now shown outside the end of each bar:

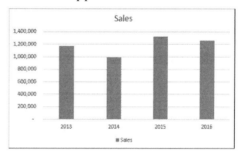

4   **Switch off the data labels.**

    1. Activate the chart by clicking just inside the chart's border.

    2. Click: Chart Design→Chart Layouts→Add Chart Element→
        Data Labels→None.

5   **Add a *Data Table* element to the bottom of the chart.**

    1. Activate the chart by clicking just inside the chart's border.

    2. Click: Chart Design→Chart Layouts→
        Add Chart Element→Data Table→With Legend Keys.

    A table is displayed below the chart:

	2013	2014	2015	2016
■ Sales	1,176,787	995,720	1,324,534	1,260,340

6   **Save your work as *Annual Sales Summary-2.***

Lesson 5-18: Highlight specific data points with color and annotations

A single value within a data series is often referred to as a *data point.*

Sometimes you will want to emphasize a specific data point in a series. For example, you may want to color a single column differently to its neighbors to emphasize some special attribute of the data point.

Color alone cannot convey why the data point is special. You will normally want to also add a text box to the chart to explain the reason for its different color.

In this lesson you'll imagine that the company is a hotel, and that 2014 was the centenary year in a competing resort, leading to an expectation of decreased sales. To mark this, you'll color the 2014 bar orange and add an annotation saying *Centenary Year* to the bar.

1 Open *Annual Sales Summary-2* from your sample files folder (if it isn't already open).

2 Change the color of the 2014 bar to orange.

    1. Click the 2014 bar once. Notice that the entire data series is selected.

    2. Click the 2014 bar once more. This time only the 2014 bar is selected.

    3. Click: Format→Shape Styles→Shape Fill→Orange, Accent 2.

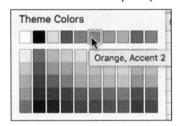

    4. The 2014 bar is now colored orange. The legend has also changed to give a further visual prompt that the orange bar relates to 2014.

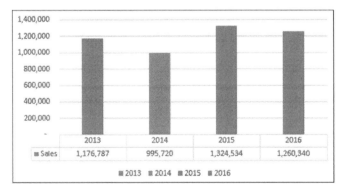

3 Add a text box above, and to the right of, the 2014 bar containing the text: **Centenary Year**

    1. Click just inside the border of the chart to activate it.

Annual Sales Summary-2

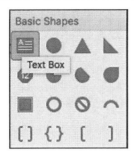

2. Click: Format→Insert Shapes→ Shapes Gallery→Basic Shapes→Text Box.

3. Click on the chart, above the orange 2014 bar, and type **Centenary**, then press **<Shift>+<Enter>** and then type **Year**. (the **<Shift>+<Enter>** key combination moves you to the next line in a text box).

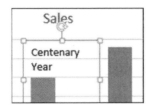

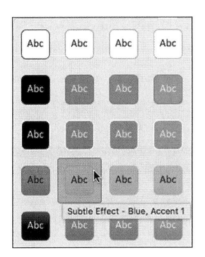

4   Add a border and fill to the text box.

Click the text box to select it and then click:

Shape Format→Shape Styles→ Shape Styles Gallery→Subtle Effect – Blue, Accent 1

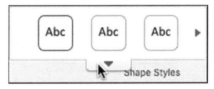

This effect is the second on row four (see sidebar).

5   Resize the text box.

Click the text box once to select it and then drag the sizing handles to resize the text box so that the text fills the box.

6   Move the text box.

Click the text box once to select it and then hover over any part of the border that is not a sizing handle. You will see the four-headed arrow cursor shape (see sidebar). When you see the four-headed arrow, click and drag to move the text box to an ideal position.

7   Add an arrow pointing from the text box to the orange 2014 bar.

1. Click the chart to activate it. (Make sure that you click just inside the border of the chart and not on the text box. The *Format* tab will not be displayed when the text box is selected).

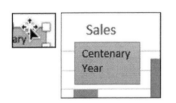

2. Click: Format→Insert Shapes→Shapes Gallery→Lines→Arrow (see sidebar)

3. Click and drag to draw an arrow pointing from the text box to the orange bar.

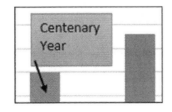

4. With the arrow selected, click: Shape Format→Shape Styles→Gallery drop-down.

5. Choose an attractive style for the arrow.

8   Save your work as *Annual Sales Summary-3.*

Lesson 5-19: Add gridlines and scale axes

In this session you'll manipulate the vertical axis of a sales chart to give two entirely different views of a company's sales. Each chart emphasizes one of the following true statements.

- It is true that sales are increasing every month.

- It is true that sales are almost completely flat.

You'll see how you can manipulate a column chart to visually convey each of these "truths" to an audience. After this session you'll never look at a chart again without paying close attention to the vertical axis!

1   Open *Sales First Quarter* from your sample files folder.

	A	B
1	Month	Sales
2	Jan	80,010
3	Feb	80,040
4	Mar	80,080

This worksheet shows sales that are almost completely flat. Sales increased by 0.04% in February and by 0.05% in March.

A twentieth of a percent increase isn't anything at all.

2   Create a chart that illustrates flat sales.

Imagine you are the sales director of the company and need to have a pep talk with your salespeople.

You want to show them a chart that demonstrates the lack of sales growth in order to motivate them to do better in April.

1. Click inside the data range.

2. Click: Insert→Charts→Column→Clustered Column.

The following chart is automatically generated:

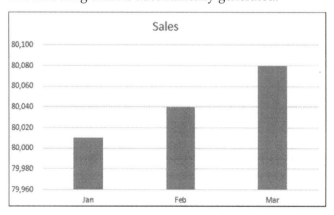

This isn't the chart you want at all. Sales look rather good!

The reason that the chart isn't as honest as it should be is because the vertical axis begins at 79,960. You're looking at the tips of columns that are very long.

To fix things up you need a more honest vertical axis; one that begins at zero.

Sales First Quarter

3. Right-click the vertical axis and select *Format Axis...* from the shortcut menu.

The *Format Axis* task pane appears.

4. Change the *Minimum* value to zero and press the **<Enter>** key.

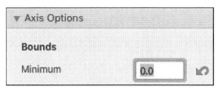

The chart now depicts a more honest representation of flat growth.

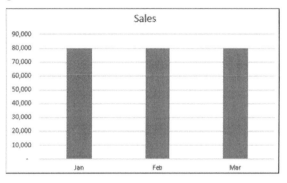

Look at the task pane and notice how Excel has automatically managed the other settings. *Major units* for gridlines (the interval between numbers on the vertical axis) have now changed to 10,000.

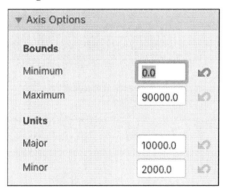

5. Change the *Minor Units* gridline value to 5000 (without a comma, as Excel has a problem with commas in this task pane). You will enable the display of minor gridline elements in a moment and will see one minor gridline between each major gridline.

3 Add minor horizontal gridlines to the chart.

1. Activate the chart by clicking just inside the chart's border.

2. Click: Chart Design→Chart Layouts→
   Add Chart Element→Gridlines→Primary Minor Horizontal.

Minor gridlines are now displayed on the chart (see sidebar).

4 Save your work as *Sales First Quarter-1*.

---

tip

Use gridlines sparingly

Too many gridlines can make a chart difficult to read.

This lesson's chart looks cluttered with minor gridlines and might even look cleaner without any gridlines.

When you do use gridlines, always choose a light color to focus attention upon foreground elements.

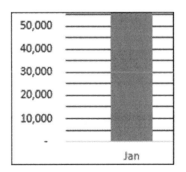

Lesson 5-20: Emphasize data by manipulating pie charts

In the last lesson you saw how a column chart could visually reinforce different characteristics of the same data.

Pie charts also offer several techniques to present data in a way that will best convey your objectives. Designers of pie charts often use the presentation methods described in this lesson to make one value in a series seem bigger or smaller in relation to its neighbors.

1   Open *Competitor Analysis* from your sample files folder.

	A	B	C
1	Splendid Supplies Competitor Analysis		
2			
3	Competitor	Annual Sales (Millions)	Market Share
4	Cheapo discount stores	22.2	28%
5	Budget supplies	16.3	21%
6	Lo Cost warehouse	24.5	31%
7	Splendid Supplies	16.2	20%

This worksheet has been compiled by Splendid Supplies to monitor the activity of their three competitors. Splendid aren't doing so well. In fact, they have the lowest market share of the four.

There's a big investor meeting coming up and Splendid would like to make their market share seem a little more impressive!

2   Create a 3-D pie chart for the range A3:B7.

1.   Select the range A3:B7.

2.   Click: Insert→Charts→Pie→3-D Pie (see sidebar).

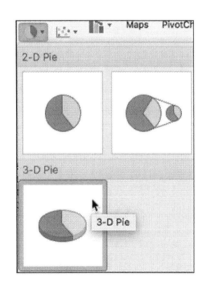

A pie chart is displayed, illustrating the market share of the four companies.

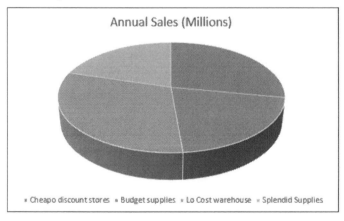

Splendid Supplies don't look very impressive on this chart. You can use a simple presentational technique to make things seem a little better.

3   Rotate the pie chart so that Splendid Supplies sales are at the front.

Because of the perspective of a 3-D pie, the slice at the front always seems the biggest (especially if you keep the perspective angle high).

1. Right-click in the plot area of the pie chart. To do this you'll need to click just outside one of the pie chart's slices.

2. Click *Format Plot Area* from the shortcut menu. If you don't see *Format Plot Area* in the shortcut menu it is because you have right-clicked in the wrong place. In this case try again, making sure that you click just outside one of the pie chart's slices.

   The *Format Plot Area* task pane appears.

3. Click the *Effects* icon  at the top of the task pane.

4. In the *3-D Rotation* section, click the *X rotation* spin button until the Splendid Supplies (yellow) slice is at the front of the pie chart (about 220 degrees).

4 Change the pie chart's perspective to emphasize Splendid Supplies' sales.

In the 3-D rotation section, click the *Perspective* spin button to make the Splendid Supplies sales seem as large as possible. I found that a setting of 35 degrees worked well.

5 Pull the Splendid Supplies slice slightly out of the pie.

A very common pie chart presentational technique is to pull the slice that you want to emphasize away from the pie chart. This slice then appears to be larger in relation to the other slices.

1. Click just inside the chart border to activate the chart.

2. Click one of the slices on the chart once to select the entire pie.

3. Click the Splendid Supplies slice once to select it.

4. Click and drag the slice slightly out of the pie.

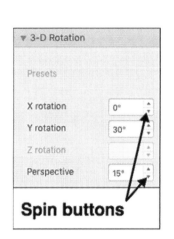

Spin buttons

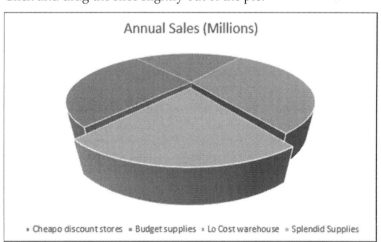

You'd never guess now that Splendid Supplies actually have the lowest market share.

6 Save your work as *Competitor Analysis-1*.

Lesson 5-21: Create a chart with two vertical axes

Sometimes you'll have two data series that are very different in magnitude but you still want to show them on the same chart.

The examples used in this lesson are *UK Average House Prices* and *Bank Base Rates*. Economists widely believe that when interest rates come down, house and commodity prices go up. Since 2008 many world governments have used low interest rates as a tool to attempt to support asset prices. To test whether this theory has succeeded, you will create a chart showing UK bank base rates and average house prices for the twelve years up to 2015.

During the twelve-year period, average house prices ranged from 148,658 to 192,852 while base rates fluctuated between 4.0% and 5.0% before a dramatic reduction to 0.5% in 2009. You need two different vertical axes to make this chart work.

1 Open *UK House Prices* from your sample files folder.

2 Create a default *Line with Markers* chart from the range.

    1. Click anywhere within the data.

    2. Click: Insert→Charts→Line→Line with Markers.

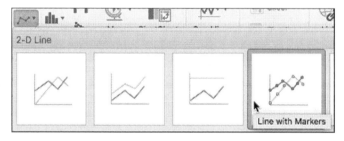

The default chart is displayed.

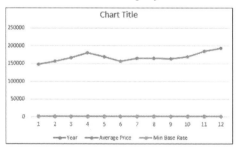

3 Remove the *Year* data series and show the years 2004 to 2015 along the *Horizontal Axis*.

You learned how to do this in: *Lesson 5-15: Create a chart with numerical axes.*

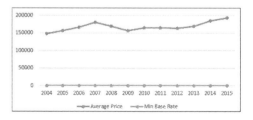

UK House Prices

4 Select the *Min Base Rate* series.

Because the *Min Base Rate* series is in almost exactly the same place as the horizontal axis, it can be difficult to select it with the mouse (though it is possible).

You may find it easier to select the chart and then click:

Format→Current Selection→Chart Elements drop down→ Series "Min Base Rate"

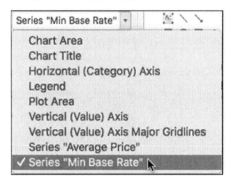

5 Move the *Min Base Rate* series to a secondary axis.

1. With the *Min Base Rate* series selected, click:

   Format→Format→Format Pane

   The *Format Data Series* task pane is displayed.

2. Click the *Series Options* icon.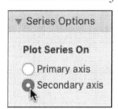

3. Click the *Secondary Axis* option button.

The chart is displayed with two vertical axes and Excel even auto-scales the new axis for you.

It is now easy to see at a glance that the UK government appears to have succeeded in their objective as the fall in house prices from 2007 to 2009 appears to have been reversed by the fall in interest rates.

6 Save your work as UK House Prices-1.

---

note

The secondary axis always appears on top of the primary axis

You can see in the example chart that when the *Min Base Rate* series (the gray line) crosses the *Average Price* series (the orange line), the gray line is on top.

There's no way to change the stacking order of the two lines.

Lesson 5-22: Create a combination chart containing different chart types

Excel allows you to allocate a different chart type to each data series. This opens up many interesting possibilities, such as superimposing a *Clustered Column* chart on top of an *Area* chart.

In this lesson you'll chart the Hawaii climate as a combination Clustered Column/Area chart with clustered columns for high/low temperature and an area chart for rainfall.

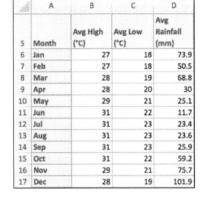

	A	B	C	D
5	Month	Avg High (°C)	Avg Low (°C)	Avg Rainfall (mm)
6	Jan	27	18	73.9
7	Feb	27	18	50.5
8	Mar	28	19	68.8
9	Apr	28	20	30
10	May	29	21	25.1
11	Jun	31	22	11.7
12	Jul	31	23	23.4
13	Aug	31	23	23.6
14	Sep	31	23	25.9
15	Oct	31	22	59.2
16	Nov	29	21	75.7
17	Dec	28	19	101.9

1   Open *Hawaii Climate-1* from your sample files folder.

This workbook documents the temperature range and rainfall in Hawaii for each month of the year.

2   Create a combination chart showing temperature as a *Clustered Column* chart type and rainfall as an *Area* chart type.

1. Click in any cell within the range.

   Because you want to chart the entire data range, there's no need to select the range of cells.

2. Click: Insert→Charts→Column→Clustered Column.

   A clustered column chart appears, showing all of the data series using the *clustered column* chart type.

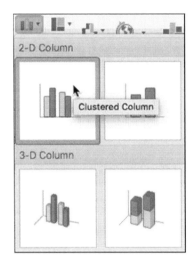

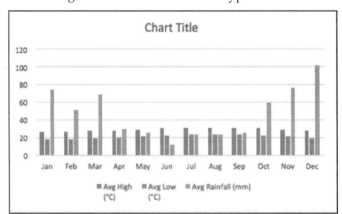

3. Select the *Avg Rainfall* series.

   This was covered in: *Lesson 5-21: Create a chart with two vertical axes*.

4. Click: Chart Design→Change Chart Type→Line→Area.

   The combination chart is created:

Hawaii Climate-1

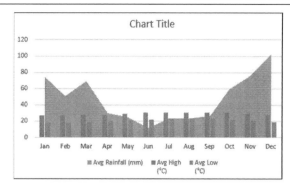

The chart isn't bad, but it could be improved. Because there is only one axis, the rainfall's *Area* chart type dominates the chart.

Adding a second vertical axis will solve this problem.

3   Add a secondary axis for rainfall.

You'll do this in the same way as you did in: *Lesson 5-21: Create a chart with two vertical axes.*

1. Select the *Avg Rainfall* data series.

2. Click: Format→Format→Format Pane.

3. Click the *Series Options* tab within the *Format Data Series* task pane.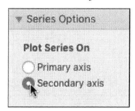

4. Click *Secondary Axis*.

▼ Series Options

Plot Series On
○ Primary axis
◉ Secondary axis

4   Add *Axis Title* elements and give them (along with the *Chart Title* element) appropriate names.

You learned how to do this in: *Lesson 5-9: Move, re-size, add, position and delete chart elements* and *Lesson 5-5: Add and remove chart elements using Quick Layout.*

The chart now looks professional:

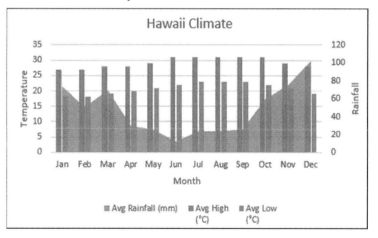

5   Save your work as *Hawaii Climate-2*.

Lesson 5-23: Add a trend line

> It is impossible to demonstrate empirically that a cause produces an effect. Just because the sun has risen every day since the beginning of the Earth does not mean that it will rise again tomorrow. However; it is impossible to go about one's life without assuming such connections, and the best that we can do is to maintain an open mind and never presume that we know any laws of causality for certain.
>
> *David Hume (1711-1776),*
> *Scottish philosopher, economist, and historian.*
> *From "An Enquiry Concerning Human Understanding".*

Trend analysis applies the science of mathematics to the art of fortune telling.

If a value has been increasing for a long time, trend analysis would suggest that it will go on increasing. Some would say that the reverse is true, but Excel remains healthily optimistic that it is possible to predict the future from the past!

Excel provides several different types of trend analysis. You're going to use a linear trend line and a two-period moving average to decide whether it would have been a good idea to buy a house in 2016.

1   Open *UK House Prices-1* from your sample files folder (if it isn't already open).

2   Remove the *Min Base Rate* data series from the chart.

     This was covered in: *Lesson 5-13: Change source data using the Select Data Source dialog tools.*

3   Format the vertical axis so that it plots values between 145,000 and 205,000.

     You learned how to do this in: *Lesson 5-19: Add gridlines and scale axes.*

4   Add a linear trend line element to forecast where property prices will be in the year 2020

     1. Activate the chart by clicking just inside the chart's border.

     2. Click: Chart Design→Chart Layouts→Add Chart Element→ Trendline→Linear.

     3. Select the new trend line, either by clicking on it or by using the Ribbon.

     4. If the *Format Trendline* task pane isn't already visible, display it by clicking: Format→Format→Format Pane.

     5. Click the *Trendline Options* icon.

     6. Make sure that the *Linear* type is selected (this is the default).

     7. As 2020 is 5 periods after 2015, enter **5** in the *Forecast Forward* text box and then press the **<Enter>** key.

UK House Prices-1

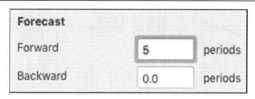

8. Select the chart and then click and drag one of the right-hand sizing handles to make the chart wider.

Notice the trend line shown on the chart.

Excel isn't very confident that your new house will be a great investment, and predicts that it won't be worth any more than you've paid for it in five years' time (though David Hume would have advised you that Excel may well be wrong).

5   Remove the trend line.

1.   Click on the trend line to select it.

2.   Press the **<Delete>** key on the keyboard.

6   Add a two-period moving average.

Moving averages are one of the most loved instruments of speculators who predict the future values of shares, currencies and commodities based entirely upon charts. The theory is that when the price crosses beneath the moving average it is time to sell.

1.   Activate the chart.

2.   Click: Chart Design→Chart Layouts→Add Chart Element→ Trendline→Moving Average.

This time the analysis shows that you should have sold in 2008 and then re-purchased in 2010. In 2015, Excel's advice is to hold.

7   Save your work as *UK House Prices-2*.

Lesson 5-24: Add a gradient fill to a chart background

When you prepare a chart for a PowerPoint presentation, or for inclusion in a high quality color publication, you want the chart to look professional and interesting. A *Gradient* background fill will put the finishing touch to your chart so that it looks like it was produced by a professional graphic artist.

1   Open *World Sales* from your sample files folder.

2   Create a *Clustered Column* chart from the entire range.

　　　1.　Click anywhere in the range.

　　　2.　Click: Insert→Charts→Column→Clustered Column.

　　　The chart is created:

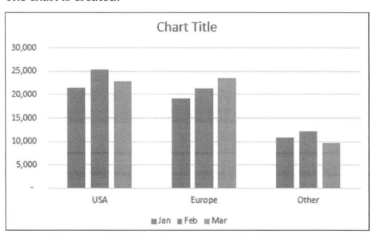

3   Switch Rows/Columns to transpose the *Legend* and *Regions*.

You learned how to do this in: *Lesson 5-12: Understand Data Series and Categories.*

The regions are now listed in the legend and the months are shown along the horizontal axis.

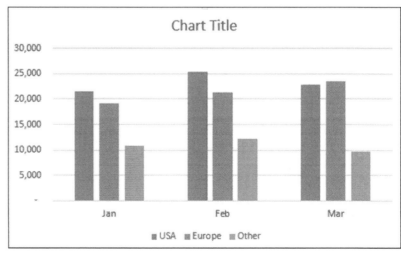

World Sales

4   Add a gradient fill to the chart background.

1. Right-click on the *Chart Area* element (just inside the border of the chart).

2. Click *Format Chart Area* from the shortcut menu.

    The *Format Chart Area* task pane appears.

3. Click the *Fill & Line* icon.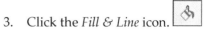

4. Click the *Fill* menu item.

5. Click the *Gradient Fill* option button.

6. Choose one of the options from the *Preset gradients* drop-down menu (I chose *Light Gradient – Accent 4*).

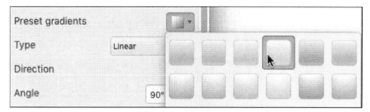

7. Explore the *Type/Direction/Angle/Transparency* and other settings until you are happy with the fill.

8. Click the *Close* button to close the *Format Chart Area* task pane.

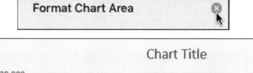

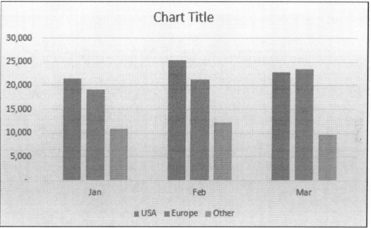

5   Save your work as *Gradient Fill*.

Lesson 5-25: Create your own chart templates

If you use charts a lot, you may find yourself applying the same fonts, fills, layouts and other attributes over and over again. If you find this happening, it is time to create a chart template.

Chart templates can be used just like the built-in gallery charts. You can use templates to create a unique, personal, or corporate chart style that will enable you to produce consistently styled work.

In this lesson you'll develop a useful chart template with larger fonts to enable them to be more readable when incorporated into a PowerPoint presentation. You can then use this template in future for any chart that is destined to be used in a presentation.

1   Open *Gradient Fill* from your sample files folder (if it isn't already open).

2   Increase the font size of the *Chart Title* element to 28 Points.

    1.   Select the *Chart Title* element

    2.   Click: Home→Font→Font Size Drop-Down→28 Points.

3   Increase the font size of the *Vertical (Value) Axis*, *Horizontal (Category) Axis* and *Legend* elements to 14 points.

Select each element in turn and set the font size in the same way as in the previous step.

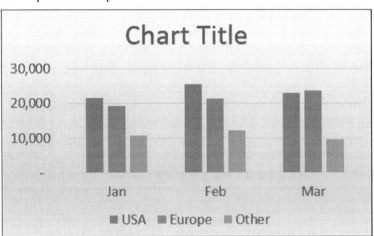

The chart now has labels that will be readable by viewers at the back of the room when projected onto a screen.

4   Save the chart design as a template.

    1.   Right-click in the *Chart Area* (just inside the border of the chart).

    2.   Select *Save as Template…* from the shortcut menu.

    3.   Type **PowerPoint Clustered Column with Title and Gradient Fill** into the *Save As* box.

    4.   Click the *Save* button.

5   Delete the chart.

Gradient Fill

Click once, just inside the border of the chart, to select it and then press the **<Delete>** key.

6   Create a new chart from the template.

1.   Click anywhere inside the data range A1:D4.

2.   Click: ■→Insert→Chart→Templates

Your chart template is displayed, along with any other chart templates that you might have saved previously.

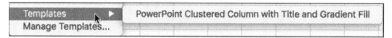

3.   Click *PowerPoint Clustered Column with Title and Gradient Fill.*

This is the template that you just saved.

When you click, a chart is displayed with all of the attributes of your template.

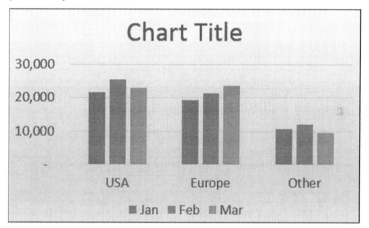

7   Save your work as *PowerPoint Template.*

Session 5: Exercise

1   Open *Exercise 5* from your sample files folder.

2   Click any cell in the range A3:F8.

3   Click: Insert→Charts→Column→Clustered Column.

     The chart looks strange at first, as there are many errors to correct.

4   Switch rows and columns so that the European country names are shown in the *Legend*.

5   Use the *Select Data Source* dialog to remove the *Year* series and place the years along the *Horizontal (Category) Axis*.

6   Change the scale of the vertical axis so that it has a *Minimum* value of 15 and a *Maximum* value of 50.

7   Format the *Legend* so that a solid line black border appears around it.

8   Change the chart's source data so that sales are only shown for the UK, Spain and Italy.

9   Increase the font size of the legend to 12 points.

10   Change the *Chart Title* text to: *European Sales*

11   Add a gradient fill to the *Chart Area* element, using the 5th preset gradient option.

12   Save your work as *Exercise 5-1*.

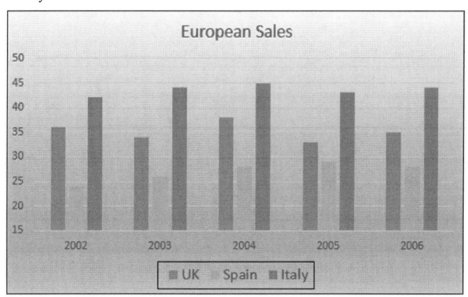

Exercise 5

If you need help slide the page to the left

Session 5: Exercise answers

These are the questions that students find the most difficult to answer:

Q 11	Q 8	Q 6	Q 5
1. Right-click just inside the border of the chart and click *Format Chart Area...* from the shortcut menu. 3. Choose the *Fill & Line* icon in the *Format Chart Area* task pane. 4. Click the *Fill* menu item. 5. Click the *Gradient Fill* option button. 6. Click *Preset gradients* and select the 5th option on the top row. This was covered in: *Lesson 5-24: Add a gradient fill to a chart background.*	1. Right-click just inside the border of the chart and click *Select Data...* from the shortcut menu. 2. Click the *France* item in the *Legend entries (Series)* list and click the *Remove* button. 3. Repeat the process to remove the *Germany* series. 4. Click the *OK* button. This was covered in: *Lesson 5-13: Change source data using the Select Data Source dialog tools.*	1. Click the vertical axis to select it. 2. Click: Format→Format→ Format Pane 3. Click the *Axis Options* icon in the *Format Axis* task pane. 4. Type the value **15** in the *Minimum* text box and press the **<Enter>** key. Make sure that **50** is shown in the *Maximum* value text box. This was covered in: *Lesson 5-19: Add gridlines and scale axes.*	1. Right-click just inside the border of the chart and click *Select Data...* from the shortcut menu. 2. Click the *Year* item in the *Legend entries (Series)* list and then click the *Remove* button. 3. Click in the *Horizontal (Category) axis labels* box. 4. Select cells A4:A8. 5. Click the *OK* button. This was covered in: *Lesson 5-15: Create a chart with numerical axes.*

If you have difficulty with the other questions, here are the lessons that cover the relevant skills:

1 Refer to: *Lesson 1-7: Download the sample files and open/navigate a workbook.*

2 Refer to: *Lesson 1-7: Download the sample files and open/navigate a workbook.*

3 Refer to: *Lesson 5-2: Create a simple chart with two clicks.*

4 Refer to: *Lesson 5-12: Understand Data Series and Categories.*

7 Refer to: *Lesson 5-7: Manually format a chart element.*

9 Refer to: *Lesson 5-7: Manually format a chart element.*

10 Refer to: *Lesson 5-5: Add and remove chart elements using Quick Layout.*

12 Refer to: *Lesson 1-8: Save a workbook.*

Session Six: Working with Multiple Worksheets and Workbooks

> There are no big problems; there are just a lot of little problems.
>
> *Henry Ford (1863-1947)*
> *American industrialist and pioneer of assembly-line production*

Henry Ford knew that big problems are really just a lot of little problems bundled together.

Often you will find that a worksheet is getting over-complicated and difficult to work with. This session will give you the skills needed to quickly break one very complex worksheet into many smaller and easier to manage worksheets.

This session will also show you how to view different parts of large worksheets at the same time and how to create cross-worksheet formulas that summarize data from several different worksheets.

Session Objectives

By the end of this session you will be able to:

- View the same workbook in different windows
- Duplicate worksheets within a workbook
- Move and copy worksheets from one workbook to another
- Hide and unhide a worksheet
- Create cross worksheet formulas
- Understand worksheet groups
- Use find and replace

Lesson 6-1: View the same workbook in different windows

Sales First Quarter 2016

Excel allows you to view the same worksheet in two separate worksheet windows. This is useful when you need to compare different areas of the same worksheet.

1   Close any Excel workbooks that are currently open.

2   Open *Sales First Quarter 2016* from your sample files folder.

This workbook has only one worksheet containing 242 rows of data.

3   Open a new window to see February 2016 and January 2016 sales at the same time.

Click: ⌘→Window→New Window.

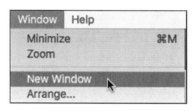

Nothing seems to happen, except that the Title bar now reads: *Sales First Quarter 2016:2* (see sidebar if this isn't appearing for you).

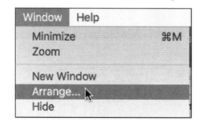

Two views of the same workbook are now open at the same time but, because they are both maximized, you can only view one at a time which isn't very useful.

4   View both windows at the same time.

Click: ⌘→Window→Arrange.

The *Arrange Windows* dialog appears.

5   Select the *Horizontal* option and then click the *OK* button.

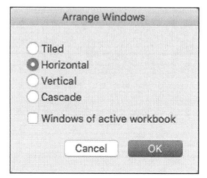

Both windows are displayed, one below the other. You are able to freely scroll to any position in either window.

You will now appreciate the importance of closing any open workbooks in step 1. If you had several workbooks open, you would now be viewing all of them in multiple windows.

In the screenshot below I've scrolled the bottom window down to see February sales:

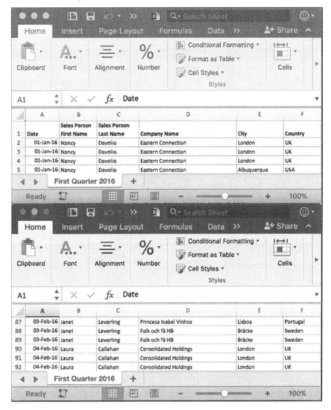

It's important to realize that you are not looking at two different worksheets, but two different views of the same worksheet.

If you change a value in one of the views, you'll immediately see the changed value in the other.

6 **Close the *Sales First Quarter 2016:2* window and maximize the *Sales First Quarter 2016:1* worksheet.**

1. Click in the *Sales First Quarter 2016:2* window. Notice how the title bar and border changes color to indicate that this is now the active window.

2. Click the *Close* button in the top left corner of the worksheet.

3. Hold the **<Alt>** key and click the *Zoom* button in the top left corner of the *Sales First Quarter 2016* worksheet.

Lesson 6-2: Duplicate worksheets within a workbook

In this lesson you're going to disassemble a large worksheet and make it into three smaller worksheets.

You'll often find that data is easier to work with if you divide it into logically separated sections.

1   Open *Sales First Quarter 2016* from your sample files folder.

This workbook shows all sales completed in January, February and March 2016. Your task will be to split them into separate months.

2   Create a new worksheet and name it *January*.

This skill was covered in: *Lesson 1-11: View, move, add, rename, delete and navigate worksheet tabs.*

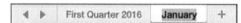

3   Select every cell in the *First Quarter 2016* worksheet.

1.   Click the *First Quarter 2016* worksheet tab.

There's a special button at the top left corner of every worksheet called the *Select All* button.

	A	B	C
1	Date	Sales Person First Name	Sales Person Last Name
2	01-Jan-16	Nancy	Davolio

2.   Click the *Select All* button to select every cell in the worksheet.

4   Copy all selected cells.

The easiest way to do this is to right-click within the selected range and then click *Copy* from the shortcut menu.

5   Paste the copied cells into the *January* worksheet, beginning at cell A1.

Click the *January* tab, right-click in cell A1 and select *Paste* from the shortcut menu.

6   Create another copy of the worksheet using *Move or Copy*.

Excel provides a simpler way to duplicate a worksheet.

1.   Right-click the *First Quarter 2016* worksheet tab and choose *Move or Copy…* from the shortcut menu.

The *Move or Copy* dialog appears.

2.   Select *(move to end)* in the *Before sheet* list.

3.   Check the *Create a copy* check box.

note

Other ways to select all cells

Select All is a very common requirement and it is well worth remembering the keyboard shortcut:

<Cmd>+<A>

It's a shortcut I use every day!

If the active cell is inside a range, this keyboard shortcut will select every cell within the range rather than every cell within the worksheet.

Sales First Quarter 2016

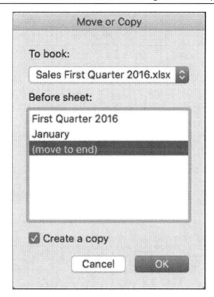

4. Click the *OK* button.

    Notice that Excel has named the new worksheet: *First Quarter 2016 (2).*

7 Change the name of the new worksheet to *February*.

This skill was covered in *Lesson 1-11: View, move, add, rename, delete and navigate worksheet tabs.*

8 Create another copy of the worksheet using *drag and drop*.

There's an even quicker way to create a duplicate worksheet.

1. Click once on the *First Quarter 2016* tab to select it.

2. Hold down the **<Alt>** key.

3. Click and hold the mouse button on the *First Quarter 2016* tab.

    The cursor changes shape to a page with a plus sign:

4. Drag to the right until you see a black insertion arrow to the right of the *February* tab.

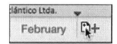

    When you release the mouse button, another copy of the worksheet is created.

9 Change the name of the new worksheet to *March*.

10 Remove rows from the January, February and March workbooks so that only the named month's transactions remain.

This was covered in: *Lesson 3-1: Insert and delete rows and columns.*

11 Save your work as *Sales First Quarter 2016-1*.

Lesson 6-3: Move and copy worksheets from one workbook to another

In *Lesson 6-2: Duplicate worksheets within a workbook,* you worked with a single workbook.

It is also possible to move and copy worksheets between different workbooks using a similar technique.

1 Close any workbooks that are currently open.

2 Open *Sales First Quarter 2016-1* from your sample files folder.

3 Open *First Quarter Sales and Bonus* from your sample files folder.

4 Arrange the windows *Horizontally* in the Excel window.

Click: ⌘→Window→Arrange→Horizontal.

The two workbooks are now shown together.

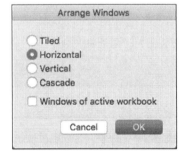

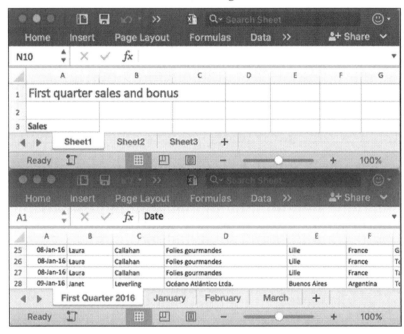

5 Rename *Sheet1* in the *First Quarter Sales and Bonus* workbook to *Bonus.*

This was covered in: *Lesson 1-11: View, move, add, rename, delete and navigate worksheet tabs.*

First Quarter Sales and Bonus

Sales First Quarter 2016-1

6 Hold down the **<Alt>** key and drag and drop the *Bonus* sheet from the *First Quarter Sales and Bonus* workbook to the *Sales First Quarter 2016-1* workbook.

A copy of the *Bonus* worksheet is created in the *Sales First Quarter 2016-1* workbook.

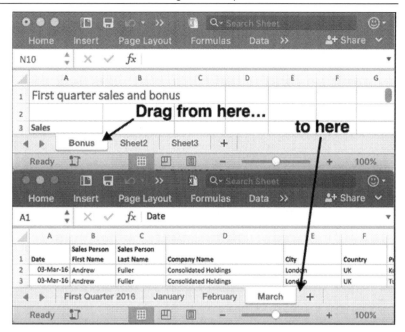

7 Drag and drop the *Sheet3* worksheet from the *First Quarter Sales and Bonus* workbook to the *Sales First Quarter 2016-1* workbook.

You will have to click the *First Quarter Sales and Bonus* workbook once to activate it before you can drag and drop the sheet tab.

This time, because you didn't hold down the **<Alt>** key, the worksheet is moved rather than copied.

8 Change the name of the copied worksheet from *Sheet3* to *Summary*.

This skill was covered in: *Lesson 1-11: View, move, add, rename, delete and navigate worksheet tabs.*

9 If necessary, move the worksheet tabs in the *Sales First Quarter 2016-1* workbook so that they appear in the following order:

This was covered in: *Lesson 1-11: View, move, add, rename, delete and navigate worksheet tabs.*

10 Maximize the *Sales First Quarter 2016-1* workbook window.

This was covered in: *Lesson 1-6: Understand Full Screen view.*

11 Save your work as *Sales First Quarter 2016-2*.

note

Hiding and unhiding a worksheet using the Ribbon and Menu Bar

The right-click method is far faster than using the Ribbon but here's how it can be done:

To *Hide* a worksheet

Click:

Home→Cells→Format→ Hide & Unhide→Hide Sheet

To *Unhide* a worksheet

Click:

Home→Cells→Format→ Hide & Unhide→Unhide Sheet

Then select the sheet that you want to hide/unhide from the dialog and click the OK button.

You can also use the following Menu Bar commands:

⌘→Format→Sheet→Hide
⌘→Format→Sheet→Unhide

Sales First Quarter 2016-2

Lesson 6-4: Hide and unhide a worksheet

Sometimes you'll want to prevent users from viewing and changing one or more worksheets.

In this case you will want to *Hide* the worksheet.

A hidden worksheet becomes invisible to the user but is still there. You can bring back hidden worksheets by *Unhiding* them.

1 Open *Sales First Quarter 2016-2* from your sample files folder (if it isn't already open).

In this workbook you may not want viewers to see the *First Quarter 2016* worksheet, as the information is already contained in the *January/February/March* worksheets.

You might also want to hide the *Bonus* worksheet as it contains confidential information. Note that you should not rely upon hidden worksheets to secure confidential information (see sidebar).

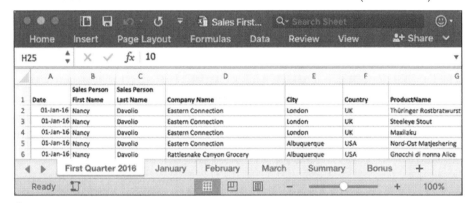

2 Select the *First Quarter 2016* and *Bonus* worksheets.

1. Click on the *First Quarter 2016* worksheet tab.

2. Hold down the **<Cmd>** key.

3. Click on the *Bonus* worksheet tab.

   Both worksheet tabs should now be highlighted:

3 Hide the *First Quarter 2016* and *Bonus* worksheets.

The easiest way to do this is to right click either of the selected tabs and then click *Hide* from the shortcut menu.

The worksheets vanish.

It's also possible to do this less efficiently from the Ribbon or Menu Bar (see sidebar).

4 Unhide the *Bonus* worksheet.

Excel will never allow you to hide all of the worksheets, so this method of unhiding sheets will always work.

1. Right-click on any of the visible worksheet tabs.

2. Click *Unhide* from the shortcut menu.

    The *Unhide* dialog is displayed:

3. Click *Bonus* and then click the *OK* button.

    You can also unhide the worksheets less efficiently by using the Ribbon (see facing page sidebar).

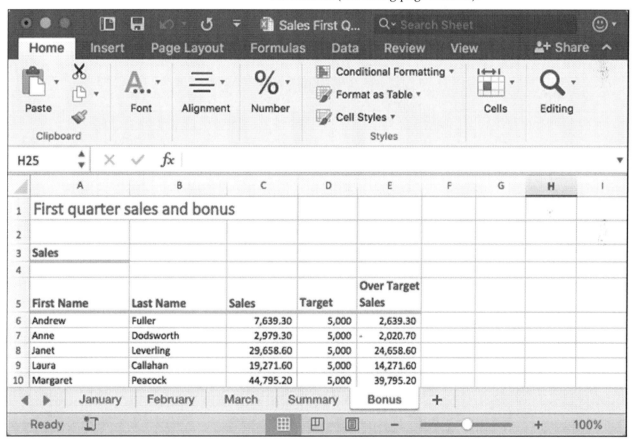

5   Save your work as *Sales First Quarter 2016-3*.

Lesson 6-5: Create cross worksheet formulas

You'll often want to summarize information from multiple worksheets within a workbook.

This can be done by simply prefixing the cell reference with the worksheet name followed by an exclamation mark.

1   Open *Sales First Quarter 2016-3* from your sample files folder (if it isn't already open).

2   Select the *January* tab and scroll to the bottom of the range.

3   Type the word **Total:** into the first empty cell in column G (cell G87).

4   Right-align cell G87.

      This was covered in: *Lesson 4-5: Horizontally align the contents of cells.*

5   Bold-face all of row 87.

      This was covered in: *Lesson 2-6: Select adjacent and non-adjacent rows and columns.*

6   Use AutoSum to add totals to columns H and J.

      This was covered in: *Lesson 2-3: Use AutoSum to quickly calculate totals.*

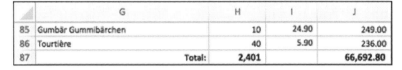

	G	H	I	J
85	Gumbär Gummibärchen	10	24.90	249.00
86	Tourtière	40	5.90	236.00
87	Total:	2,401		66,692.80

7   Add similar totals to the *February* and *March* worksheets.

8   Select the *Summary* tab.

9   Type the text: **First Quarter Summary** into cell A1 and apply the *Title* cell style.

      This was covered in: *Lesson 4-10: Use cell styles and change themes.*

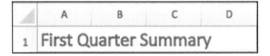

	A	B	C	D
1	First Quarter Summary			

10   Type **Month**, **Units** and **Price** into cells A3, B3 and C3.

11   Type **Jan** into cell A4 and then AutoFill down two cells to add Feb and Mar.

      This was covered in: *Lesson 2-14: Use AutoFill for text and numeric series.*

12   Apply the *Heading 2* style to cells A3:C3.

Sales First Quarter 2016-3

13 Apply the *Heading 4* style to cells A4:A6.

	A	B	C	D
1	First Quarter Summary			
2				
3	Month	Units	Price	
4	Jan			
5	Feb			
6	Mar			

14 Add a formula to cell B4 to display the total units sold in January.

1. Click cell B4.

2. Press the equals key on your keyboard (=) to begin a formula.

3. Click on the *January* tab. ▢ January ⟋ February ▢

4. Scroll to the bottom of the screen using the scroll bars or arrow keys, being careful not to click on any cell.

5. Click on cell H87 (the cell with the total units in it).

6. Press the **<Enter>** key on the keyboard.

The total is shown on the *Summary* sheet.

	A	B	C
3	Month	Units	Price
4	Jan	2401	

important

You must use quotation marks if a worksheet name contains spaces

The example worksheet names used in this session do not contain any spaces.

If you had a worksheet called *January Sales* you would have to construct your formula like this:

='January Sales'!K22

Because worksheet names with spaces are more difficult to work with, many Excel users prefer to name their sheets without spaces by capitalizing the first letter of every word.

Example:

JanuarySales
EuropeIncludingSouthAfrica

15 Use the same technique to add summary totals to **Units** and **Price** for all three months.

	A	B	C
3	Month	Units	Price
4	Jan	2401	66692.8
5	Feb	2132	41207.2
6	Mar	1770	39979.9

16 Examine the formulas that Excel has created.

Click in cell B4 and then look at the formula bar at the top of the screen. Note that the formula is:

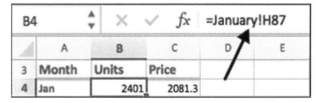

The formula is simply the worksheet name, followed by an exclamation mark, followed by the cell reference.

Note the important sidebar information regarding worksheet names that contain spaces.

17 Save your work as *Sales First Quarter 2016-4*.

Lesson 6-6: Understand worksheet groups

A very interesting (and little known) feature of Excel is its ability to group worksheets into a three-dimensional array of worksheet cells.

When worksheets are grouped, it is possible to perform a single operation upon all of the worksheets in the group. This can be very useful when you need to:

- Print out all of the worksheets in the group.

- Enter data into the same cell for all worksheets in the group.

- Apply formatting to the same cell or range for all worksheets in the group.

1   Open *Widget Supplies Price List* from your sample files folder.

The formatting of this workbook leaves a lot to be desired. It consists of three worksheets all showing similar information but lacking any style.

	A	B	C	D	E	F	G
1	Price List						
2	Prices Effec	20th March 2016					
3	When calculating prices the following exchange rates will be used						
4							
5		USD	GBP	EUR	JPY		
6	USD	1	1.49367	1.08498	0.00816		
7							
8	Description	Dollars	Pounds	Euros	Yen		
9	Standard w	3.75	2.510595	3.456285	459.5588		
10	Premium w	5.5	3.682206	5.069218	674.0196		
11	De-luxe gol	7.95	5.322461	7.327324	974.2647		

You're going to use the magic of grouping to format all three worksheets at the same time.

2   Select all three worksheets to create a worksheet group.

1. Click the *Widgets* worksheet tab.

2. Hold down the **<Shift>** key and click the *Sprockets* worksheet tab.

All three tabs now have a white background to show that they are selected.

Something else has also happened. The title bar at the top of the screen now indicates that the worksheets form a worksheet group.

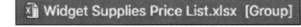

3   Apply formatting to the *Sprockets* worksheet to make it look attractive.

---

note

Selecting non-contiguous worksheets

Non-contiguous simply means *not next to each other*.

When the worksheet tabs aren't next to each other, hold down the **<Cmd>** key and click each in turn. If you make a mistake you can **<Cmd>+<Click>** a second time to de-select one tab.

You can be even cleverer and use a combination of **<Shift>+<Click>** and **<Cmd>+<Click>** when some of the tabs are next to each other and others are not.

Widget Supplies Price List

When you have grouped every worksheet in a workbook, you have a little problem. You can't switch between worksheets and still keep the group selected. As soon as you click a selected sheet the other two are de-selected.

To work-around this you'll have to insert a new blank worksheet. The sheet's only purpose is to allow you to switch between sheets in the selected group.

1. Add a worksheet called *Dummy*.

2. Select the *Widgets, Grommets* and *Sprockets* group as before.

3. Click on the *Sprockets* tab. The group remains selected and the *Sprockets* worksheet is now active.

4. Apply the comma style to the range B9:E11. This was covered in: *Lesson 4-3: Format numbers using built-in number formats.*

5. Adjust the widths of all columns so that they fully display their contents. This was covered in: *Lesson 2-9: Re-size rows and columns.*

6. Apply the *Title* style to cell A1, the *Heading 4* style to cells A2, A6 and A9:A11 and the *Heading 3* style to cells B5:E5 and A8:E8. This was covered in: *Lesson 4-10: Use cell styles and change themes.*

7. Click on each of the other two tabs to ensure that columns are also wide enough for their contents. Adjust if needed.

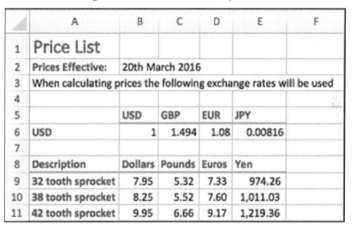

4   With the group still selected, change some exchange rates and the *Prices Effective* date.

I saved the best bit for last. You can now update the exchange rates for all three price lists at the same time. This would be regularly needed as exchange rates fluctuate. When a group of worksheets are selected, any change made to one worksheet is also made to all of the others.

5   Save your work as *Widget Supplies Price List-1*.

Lesson 6-7: Use find and replace

Excel's find and replace tool is amazingly powerful. There are several special features that can massively shorten many common tasks.

This lesson will explore all of the special features and suggest useful ways in which they can be used to solve real-world problems.

1 Open *Sales First Quarter 2016-4* from your sample files folder.

2 Use *Find and Replace* to change the text *Davolio* to *O'Reilly* throughout the workbook.

Nancy Davolio has married Sean O'Reilly and she is very proud of her new name. She's made a special request for you to change her name throughout the workbook too!

1. Click: ⌘→Edit→Find→Replace.

The *Replace* dialog is displayed.

2. Type **Davolio** in the *Find what:* text box and **O'Reilly** in the *Replace with:* text box.

3. You don't want to only look in the current worksheet, but in all of the worksheets in this workbook, so select the *Within: Workbook* option.

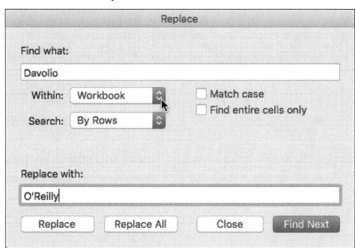

4. Click the *Find Next* button. The first instance of *Davolio* is found on the worksheet.

5. Click the *Replace* button to replace just this one instance. The cursor moves to the next instance found.

---

note

Wildcard searches

Sometimes you will only have a partial idea of what you need to find.

In this case you can use the wildcard characters – the asterisk (*) and the question mark (?).

The asterisk means that any number of wildcard letters can occur between the letters.

The question mark means that one wildcard letter can occur for each question mark.

It is easiest to show how wildcards work with a few examples:

C*g Finds **Containing**
     Finds **Citing**
     Finds **Changing**

S??d Finds **Said**
     Finds **Sand**
     Finds **Seed**
     Doesn't Find **Sound**
     Doesn't Find **Surround**
     Doesn't Find **Sad**

6. Click *Replace All* to replace all remaining instances of *Davolio* with *O'Reilly*. Excel prompts that it has made 28 replacements.

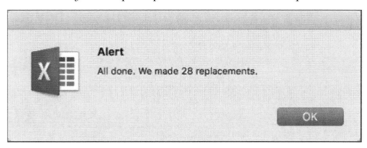

Alert

All done. We made 28 replacements.

OK

7. Click the *OK* and *Close* buttons to close both dialogs.

8. Examine the worksheets. Notice that Nancy's surname has now changed in every worksheet.

	A	B	C	D	E
		Sales Person	Sales Person		
1	Date	First Name	Last Name	Company Name	City
2	01-Jan-16	Nancy	O'Reilly	Eastern Connection	London
3	01-Jan-16	Nancy	O'Reilly	Eastern Connection	London
4	01-Jan-16	Nancy	O'Reilly	Eastern Connection	London
5	01-Jan-16	Nancy	O'Reilly	Eastern Connection	Albuquerque
6	01-Jan-16	Nancy	O'Reilly	Rattlesnake Canyon Grocery	Albuquerque
7	01-Jan-16	Nancy	O'Reilly	Rattlesnake Canyon Grocery	Albuquerque
8	01-Jan-16	Nancy	O'Reilly	Rattlesnake Canyon Grocery	Albuquerque

3 Save your work as *Sales First Quarter 2016-5.*

Session 6: Exercise

1 Close any workbooks that are open.

2 Open *Exercise 6* from your sample files folder.

3 View two copies of the worksheet in different windows stacked horizontally.

4 Scroll one of the windows so that the first USA sale is visible in the first row.

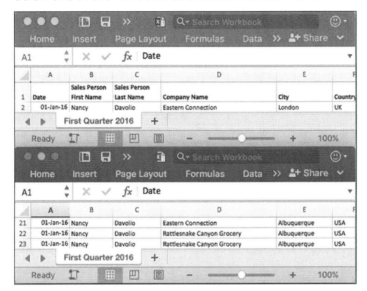

5 Close the *Exercise 6:2* window and maximize the *Exercise 6:1* window.

6 Make two duplicate copies of the *First Quarter 2016* worksheet and name them *USA* and *UK*.

7 Delete all of the non-USA rows from the USA worksheet and all of the non-UK rows from the UK worksheet.

8 Hide the *First Quarter 2016* worksheet tab.

9 Use AutoSum to create totals at the bottom of columns H and J (*Quantity* and *Total*) for both the *USA* and *UK* worksheets.

10 Add a new worksheet and name it *Summary*.

11 Complete the summary sheet as illustrated below using cross-worksheet formulas to calculate the totals.

	A	B	C	D
1	USA and UK Sales Summary			
2				
3	Country	Units	Sales	
4	USA	913	26,572.20	
5	UK	379	7,299.40	
6	Total	1292	33,871.60	

12 Save your work as *Exercise 6-End*.

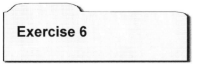

Exercise 6

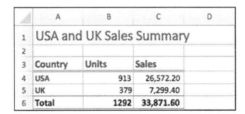

If you need help slide the page to the left

Session 6: Exercise answers

These are the questions that students find the most difficult to answer:

Q 11	Q 8	Q 6	Q 3 and 4
In the example the following styles were used: A1 Title A3:C3 Heading 2 A4:A5 Heading 4 A6:C6 Total 1. Click cell B4 and type an equals sign into it (=). 2. Click the *USA* tab. 3. Use the scroll bars to make the total cell (cell H27) visible, being careful not to click on any of the cells within the worksheet. 4. Click cell H27 and then press the **<Enter>** key. This was covered in: *Lesson 6-5: Create cross worksheet formulas.*	1. Right-click the *First Quarter 2016* worksheet tab. 2. Click *Hide* from the shortcut menu. This was covered in: *Lesson 6-4: Hide and unhide a worksheet.*	1. Click on the *First Quarter 2016* worksheet tab to select it. 2. Hold down the **<Alt>** key. 3. Click and drag the *First Quarter 2016* worksheet tab to the right. 4. Double-click the duplicated worksheet's tab and type the tab's new name. This was covered in: *Lesson 6-2: Duplicate worksheets within a workbook.*	1. Click: ⌘→Window→ New Window 2. Click: ⌘→Window→Arrange 3. Click the *Horizontal* option in the *Arrange Windows* dialog. 4. Click the *OK* button. 5. Scroll one of the windows to the first USA sale (row 21). This was covered in: *Lesson 6-1: View the same workbook in different windows.*

If you have difficulty with the other questions, here are the lessons that cover the relevant skills:

1   Refer to: Lesson 1-5: Minimize, re-size, move and close the Excel window.

2   Refer to: Lesson 1-7: Download the sample files and open/navigate a workbook.

5   Refer to: Lesson 6-1: View the same workbook in different windows.

7   Refer to: Lesson 3-1: Insert and delete rows and columns.

9   Refer to: Lesson 2-3: Use AutoSum to quickly calculate totals.

10   Refer to: Lesson 1-11: View, move, add, rename, delete and navigate worksheet tabs.

12   Refer to: Lesson 1-8: Save a workbook.

Session Seven: Printing Your Work

> The greatest misfortune that ever befell man was the invention of printing.
>
> *Benjamin Disraeli, British Prime Minister and Novelist (1804-1881).*

As the world of commerce moves nearer to the paperless office, printing will become less important.

In the last few years, screen and rendering technology have improved to the extent that I now prefer to read on-screen rather than from paper.

Apple now claim that their "retina" display has such a high pixel density that the human eye is unable to notice pixelation at a typical viewing distance. This suggests that there is no longer any quality advantage in printing on paper.

Perhaps the world is not far away from a time when all communication will be done electronically, but in today's world, paper printed documents are still used in many areas of business.

Excel has a range of tools that will allow you to present your work as polished and professional printed reports. This session will give you all of the skills you need to control every aspect of printing your work on paper.

Session Objectives

By the end of this session you will be able to:

- Print Preview and change paper orientation

- Use Page Layout view to adjust margins

- Use Page Setup to set margins more precisely and center the worksheet

- Set paper size and scale

- Insert, delete and preview page breaks

- Add auto-headers and auto-footers and set the starting page number

- Add custom headers and footers

- Specify different headers and footers for the first, odd and even pages

- Print only part of a worksheet

- Add row and column data labels and grid lines to printed output

- Print several selected worksheets and change the page order

Lesson 7-1: Print Preview and change paper orientation

1 Open *Sales Report* from your sample files folder.

Make sure that you open the Session 7 *Sales Report* file as there's also a sample file of the same name in an earlier session.

2 *Print Preview* the worksheet to see how it will look on paper.

1. Click: ⌘→File→Print.

The *Print* dialog appears, showing a preview of the printed page in the left-hand pane.

2. Click the *Next Page* and *Previous Page* buttons to page through the document.

Notice that the paper isn't wide enough to show all of the columns. Excel tries to help out by printing the left-most columns across the first five or six pages followed by the right-most columns on the next five or six pages.

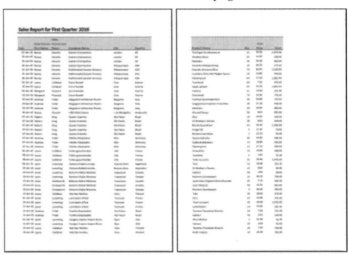

You would have to take the two pages, cut them with scissors, and tape them together in order to see all of the rows and columns.

3 Click *Show Details* to display all printing options.

Most of the printing options are hidden by default, but clicking *Show Details* will display them.

If the complete set of options is already visible, you'll see the *Hide Details* button instead.

Sales Report

4   Change the paper orientation to *Landscape* in order to print more columns on each sheet of paper.

Click the *Landscape* icon next to *Orientation.*

In *Landscape* orientation, the paper is printed as if it had been put into the printer sideways.

The printout is very nearly there now, but there is still a problem with the last column, which prints out all on its own.

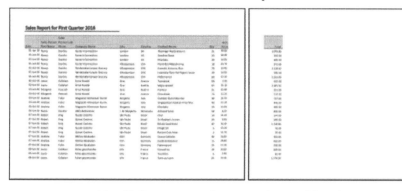

You'll discover a solution to this problem later in: *Lesson 7-2: Use Page Layout view to adjust margins.*

5   Print a copy of the worksheet.

If you'd like to save the forests (and save the cost of sixteen sheets of paper), you may wish to skip this step.

Click the *Print* button.

Even if you didn't actually print the worksheet, I'm sure you will believe that the printout would not have been very good. You'd be back to the scissors and tape if you wanted the pages to show that missing last column.

The printout would have been in *Landscape* orientation because you've told Excel to do that.

6   Save your work as *Sales Report-1.*

important

If you are in North America or Canada, you may see a slightly different printout

If you are in North America or Canada, your printer will probably contain Letter size paper.

The sample file has been set up for A4 size paper.

You'll still be able to complete all lessons in this session, but you may find that the screenshots and any hard copies printed are slightly different to that shown in the book.

International differences in paper sizes will be discussed in depth in the sidebar: "A4 and Letter Paper Size" in: *Lesson 7-4: Set paper size and scale.*

Lesson 7-2: Use Page Layout view to adjust margins

You discovered how to change between Excel's "views" in: *Lesson 1-15: Understand views.*

Page Layout View is a bit like *Print Preview,* as you can see just how your page prints. The big difference is that, unlike *Print Preview,* you can edit a worksheet in this view. You can also set up many page layout features including margins, headers, footers and page numbering.

You'll be exploring all of this view's features in coming lessons. This lesson will focus upon changing the page margins (the blank areas at the top, bottom, left and right of the printout).

1 Open *Sales Report-1* from your sample files folder (if it isn't already open).

2 Display *Page Layout* view.

The fastest way to do this is to click the *Page Layout* button on the status bar at the bottom right of the screen.

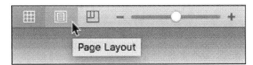

See sidebar for alternative ways to switch to *Page Layout* view.

Page Layout view shows almost exactly how the worksheet will print.

The missing *Total* problem is immediately obvious.

3 Make sure that the rulers are visible.

Unless you've turned them off, you'll see a ruler at the top and left of the page that contains the active cell.

Click cell A1, to make it the active cell, and look for the rulers.

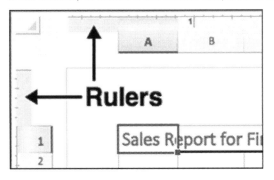

note

Switching to Page Layout view using the Ribbon or Menu Bar

As well as using the buttons on the status bar, you can also switch to Page Layout view using the Ribbon and Menu Bar.

On the Ribbon, use:
View→Workbook Views→
Page Layout

On the Menu Bar, use:
→View→Page Layout

Sales Report-1

If you don't see the rulers, switch them on by clicking:

View→Show→Ruler

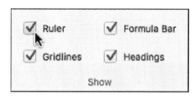

4   Adjust the left margin using the rulers.

1.   Select column A.

Notice how a portion of the ruler above column A is shaded green. This gives you a visual indication of where the margin begins.

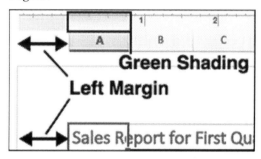

2.   Hover the mouse cursor over the left-hand side of the ruler's green shaded section.

The cursor shape changes to a double-headed arrow.

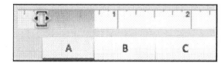

3.   When you see the double-headed arrow, click and drag to the left to reduce the margin to about one centimeter (see sidebar if the ruler doesn't display in centimeters).

You won't be able to set the margins precisely this way, so just make a rough estimate of the right size so that all of the columns fit on the page. You'll learn how to set the margins precisely in the next lesson.

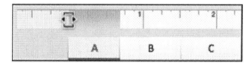

All of the columns now fit onto one page.

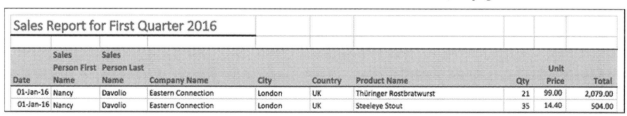

Sales Report for First Quarter 2016									
Date	Sales Person First Name	Sales Person Last Name	Company Name	City	Country	Product Name	Qty	Unit Price	Total
01-Jan-16	Nancy	Davolio	Eastern Connection	London	UK	Thüringer Rostbratwurst	21	99.00	2,079.00
01-Jan-16	Nancy	Davolio	Eastern Connection	London	UK	Steeleye Stout	35	14.40	504.00

5   Save your work as *Sales Report-2*.

Lesson 7-3: Use Page Setup to set margins more precisely and center the worksheet

In the last lesson you adjusted the left margin using the horizontal ruler, and that's often the best way. It is quick and easy and you can immediately see the results of the change on the printed output.

Sometimes you will want the pages in your report to have precise margins. This would be the case when you were going to insert the report into another report (perhaps prepared in Word) and you need the margins to be consistent throughout the publication.

Another common requirement is the need to center the report on the printed page.

1 Open *Sales Report-2* from your sample files folder (if it isn't already open).

2 Display *Page Layout* view (if you aren't already in it).

This was covered in: *Lesson 7-2: Use Page Layout view to adjust margins.*

3 Set the margins to the *Narrow* preset.

1. Click: Page Layout→Page Setup→Margins.

A rich menu appears, showing three preset margin setups along with an option to customize margins.

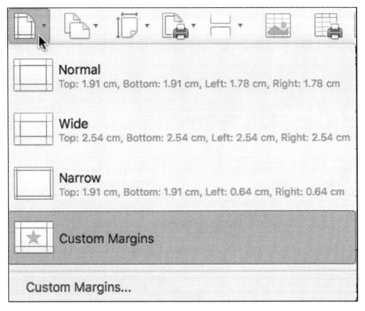

2. Click the *Narrow* option to apply left and right margins of 0.64cm.

Notice that all of the margins have now changed to the *Narrow* specification.

Sales Report-2

4 Set a custom left and right margin of exactly one centimeter.

Imagine that this report will be bound within another that uses margins of one centimeter.

Since there's no suitable preset, you'll have to apply the margins manually using the *Custom Margins* options.

1. Click:

    Page Layout→Page Setup→Margins→Custom Margins...

    The *Page Setup* dialog appears with the *Margins* tab selected.

2. Type directly into the text boxes, or use the spin buttons, to set the left and right margins to exactly one centimeter.

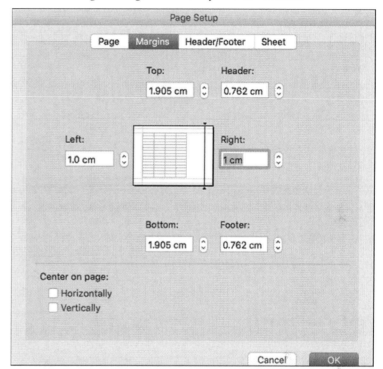

3. Click the *OK* button.

5 Horizontally center the printout on the page.

The page would look better centered.

1. Bring up the *Page Setup* dialog again by clicking:

    Page Layout→Page Setup→Margins→Custom Margins...

2. Check the *Center on page Horizontally* check box.

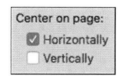

3. Click the *OK* button.

    The page is now perfectly centered, both on the screen and on any hard copy printed.

6 Save your work as *Sales Report-3.*

Lesson 7-4: Set paper size and scale

Imagine that *Landscape* orientation isn't an option for you.

You need *Portrait* orientation and you simply must get all of the columns on each page.

There's only two ways you can achieve this.

1. Buy some bigger paper. As long as your printer can accept it, you will have a larger area upon which to print.

2. Print everything in a smaller font.

The second option often works well (as long as you have good eyesight).

You'll be relieved to know that you don't have to manually re-format every font on the page. You can automatically scale the existing fonts to fit.

1   Open *Sales Report-3* from your sample files folder (if it isn't already open).

2   Display *Page Layout* view (if you aren't already in it).

This was covered in: *Lesson 7-2: Use Page Layout view to adjust margins*.

3   Change the paper orientation back to *Portrait*.

Click: Page Layout→Page Setup→Orientation→Portrait.

Notice that the columns no longer fit upon one sheet of paper.

City	Country		Product Name
London	UK		Thüringer Rostbratwurst
London	UK		Steeleye Stout

4   Change the paper size to A3.

You will not see an A3 paper option if there are no printer drivers installed on your computer that support A3 (see sidebar).

Click: Page Layout→Page Setup→Size→A3 297 x 420 mm.

In the USA and Canada, the nearest equivalent of A3 is Ledger (ANSI B) 17X11 (see sidebar on the facing page for more on this). For the purposes of this lesson you should still set the size to A3 if you are able to.

That works fine. All columns now fit across one sheet of A3 paper.

But what if you don't have an A3 printer, or if the report has to fit on a sheet of A4 (or Letter sized) paper?

5   Change the paper size to A4 (or Letter) sized.

In every country in the world except the USA and Canada the normal business paper size is A4.

important

The paper sizes that are available depend upon the printer drivers installed on your computer

Excel sensibly restricts your choice of paper sizes to those that are supported by your printer(s).

If you do not have a printer driver installed that supports A3 paper, you will not see this in the list when you click:

Page Layout→Page Setup→Size

Sales Report-3

In the USA and Canada, the slightly narrower and longer Letter size (or ANSI A) is the most common.

Click: Page Layout→Page Setup→Size→A4 210 x 297 mm.

6   **Make the report fit on a sheet of A4 (or Letter size) paper by scaling the print.**

1. Click Page Layout→Page Setup→Page Setup.

    The *Page Setup* dialog appears.

2. Click the *Page* tab if it isn't already selected.

3. Click the *Adjust to* spin button to scale the workbook down to 70% of its original size.

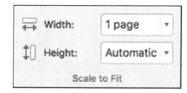

4. Click the *OK* button.

All of the columns now fit on a single page in Portrait orientation.

Bear in mind that, even though it fits on the page, the information on the page may not be very easy to read at such a small type size.

Another method of achieving the same result would have been to use the Page Layout→Scale to Fit→Width menu to scale the page to the width of *1 page*.

The advantage of this approach is that the content will perfectly fit between the page margins. This will look better and will avoid the need to center the printout on the page.

7   **Save your work as *Sales Report-4*.**

Lesson 7-5: Insert, delete and preview page breaks

After you've either printed a worksheet (or entered *Page Layout* view and then returned to *Normal* view), you will see thin dotted lines indicating where the page will break.

Sometimes you need to take control of page breaks. This lesson will show you how.

1 Open *Sales Analysis Chart* from your sample files folder.

Note that no page breaks are shown. This is because the worksheet has never been printed or previewed.

2 Use the *Print* dialog to Print Preview the worksheet.

Click: ↝File↝Print.

The preview reveals that the printout will cut the pie chart in half:

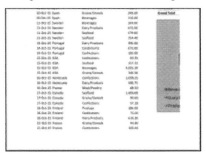

You need to solve this problem by inserting a vertical page break.

3 Close the *Print* dialog and notice that page breaks are shown as dotted lines.

Click the *Cancel* button on the *Print* dialog and notice the dotted lines showing the vertical and horizontal page breaks.

If you don't see any dotted lines, somebody may have disabled them. See the sidebar for instructions on how to switch them back on.

Vertical Break

C	D	E	F
Beverages	310.00		
Beverages	304.00		
Dairy Products	672.00		

It is immediately clear where the problem lies. The vertical break needs to occur at the left of column E to solve the problem.

4 Insert a page break to the left of column E.

1. Click cell E1. It is important to choose row 1, otherwise both a horizontal and vertical page break would be inserted.

2. Click: Page Layout↝Page Setup↝Breaks↝Insert Page Break.

A solid line appears to the left of the active cell to show the new position of the vertical page break. When you see a solid

Sales Analysis Chart

line (rather than a dotted line) you know that the break was manually inserted (rather than automatically added by Excel).

5   Confirm that the worksheet will now print correctly.

1. Click: ⌘→File→Print to see a preview of how the worksheet will print (or view the page in *Page Layout* view) and move to the last page in the printout to confirm that the worksheet will now print correctly.

2. Click the *Cancel* button to close the *Print* dialog.

6   Insert a horizontal page break above row 78.

Row 78 displays the first sale for November 2015.

75	31-Oct-15	Germany	Beverages	216.00
76				37,515.73
77				
78	01-Nov-15	USA	Condiments	616.00

For presentational reasons you want November's sales to begin on a new page, so you need to insert a page break above row 78.

1. Click in cell A78. It's important to click in column A, otherwise both a horizontal and vertical page break would be inserted to the left of, and above the active cell.

2. Click: Page Layout→Page Setup→Breaks→Insert Page Break.

    A solid line appears above the active cell (row 78) to show the position of the new (manually inserted) horizontal page break.

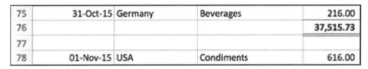

7   Confirm that the worksheet will now print correctly.

View the page in *Page Layout* view.

The page now breaks at row 77 and a new page begins for row 78.

8   Remove the horizontal page break above row 78.

1. Return to *Normal* view and click anywhere in row 78 except cell E78. If you were to select cell E78 you would remove both the horizontal and vertical page breaks.

2. Click: Page Layout→Page Setup→Breaks→ Remove Page Break.

    The solid line disappears, indicating that the page will no longer break before row 78.

9   Save your work as *Sales Analysis Chart-1*.

note

Resetting all page breaks

Sometimes you might want to reset all of the page breaks back to their default locations.

You can do this by clicking:

Page Layout→
Page Setup→Breaks→
Reset All Page Breaks

note

Page Break Preview has returned in Excel 2019 for Mac

The *Page Break Preview* feature was available in Excel 2004 for Mac, but was removed with the release of Excel 2008.

Excel 2019 for Mac brings back the *Page Break Preview* feature, although users of Excel 365 received this feature a little earlier via an update.

Lesson 7-6: Adjust page breaks using Page Break Preview

In the last lesson you learned how to adjust page breaks in *Normal* view. Many users also like to adjust page breaks in *Page Layout* view.

Microsoft recommends that you don't use either. There's a purpose-built view just to handle page breaks called *Page Break Preview* view.

I tie my tongue in knots during my classes just trying to say *Page Break Preview view*!

This view allows you to click and drag page breaks (something that you can't do with the other views).

1   Open *Sales Analysis Chart-1* from your sample file folder (if it isn't already open).

2   Display *Page Break Preview* view.

Click the *Page Break Preview* button at the bottom right of the screen.

You can also select this view from the Ribbon by clicking:

View→Workbook Views→Page Break Preview

Page Break Preview

Just like *Normal* view, *Page Break Preview* allows you to see which breaks are manual and which are automatic. Breaks shown as solid lines were manually inserted. Breaks shown as dotted lines were automatically inserted by Excel.

	A	B	C	D	E
50	22-Oct-15	Ireland	Dairy Products	200.00	
51	22-Oct-15	Ireland	Dairy Products	122.88	
52	22-Oct-15	Ireland	Produce	1,628.16	
53	23-Oct-15	Portugal	Condiments	285.12	

Notice that your manually inserted vertical break (to the left of column E) is shown as a solid line, while Excel's automatic page break (after row 51) is shown as a dotted line.

3   Move the automatic break from between rows 103 and 104 to between rows 77 and 78.

1.   Move the mouse cursor over the dotted blue line between rows 103 and 104 until you see the double-headed arrow cursor shape.

| 103 | 14-Nov-15 | Mexico | Meat/Poultry | 396.00 | |
| 104 | 15-Nov-15 | UK | Beverages | 90.00 | |

2.   When you see the double-headed arrow, click and drag to move the page break up the page so that the line is between rows 77 and 78.

Sales Analysis
Charts-1

When you release the mouse button, the page break is shown as a solid blue line.

77					
78	01-Nov-15	USA		Condiments	616.00

4 Automatically scale the sheet so that all of November's sales fit on one sheet.

An interesting feature of *Page Break Preview* is its ability to scale a page to fit the paper. You did this manually in: *Lesson 7-4: Set paper size and scale*. The process is far more intuitive in this view.

1. Scroll to row 129. Notice that there is an automatic page break between rows 129 and 130.

2. Drag this page break to a new position between rows 145 and 146.

   Excel hasn't inserted another automatic break anywhere in Page 3 even though Page 3 is now a lot longer than it was before. The only way that Excel can possibly print Page 3 is by automatically scaling it down to fit the page.

3. Click: File→Print to print preview the worksheet and notice that the fonts for the entire report have been reduced. Excel cannot scale a single page in isolation; it scales all pages to keep the font size of all report pages consistent.

4. Click the *Cancel* button to close the *Print* dialog.

5 Remove all manually applied page breaks.

Excel's automatic scaling system means that it is easy to lose track of what is happening. Sometimes you want to set everything back to the way it used to be and start again.

Click: Page Layout→Page Setup→Breaks→Reset All Page Breaks.

All manual page breaks disappear and Excel's automatic page breaks reappear.

6 Save your work as *Sales Analysis Chart-2*.

Lesson 7-7: Add auto-headers and auto-footers and set the starting page number

Headers and footers are displayed at the top and bottom of each printed page.

If you are printing a long report it is very useful to add page numbers. Other items commonly added to page headers and footers include:

- A title.
- The date and time that the report was printed.
- The report author's name.
- The name of the Excel file that was used to generate the report.
- The full path to the Excel file.
- A company logo.
- Copyright notices.
- A distribution list or the security level of the document (for example you may want to include the word: *Confidential*).

1   Open *Sales Report-4* from your sample files folder.

2   Display *Page Layout* view (if you aren't already in it).

This was covered in: *Lesson 7-2: Use Page Layout view to adjust margins*.

3   Click in the page header area at the top of the screen.

The page header area contains the text: *Add header*.

Add header

When you click in this area, a new tab appears on the Ribbon.

Header & Footer

You will use this tab to access Excel's *Auto Header and Footer* feature.

4   Add an Auto Header that will display page numbers at the top of each page in the format: *Page 1*.

When you click in the header area you are able to access the *Header & Footer* tab.

1.   Click: Header & Footer→Header & Footer→Header.

2.   Choose the option *Page 1* (see sidebar). Page numbers are now shown at the top of each page (you may need to scroll up and down the page to see the page number update).

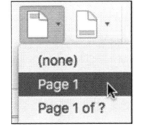

Sales Report-4

5 Add an Auto Footer to show the filename at the bottom of the page.

1. Click in the *Add footer* area at the bottom of the page.

2. Click: Header & Footer→Header & Footer→Footer.

3. Choose the *Sales Report-4.xlsx* item from the drop-down list (see sidebar).

The filename is now shown at the bottom of every page in the report (you may need to scroll up and down the page to see the footer update).

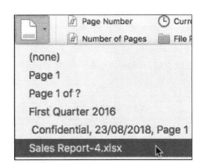

Rio de Janeiro	Brazil	Original
Torino	Italy	Gumbär
Sales Report-4.xlsx		

6 Change the page numbering so that numbering begins at page ten.

It is very common to print an Excel report and then collate it into another report (perhaps produced using Word). If the pages were to be inserted after page 9, you would want Excel to begin numbering at page 10.

1. Click: Page Layout→Page Setup→Page Setup.

2. Click the *Page* tab and type the number 10 into the *First page number* text box.

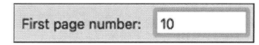

3. Click the *OK* button.

Page numbering now begins at Page 10.

7 Save your work as *Sales Report-5*.

Lesson 7-8: Add custom headers and footers

Auto-headers and footers provide a quick and convenient method when your needs are simple. Custom headers allow you to combine your own text with report fields (such as page numbers). You are also able to add text to three different sections in the header and footer areas (Left, Right and Center).

1 Open *Sales Report-5* from your sample files folder (if it isn't already open).

2 Display *Page Layout* view (if you aren't already in it).

This was covered in: *Lesson 7-2: Use Page Layout view to adjust margins*.

3 Click on the *Page Header* area.

Notice that when you click the *Page Header* area the contents change from **Page 10** to **Page &[Page]**.

The Ampersand (&) is called an *escape character*. It tells Excel that whatever text follows is a *field* rather than literal text. The field *&[Page]* tells Excel to insert the current page number.

4 Change the page header to: *The Gourmet Food Company*.

Click in the center of the header area (where you currently see the page number) and type **The Gourmet Food Company**

5 Place the date and time in the left-hand part of the page header.

There's no Auto-header for date and time. In this case you'll have to create your own custom header field.

1. Click in the **left-hand** section of the header area.

2. Type the text **Printed on:** followed by a space.

3. Click: Header & Footer→
   Header & Footer Elements→Current Date.

4. Type a space followed by **at:** and then another space.

5. Click: Header & Footer→
   Header & Footer Elements→Current Time.

The left-hand section of the header bar now contains the following text:

> **note**
>
> ### How to include an ampersand in a header or footer
>
> In the header and footer area, the ampersand (&) denotes the beginning of a field.
>
> Sometimes you will need to put an ampersand into header text. For example, your company might be called:
>
> *Marks & Spencer*
>
> To do this you need to incorporate a double ampersand into the header to tell Excel to print the ampersand. You would need to type:
>
> **Marks && Spencer**

> **note**
>
> ### Headers and footers may have multiple lines
>
> You can make your header and footer information span as many lines as you need. Press the <Enter> key when you want to move to a new line.
>
> If you use many lines, it may be necessary to adjust the top margin as the header can sometimes overlap the worksheet.

> **Sales Report-5**

note

Adding a graphical header

Sometimes you will need a page header that requires more sophisticated formatting than Excel is capable of. The solution is to create the header as a graphic using a program such as Adobe Photoshop.

When the graphic has been prepared click:

Header & Footer→
Header & Footer Elements→
Picture

You are then able to insert the graphic into the header.

When a graphic appears in the header the *Format Picture* button in the *Header & Footer Elements* group becomes available.

When you click away from the header section, the date and time are displayed. The date is displayed in a format dictated by the locale of your computer. In this example it is the date: 23rd Aug 2018 displayed in UK format (day/month/year):

Printed on: 23/08/2018 at: 16:05

6   Place the page number on the right-hand side of the page header.

There is an *Auto Header* for this purpose but you can't use it. Auto headers may only be used in the center section of the header. You'll have to make your own using the *Header & Footer Elements* just as you did for the date and time.

1. Click in the right-hand part of the page header and type **Page:** followed by a space (the last space may not appear on screen but don't worry, it is there).

2. Click: Header & Footer→
    Header & Footer Elements→Page Number.

3. The right-hand section of the header bar now contains the following text:

    Page: &[Page]

    When you click away from the header section, the current page number is displayed:

    Page: 10

Printed on: 23/08/2018 at: 16:10   The Gourmet Food Company   Page: 10

note

Good design practice

It is always a good idea to restrict your font choice to one of the two provided by the current theme.

This allows fonts to automatically change when you change the theme.

Themes were covered in: *Lesson 4-9: Understand themes.*

7   Apply an attractive format to the page header section.

1. Click the left-hand section of the header. The text is automatically selected.

    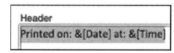

    Header
    Printed on: &[Date] at: &[Time]

2. Click: Home→Font→Font and set the font face to *Calibri Light, 10 Point*. Note that, following good design practice, this is one of the two theme fonts (see sidebar).

3. Click: Home→Font→Font Color and set the color to the *Blue-Gray, Text 2* theme color (the 4th color on the top row of theme colors).

4. Apply the same format to the right-hand section of the header.

5. Format the center section of the header as *Calibri Light, 28 point, Blue-Gray, Text 2.*

Printed on: 05/10/2017 at: 11:16   The Gourmet Food Company   Page: 10

8   Save your work as *Sales Report-6.*

Lesson 7-9: Specify different headers and footers for the first, odd and even pages

If you look at the pages in this book, you'll notice that there's a different header and footer for odd and even pages. The first page of each session is also different.

If the sample worksheet needed to be inserted into a publication similar to this one, you'd need to specify three different headers and footers; one for odd pages, one for even pages, and one for the first page.

1   *Open Sales Report-6 from your sample files folder (if it isn't already open).*

2   Display *Normal* view (if you aren't already in it).

    Click the *Normal* view button at the bottom right of the screen.

3   Insert five blank rows above row 1.

    This was covered in: *Lesson 3-1: Insert and delete rows and columns.*

4   Insert a manual page break above row 6.

    This was covered in: *Lesson 7-5: Insert, delete and preview page breaks.*

    A dotted line appears above row 6.

    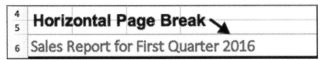

5   Merge and center cells A2:J2 and enter the text: **Sales Report Jan-Mar 2016** into the merged cell.

    This was covered in: *Lesson 4-6: Merge cells, wrap text and expand/collapse the formula bar.*

6   Apply the *Title* style to the newly added text.

    This was covered in: *Lesson 4-10: Use cell styles and change themes.*

7   Merge and center cells A3:J3 and enter the text: **Private & Confidential**

8   Apply the *Heading 4* style to the newly added text.

9   Apply a fill color of *Blue, Accent1, Lighter 80%* to cells A2:A3.

10   Resize row 1 so that it is about 200 pixels deep.

11   Open the Print dialog to see a print preview.

    Click: ⌘→File→Print.

Sales Report-6

You can see that you've created a cover sheet for the report. It doesn't look bad, but the header and footer are spoiling things. You need to suppress the header and footer from the cover sheet.

12 Remove the header and footer from the first (cover) page.

1. Click the *Cancel* button to close the *Print* dialog.

2. Change the view to *Page Layout* view.

3. Click in the *Header* area of the first page.

4. Click: Header & Footer→
    Options→Different First Page.

    The header and footer information vanishes from the cover page.

13 Set a different odd and even page header and footer.

1. Click in the *Header* area.

2. Click Header & Footer→
    Options→Different Odd & Even Pages.

    The header and footer information vanishes from odd pages but remains on even pages.

14 Remove all header and footer information.

You're going to replace the existing page header and footer, so delete the contents of all header and footer sections.

15 Add odd and even page footers so that the page number appears on the right of all odd pages and on the left of all even pages.

If you look at the footer of this book, you will see that the page numbers are arranged in this manner.

1. Click in the footer area of any of the pages except the first page.

    Notice that when you click in the footer area, Excel indicates which footer you are editing (odd or even).

2. Insert a page number into the odd and even page footer areas.

If you're wondering why Excel thinks that even pages are odd, and odd pages are even, see the sidebar for an explanation.

While a cover page is useful in all reports, the different odd and even page headers will only improve the presentation of reports that will be printed on both sides of the paper and then bound.

16 Save your work as *Sales Report-7*.

note

Print areas do not have to be contiguous

You may want to print several different sections from your worksheet.

Simply select the non-contiguous (non-adjacent) ranges (covered in: *Lesson 2-7: Select non-contiguous cell ranges and view summary information*) and then use either of the techniques discussed in this lesson to print the selected cells.

trivia

Origins of the term: "One-off"

Many years ago, I studied engineering and spent part of my time discovering the joys of lathes, milling machines, grinders and all of the other paraphernalia found in machine shops.

Sometimes I would wander around the factory where the lathe operators would sit next to their machines – usually reading a book.

They would have a specification drawing next to them with something like "600 Off" written on it. This would mean that they would make 600 parts to the defined specification.

A *One-off* would be quite unusual as it would be expensive to set-up the lathe to produce just one part.

The term "one-off" is now commonly used in the UK to describe something that happens, or is made, only once.

Sales Report-7

Lesson 7-10: Print only part of a worksheet

Sometimes you will want to print a selection of cells from a worksheet.

Excel provides two ways to do this. The first method is applicable when the requirement is a one-off. In other words, the next time you print, the entire worksheet will be printed in the usual way.

The second method involves setting a print area. If you then save the worksheet, the defined print area will remain until you clear the print area.

In this lesson you'll explore both methods.

1 Open *Sales Report-7* from your sample files folder (if it isn't already open).

2 Display *Normal* view (if you aren't already in it).

Click the *Normal* view button at the bottom right of the screen.

Imagine that you need to print a listing for all of January's sales.

3 Select all of the transactions for January 2016 (cells A8:J93).

4 Print only the selected cells.

1. Click: ⌘→File→Print.

   The *Print* dialog is displayed.

2. Click the *Print* drop-down menu.

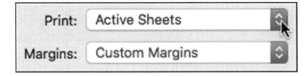

   If this isn't visible, click the *Show Details* button to display all print settings.

3. Select *Selection* from the drop-down list:

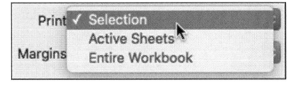

   Notice that only January transactions (cells A8:J93) are now displayed in the print preview on the left.

   If you were to click the *Print* button at this stage, only January sales would be printed.

5 Close and re-open the *Print* dialog.

1. Click *Cancel* to close the *Print* dialog.

note

Setting the Print Area with the Menu Bar

You can also set the Print Area by clicking:

🍎→File→Print Area→
Set Print Area

note

The print area is implemented using a named range

Excel has a feature called "named ranges". The definition and use of named ranges is an expert-level skill covered in the next book in this series: *Learn Excel 2019 for Mac Expert Skills with The Smart Method*.

When you set a print area, Excel simply creates a sheet-level named range called *Print Area* for the currently active worksheet. Each worksheet can have its own print area.

If you do progress to become an Excel Expert, it is possible to define this named range manually and to use it in formulas.

2. Click: 🍎→File→Print to reopen the *Print* dialog.

    Notice that the print settings have reverted to *Print Active Sheets*.

    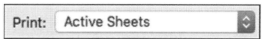

    In other words, the instruction to only print the selected cells is lost when the dialog is closed.

    But consider the case of a worksheet where you will only ever want to print a selected range. In this case you'd like the print settings to be saved with the workbook.

6   Set the print area to cells (A8:J93).

    1. Click the *Cancel* button to close the *Print* dialog.

    2. Select cells A8:J93.

    3. Click: Page Layout→Page Setup→Print Area→Set Print Area.

        When you set the print area it remains set even if you close and re-open the workbook.

    4. Click: 🍎→File→Print to re-open the *Print* dialog.

        Notice that only January sales are shown in the preview in the left pane of the window.

7   Save, close and re-open the workbook and then open the *Print* dialog.

    1. Save and close *Sales Report-7*.

    2. Re-open *Sales Report-7*.

    3. Click: 🍎→File→Print to reopen the *Print* dialog.

        Notice that only January sales are still shown in the preview in the right pane of the window, proving that the print area was saved with the workbook

8   Clear the print area.

    1. Click the *Cancel* button to close the *Print* dialog.

    2. Click: Page Layout→Page Setup→Print Area→Clear Print Area.

9   Examine the print preview to prove that the full worksheet will be printed in future.

    Click: 🍎→File→Print to open the *Print* dialog.

    Notice that the cover sheet, along with all sales, are now shown in the preview in the left pane of the window.

10 Save *Sales-Report 7*.

Lesson 7-11: Add row and column data labels and grid lines to printed output

1 Open *Sales Report-7* from your sample files folder (if it isn't already open).

2 View the worksheet in *Page Layout* view.

There's a slight problem with this worksheet. The first page is easy to understand, as it has a column header row to indicate which data is in each column (such as Date, City and Company Name):

Sales Report for First Quarter 2016				
	Sales Person First	Sales Person Last		
Date	Name	Name	Company Name	City
01-Jan-16	Nancy	Davolio	Eastern Connection	London
01-Jan-16	Nancy	Davolio	Eastern Connection	London

The second page isn't so easy to understand because the column header row is missing:

23-Jan-16	Michael	Suyama	Gourmet Lanchonetes
23-Jan-16	Michael	Suyama	Gourmet Lanchonetes
23-Jan-16	Robert	King	Mère Paillarde
23-Jan-16	Robert	King	Mère Paillarde

3 Add column headings to each printed page.

1. Click: Page Layout→Page Setup→Print Titles.

   The *Page Setup* dialog is displayed with the *Sheet* tab selected.

2. Click inside the *Rows to repeat at top* text box.

3. Select all of row 8 by clicking anywhere in row 8.

   The row reference appears in the dialog.

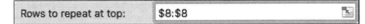

   Rows to repeat at top: $8:$8

   Note that you could enter these manually if you wanted to. For example, to print rows 6 to 8 on each page you would enter: **6:8** (or **$6:$8**).

   The dollar signs denote an absolute reference. You learned about absolute references in: *Lesson 3-11: Understand absolute and relative cell references.*

4. Click the *OK* button.

   Notice that the column headings now appear at the top of every page in the printout.

		Sales Person First	Sales Person Last	
	Date	Name	Name	Company Name
72	23-Jan-16	Michael	Suyama	Gourmet Lanchonetes
73	23-Jan-16	Michael	Suyama	Gourmet Lanchonetes

Sales Report-7

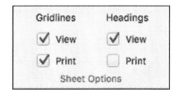

4   Add gridlines to the printout.

Sometimes it is difficult for the eye to track across printed lines. For this type of report, it is useful to print gridlines onto the printed page in a similar way to the ones displayed on the worksheet.

Click: Page Layout→Sheet Options→Gridlines→Print.

5   Open the *Print* dialog to preview how the workbook will print.

Click: ▸→File→Print to open the *Print* dialog.

The preview in the left-hand pane shows that gridlines will be printed upon each page:

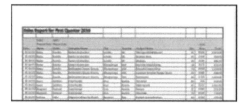

6   Add row and column headings to the printout.

You may want to send a printed worksheet to a colleague and then discuss it on the telephone. It might be useful to be able to ask "what do you think of the value in cell H11?" This isn't possible because row and column headings are not normally shown on the printed page.

1.   Click the *Cancel* button to close the *Print* dialog.

2.   Click: Page Layout→Sheet Options→Headings→Print.

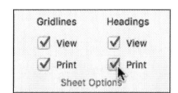

7   Open the *Print* dialog to preview how the workbook will print.

Click: ▸→File→Print to open the *Print* dialog.

The preview in the left-hand pane shows that row and column headings will be printed upon each page:

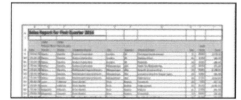

8   Remove the gridlines and column headings from the printout.

1.   Click the *Cancel* button to close the *Print* dialog.

2.   Clear the check boxes that were ticked in the previous steps.

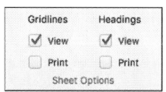

9   Save your work as *Sales Report-8*.

Lesson 7-12: Print several selected worksheets and change the page order

1   Open *Palace Hotel Bar Activity* from your sample files folder.

2   Change the view to *Page Break Preview* and examine how the workbook will print.

Click the *Page Break Preview* button at the bottom right of the screen.

Notice that the worksheet prints first downward (listing all activity between 11:00 AM and 4:00 PM for all days).

When it reaches the bottom of the list, it moves across to print all activity between 5:00 PM and 10:00 PM and so on.

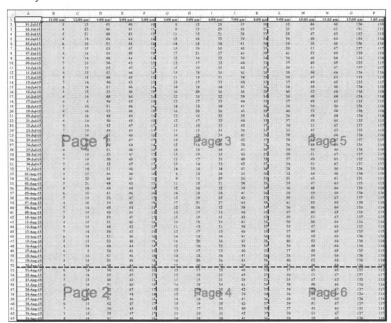

But what if you don't want to print in this order? Perhaps you would like to first print all activity for all times. In other words, you want the above display to make the existing Page 3 into Page 2.

3   Change the print order to *Over, then down*.

1.   Click: Page Layout→Page Setup→Page Setup.

![Page Setup ribbon group showing Print Area, Breaks, Background, Print Titles, Page Setup, Width, Height]

Palace Hotel Bar Activity

2.   Click the *Sheet* tab.

3.   Click the *Over, then down* option button.

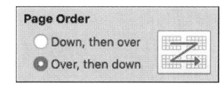

4.   Click the *OK* button.

You can see that the page order has now changed.

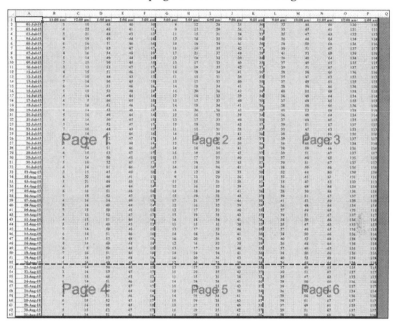

4   Print the headcount for Jul-Aug and Nov-Dec in one printout.

You can print several worksheets at the same time and they needn't be adjacent.

1.   Click the *Jul-Aug* tab.

2.   Hold down the **<Cmd>** key and click the *Nov-Dec* tab.

Both tabs are now colored white

3.   Click: ⌘→File→Print.

4.   Note that when more than one sheet is selected, the *Print* menu has the *Print Active Sheets* option selected by default.

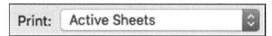

5.   Click the *Next Page* button at the bottom below the print preview to confirm that the contents of the *Jul-Aug* and *Nov-Dec* worksheets would have been printed.

6.   Click the *Cancel* button to close the *Print* dialog.

5   Save your work as *Palace Hotel Bar Activity-1*.

Session 7: Exercise

1 Open *Exercise 7* from your sample files folder.

2 Switch to *Page Layout* view.

3 Change the left margin to about 1.0 cm using the click and drag method.

4 Click: Page Layout→Page Setup→Margins and use the *Custom Margins...* option to set top and bottom margins to precisely 2.0 cm and the left and right margins to precisely 1.0 cm.

5 Horizontally center the printout on the page.

6 Change the page orientation to landscape.

7 Insert a horizontal page break between rows 27 and 28.

8 Add an auto-header to match the following:

> Page 1 of 3

9 Make the data labels in row 1 repeat on every page.

10 Set the print area to A1:J12 and then open the *Print* dialog to prove that only these cells would be printed.

11 Clear the print area.

12 Add gridlines to the printout.

13 Open the *Print* dialog to prove that gridlines would be printed.

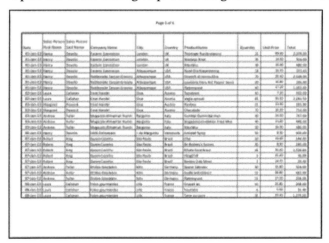

14 Save your work as *Exercise 7-End*.

Exercise 7

If you need help slide the page to the left ➡

Session 7: Exercise answers

These are the questions that students find the most difficult to answer:

Q 10	Q 9	Q 7	Q 5
1. Select cells A1:J12.	1. Click:	1. Click in cell A28.	1. Click:
2. Click:	Page Layout→	2. Click:	Page Layout→
Page Layout→	Page Setup→Print Titles	Page Layout→	Page Setup→Page Setup
Page Setup→	2. Click in the *Rows to repeat at top* text box.	Page Setup→	
Print Area→	3. Either click in row 1 with the mouse or type 1:1 into the box.	Breaks→	2. Click the *Margins* tab.
Set Print Area		Insert Page Break	3. Beneath *Center on page,* check the *Horizontally* box.
	This was covered in: *Lesson 7-11: Add row and column data labels and grid lines to printed output.*	This was covered in: *Lesson 7-5: Insert, delete and preview page breaks.*	This was covered in: *Lesson 7-3: Use Page Setup to set margins more precisely and center the worksheet.*
This was covered in: *Lesson 7-10: Print only part of a worksheet.*			

If you have difficulty with the other questions, here are the lessons that cover the relevant skills:

1   Lesson 1-7: Download the sample files and open/navigate a workbook.

2,3   Lesson 7-2: Use Page Layout view to adjust margins.

4   Lesson 7-3: Use Page Setup to set margins more precisely and center the worksheet.

6   Lesson 7-1: Print Preview and change paper orientation.

8   Lesson 7-7: Add auto-headers and auto-footers and set the starting page number.

11   Lesson 7-10: Print only part of a worksheet.

12   Lesson 7-11: Add row and column data labels and grid lines to printed output.

13   Lesson 7-1: Print Preview and change paper orientation.

14   Lesson 1-8: Save a workbook.

Session Eight: Cloud Computing

> Cloud is about how you do computing, not where you do computing.
>
> *Paul Maritz, Computer Scientist and Software Executive*

In this session you will learn how *Office Online, OneDrive* and *Office Mobile* work together to enable you to access Excel, and all of your files, on any modern device, anywhere.

Cloud computing is one of the most rapidly evolving areas of Information Technology today. This session will show you how to make the most of this exciting new way of working.

Session Objectives

By the end of this session you will be able to:

- Understand Cloud Computing
- Save a workbook to a OneDrive
- Open a workbook from a OneDrive
- Understand operating systems and devices
- Understand Office versions
- Understand Excel Online
- Open a workbook using Excel Online
- Share a link to a workbook
- Edit a workbook simultaneously with other users using Excel Online

note

Cloud computing and thin clients

Office Online is a true cloud application. It was designed to be used without any software installation, on any device that supports a modern web browser.

The term "cloud computing" (in its modern context) was first used in 2006 (by the Google CEO Eric Schmidt).

There is a much older concept in the IT world called *thin client computing*.

Thin client computing allows traditional applications (written for desktop computers) to be deployed, unmodified, as cloud applications.

In the thin client model, the user doesn't use a web browser but installs a special thin client application.

The user then starts the thin client application and can effectively operate a computer located in the cloud by remote control. The user's computer sends keystrokes to the cloud computer. The cloud computer then returns a copy of the screen display back to the user.

Microsoft's *Remote Desktop Services (RDS)* and products from *Citrix Systems* are the most widely used thin client solutions.

The huge advantage of thin client implementations is that a company can continue to use the old desktop applications that they are used to.

Thin clients are very simple applications compared to sophisticated modern web browsers.

Browsers make better use of Internet bandwidth and usually provides a better user experience than thin client solutions.

Lesson 8-1: Understand cloud computing

> First to mind when asked what 'the cloud' is, a majority respond it's either an actual cloud, the sky, or something related to weather.
>
> *Citrix Cloud Survey Guide (August 2012)*

Cloud computing simply means the use of Internet-hosted files and applications

When you access Internet hosted applications such as Facebook, Twitter, Google Search, or Amazon using a web browser you are experiencing cloud computing (the Internet is often referred to as "the cloud").

You can access modern cloud applications, without installing any software, by typing a simple URL into any modern web browser. This means that cloud applications will run on any device with a modern browser (including the iPad, PC, Apple Mac and nearly all smartphones).

Cloud applications (hosted in a web browser) often have rich functionality that rivals traditional desktop applications. This has only become recently possible with the 2014 release of HTML 5 (the markup language used by modern web browsers).

It is easy to envisage a future where you will never have to install an application onto your computer. You'll simply visit the application's web site and start using it immediately. Instead of saving your files to your local hard drive, you'll save them to the cloud. Microsoft's "hard drive in the cloud" product is called *OneDrive*.

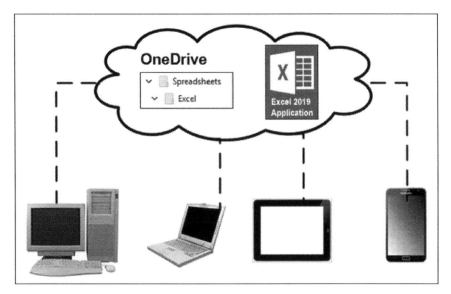

In the case of Microsoft Office, it is already possible to use a special limited-feature cloud version of Office (called *Office Online*). You'll learn about Office Online later, in: *Lesson 8-6: Understand Excel Online*.

anecdote

Latency

A long time ago (in the mid 1990's) I was involved in a very early implementation of a cloud project. It was so long ago that the term "cloud computing" wouldn't be invented for another ten years.

The multi-million-dollar project involved connecting a network of computers in Europe and Africa to a common database located in the United Kingdom.

We decided that a thin client solution (see facing page sidebar) was the most appropriate way to cater for the business requirement.

Testing went wonderfully well in European countries but when the software was rolled out to Africa there was a little problem.

The network link was routed via satellite. Satellites are placed 22,236 miles above the Earth's surface to achieve geostationary orbit.

The speed of light is approximately 186,000 miles per second. Unfortunately, this wasn't fast enough to prevent an infuriating lag between African users pressing a key and the corresponding letter appearing upon the keyboard.

This problem is referred to as *latency*.

It would have been very useful to increase the speed of light to solve the problem. Albert Einstein might have advised, however, that that wasn't an option.

Office Online requires no installation and will run in any web browser. When you use Office Online you'll typically also store your files in the cloud (in a Microsoft OneDrive).

Advantages of cloud computing

Cloud computing promises many advantages over traditional IT implementations:

- Users can work anywhere using any device. They can continue their work while at home or on the road and will always have full access to their files.

- Companies will not need a dedicated IT department as support can be outsourced to technicians working at a remote data center.

- The responsibility for backups can be delegated to the data center. This reduces the possibility of data loss after hardware failure.

- Businesses will not need to concern themselves with keeping software and anti-virus measures up-to-date.

- Access to software will usually be purchased on a subscription basis. When a given piece of software isn't needed any more, the company can simply unsubscribe. This concept is often referred to as: *Software as a Service* (SaaS).

Computers that only access cloud applications are inexpensive as they do not need powerful processors or large amounts of memory.

note

OneDrive subscriptions

Microsoft have offered a different range of OneDrive plans over the last couple of years. By the time you read this book they will probably have changed their offerings again.

In September 2018 the following plans were available:

Free: This plan is now limited to 5Gb of free storage (until early 2016 Microsoft offered 15Gb of free storage).

Visit:

http://OneDrive.com

…for all the details that you need to open a free OneDrive account

Office 365 subscribers: If you purchased Excel 2019 using a Microsoft Office 365 annual subscription, you will have 1 Terabyte of storage included as part of the Office 365 package.

Paid Subscription: If you are not an Office 365 subscriber and need more than 5Gb of storage, you can subscribe to a 50Gb plan for $1.99 per month.

Of course, as with all cloud services, the above plans can change at any time. Visit:

http://OneDrive.com

… for current pricing and availability of all Microsoft OneDrive plans.

Lesson 8-2: Save a workbook to a OneDrive

In order to complete this lesson, you will need a OneDrive account. At the time of writing (September 2017) a free 5Gb subscription was available. See sidebar for more information about different OneDrive plans.

A OneDrive can be visualized as a "hard drive in the sky". Saving a workbook to a OneDrive means you'll be able to access it from any device, anywhere in the world.

The files are usually stored on one of Microsoft's servers (accessed via the Internet). Some corporate users may prefer to store their OneDrive files on their own servers for security reasons (see sidebar facing page).

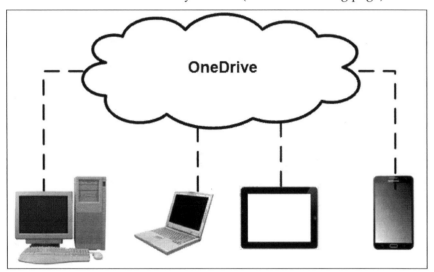

1   Open *Smartphone Sales* from your sample files folder.

2   Open the Save As dialog and switch to Online Locations.

   1.   Click: →File→Save As.

       The *Save As* dialog appears.

   2.   Click the *Online Locations* button.

       If *Online Locations* has already been selected you will see the *On my Mac* button instead.

3   Sign in to a OneDrive account if you are not already signed in.

   If you are already signed into a OneDrive account, it will appear in the left-hand pane:

   OneDrive - Personal
   mikesmart@thesmartmethod....

   If there isn't a OneDrive option, it means you need to sign in.

   To do this, click the *Add a Place* button at the bottom of the left-hand pane.

Smartphone Sales

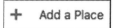

note

OneDrive security concerns

When you store a file on your local hard drive, you can be reasonably sure that nobody else can access the contents (provided that they cannot gain access to your computer).

When you upload a file to a Microsoft OneDrive server, you may worry that the file contents are vulnerable to theft.

Because a very reliable encryption method called SSL (Secure Sockets Layer) is used to transport files to and from the OneDrive, there isn't any realistic possibility of your file being intercepted when travelling to and from the Microsoft servers.

Because your files are not encrypted upon Microsoft's servers, the main security worry might be that their servers could be compromised and that your files could be accessed by others.

There are two potential solutions for users who have security concerns:

1. Encrypt your files before saving them to the OneDrive.

The *Expert Skills* book in this series comprehensively covers encryption of security-sensitive Excel files.

2. Host your own private OneDrive using *Microsoft SharePoint* along with the *OneDrive for Business* SharePoint component.

SharePoint is mainly used by corporations and is usually installed upon a corporate server by the IT department.

Once installed, *OneDrive for Business* can be used to store files on corporate servers in exactly the same way as upon Microsoft's own OneDrive servers.

After clicking the button, you'll be prompted to sign in. If you don't already have a OneDrive account, you will be given the option to create one.

4   Save the workbook to your OneDrive in a folder called: *Documents\Excel\Practice.*

1.   Click the OneDrive folder icon.

You can now see the contents of your OneDrive in the central pane.

You may see different OneDrive folders as Microsoft change the default OneDrive folders from time to time.

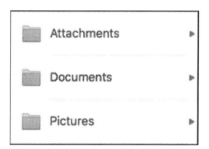

2.   Click the *Documents* folder.

The empty *Documents* folder is displayed.

In *Lesson 1-10: Pin a workbook and understand file organization,* you learned why it is a good idea to place your Excel files into a separate folder within your local *Documents* folder. You will also create an *Excel* folder beneath the *Documents* folder on your OneDrive.

3.   Click the *New Folder* button at the bottom of the dialog.

4.   Type **Excel** as the name of the new folder and click *Create.*

In *Lesson 1-10: Pin a workbook and understand file organization,* you learned why it is a good idea to further organize your Excel files within the *Excel* folder. You will create a *Practice* folder inside the *Excel* folder to do the same thing on your OneDrive.

5.   Create a new OneDrive *Practice* subfolder inside the newly created *Excel* folder.

6.   Click: *Save* to save the *Smartphone Sales* workbook into the new *OneDrive\Documents\Excel\Practice* folder.

The workbook is saved and you are returned to the main Excel screen.

5   Close Excel.

note

Beware of the "lunchtime lock"

The lunchtime lock happens when you do this:

1. Open a OneDrive file on your home computer.

2. Leave your computer switched on with the file open and go to work.

3. Open the same OneDrive file on your work computer.

When you try to open the file at work you will see a dialog telling you that the file is "locked" and cannot be worked upon.

IT staff call this problem the "lunchtime lock".

A common support problem occurs when a team member goes out to lunch, leaving a shared file open. This prevents anybody else on the team from editing the same file.

Later, in: *Lesson 8-9: Edit a workbook simultaneously with other users using Excel Online*, you'll discover how to share files using the cloud-based *Excel Online* application.

Excel Online is, in this respect, more sophisticated than the *Excel desktop application* (the version of Excel you've been using up to now) as it allows several users to read and edit a workbook at the same time. This means that the lunchtime lock scenario cannot occur.

Lesson 8-3: Open a workbook from a OneDrive

Once a workbook has been saved to a OneDrive it can be opened from absolutely anywhere, provided you are connected to the Internet.

In: *Lesson 8-7: Open a workbook using Excel Online,* you'll discover that you can also open a workbook from any device that has a web browser (even if Excel 2019 is not installed on the device). This includes smartphones and tablets such as the iPad.

In this lesson you'll consider the scenario where you have a Windows PC at your office, and another Windows PC at home.

You simply want to be able to view and edit the same workbook on both computers.

1   Close any open Excel windows and re-open Excel.

The start-up screen is displayed.

2   Open the *Smartphone Sales* sample file from your OneDrive.

1.   Click: *Open* from the left-hand menu bar.

2.   Click your *OneDrive* in the left-hand pane.

If you don't see this icon, you'll need to sign into a OneDrive. You saw how to do this in: *Lesson 8-2: Save a workbook to a OneDrive.*

You can now see your OneDrive's *Documents, Pictures* and *Public* folders on the right-hand side of the screen.

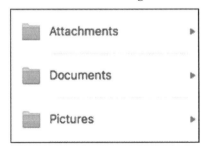

3.   Click the *Documents* folder.

You can now see the Excel sub-folder.

4.   Click the *Excel* folder.

You can now see the *Practice* sub-folder.

5.   Click the *Practice* folder.

Smartphone Sales

note

OneDrive alternatives

Excel 2019 integrates OneDrive features into the *Save As* dialog.

You can save a file to your OneDrive as easily as saving to your local hard drive.

There are similar rival services to OneDrive offered by Dropbox, Google Drive, Apple iCloud and Amazon Drive, but none integrate with Office as seamlessly as OneDrive.

note

The advantages of using a OneDrive instead of a local drive

1. You can access your workbooks from any Internet connected device, anywhere in the world.

This means that you can work with your tablet device, smartphone or laptop when travelling, without having to copy files between devices.

2. You can share files with other users without having to e-mail the files to them.

You do this by sending a hyperlink to the other user rather than the file itself.

You'll discover more about this later, in: *Lesson 8-8: Share a link to a workbook.*

3. You can collaborate more easily with other users by giving certain users the right to edit your files.

4. You can allow users who do not have Excel 2019 installed upon their device to view, or even edit, your workbook.

You'll discover more about this later, in: *Lesson 8-6: Understand Excel Online.*

You should see the previously saved *Smartphone Sales* file in the folder:

6. Double click on the *Smartphone Sales* file to open it.

7. The *Smartphone Sales* workbook opens from the OneDrive:

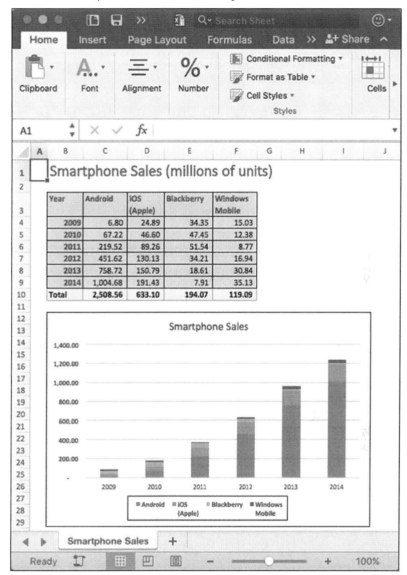

You can use this technique to open a workbook from any computer that has Excel 2019 installed.

3 Close Excel.

Lesson 8-4: Understand operating systems and devices

Excel 2019 can now run on almost all modern devices (such as computers, smartphones and tablet computers). As you'll learn in: *There are two common mobile* operating systems: *Google Android* and *Apple iOS.* *Apple iOS* is only used on Apple devices such as the iPad and iPhone.

Google Android is used on a vast number of devices from many different manufacturers.

Lesson 8-5: Understand Office versions, there are several different versions of Office (all with different features).

In order to completely understand how the different versions of Office fit into the new world of cloud computing, you'll need an overview of the devices and operating systems in common use today (or at least those that were common when this book was written in late 2018).

What is a smartphone?

A smartphone is a mobile telephone that also includes a computer and a touch screen.

What is a tablet computer?

Apple's iPad (launched in April 2010) was the first mass-market modern tablet computer. Tablet computers are also sometimes called *pad devices.* A tablet computer is similar to a very large smartphone (though most do not have telephony capability).

Screen sizes are typically 7 to 13 inches. Like a smartphone, they are usually controlled via a touchscreen. Some tablet computers (such as the Microsoft Surface and iPad Pro) have an optional detachable keyboard and mouse available as an add-on.

What is a microprocessor (or CPU)?

Desktop and laptop microprocessors

The microprocessor is the computer chip that performs all of the computer's calculations. It can be thought of as the brain of the computer. All microprocessors have an *instruction set* (sometimes called the *architecture*). Operating systems communicate with the microprocessor using this instruction set (you'll learn more about operating systems later in this lesson).

Almost all desktop computers are fitted with a powerful processor that supports the *x64 instruction set* (typically provided by a microprocessor manufactured by Intel or AMD).

trivia

The amazing success story of the iPad

As I write this sidebar (in September 2018) it is hard to believe that the iPad has not yet had its ninth birthday. It seems to have been around forever.

When the iPad went on sale in early April 2010 it was an overnight success. Apple sold 450,000 in the first week, 1 million in the first month and 19 million in the first year.

Seeing the success of Apple, many other manufacturers began manufacturing tablet computers that used the rival Android operating system.

In May 2017 it was reported that Apple's all-time worldwide iPad sales had exceeded 360 million units.

Tablet and smartphone microprocessors

Tablet computers and smartphones need to have a long battery life and light weight. A different type of (less powerful) microprocessor is typically used in this type of device that combines cool running (meaning that no fan is needed) and low power consumption. The market leader is a family of chips that support the ARM instruction set.

The Intel Atom x5, x7 and 4415Y microprocessors

The Intel Atom x5/x7 (released in March 2015) and 4415Y (released in June 2017) have both the cool-running/low power features needed for tablet computers combined with support for the x64 instruction set needed to run the full Windows 10 desktop operating system.

Microsoft wasted no time in releasing their Surface 3 tablet computer in May 2015. With an Intel Atom x7 processor, the Surface 3 runs the same full Windows 10 operating system used on desktop computers but still claims to have 10 hours of battery life.

Microsoft's Surface Go (released in August 2nd, 2018) uses the 4415Y microprocessor to power a new low-cost Windows 10 tablet that weighs in at just 522 grams.

What is an operating system?

The desktop operating systems

You are probably using Office 2019 on a desktop or laptop computer that uses the *macOS* (previously known as *OS X*) operating system.

Operating systems are the middleman between applications (such as Microsoft Office) and the computer hardware.

For example, when Excel needs to save a file it doesn't need to know anything about the make, model and type of disk drives fitted to the computer. A request is simply sent to the operating system to save the file. The operating system then handles the request.

Both the *macOS* and *Windows* operating systems (used in almost all desktop and laptop computers) were designed to use the *x64 instruction set* (typically provided by a microprocessor manufactured by Intel or AMD).

The mobile operating systems

Mobile operating systems are designed for lightweight portable devices such as mobile telephones and some tablet computers that use microprocessors that do not support the x64 instruction set.

There are two common mobile operating systems: *Google Android* and *Apple iOS*. Apple iOS is only used on Apple devices such as the iPad and iPhone.

Google Android is used on a vast number of devices from many different manufacturers.

Lesson 8-5: Understand Office versions

Office 2019 for Windows

This is the full (and most powerful) version of Office that only runs on the Windows 7, Windows 8 and Windows 10 operating systems.

We've produced a different version of this book suitable for Windows users:

Learn Excel 2019 Essential Skills for Windows with The Smart Method ISBN: 978-1-909253-34-6

Office 2019 for Mac

Microsoft produce a version of Office 2019 for Windows that runs on the *macOS* (previously known as *OS X*) operating system (used on Apple desktop and laptop computers).

You could be forgiven for thinking that the (confusingly named) *Office 2019 for Mac* (that runs under the *macOS* operating system found on Apple desktop and laptop computers) was "just the same" as *Office 2019 for Windows*.

Unfortunately, this is not the case.

The *Excel 2019 for Mac* version has a reduced feature set and a radically different user interface to the *Excel 2019 for Windows* version.

You can find more information about the differences between the Mac and Windows versions of Excel 2019 in: *Appendix A: Differences between the Windows and Mac versions of Excel 2019.*

Office Mobile

Microsoft offer a (severely) cut-down limited-feature mobile app version of the full Excel desktop application. It is designed to complement Excel 2019 desktop versions, not to replace them.

There are versions of Office Mobile to support just about every operating system. You can install Office Mobile on current versions of the *Windows 10 desktop, Windows 10 Mobile, Android* and *iOS* operating systems.

You can download the Office mobile apps free from the Windows Store (for Windows 10 devices), Google Play (for Android devices) and app store (for iPad and iPhone).

Office Mobile is free for personal use but there are some restrictions in the free version:

1. Commercial use is not allowed.

2. If the screen size is more than 10.1 inches, editing of documents is not possible.

3. Some features are not available.

If you are an Office 365 subscriber, all of the above restrictions are removed (though Office Mobile remains very limited compared to the full desktop versions of Office 2019).

Here's a screenshot from Office Mobile running on a Windows PC:

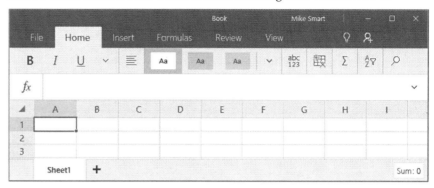

You can see that it is quite primitive when compared to the full version of Excel running on your desktop computer.

Office Online

Just like *Office Mobile*, *Office Online* is very primitive when compared to the full Excel 2019 desktop application, but it is being continuously improved and upgraded.

Office Online is a completely free cloud application designed for larger mobile devices (such as tablet computers). It is also useful when sharing documents with users that do not have an Office 2019 license or subscription. This version will be discussed in depth in: *Lesson 8-6: Understand Excel Online.*

Office Online is very different to the other Office versions as it is a *cloud application*. Cloud applications have many advantages over traditional applications (see sidebar).

Office Online is available to the public free of charge. You can access it from the Office.com website.

Office 2019 version availability (at Aug 2018)

Device	Office 2019 for Windows	Office 2019 for Mac	Office Mobile	Office Online
Windows 7 or 10 PC or tablet computer	X		X	X
Apple Mac		X		X
Apple iPad			X	X
Apple iPhone			X	X
Android Tablet			X	X
Android Phone			X	X

Note that not all Android devices are supported.

Lesson 8-6: Understand Excel Online

Excel 2019 for Windows desktop application

- Application installed on hard drive.
- Workbooks may be saved to hard drive or OneDrive.
- Only runs on Windows computers.

Smartphone Sales

Excel 2019 Application

> **note**
>
> **Perpetual license holders cannot access every Excel 2019 feature**
>
> As you discovered in: *Lesson 1-3: Check that your Excel version is up to date,* the features available in the Excel 2019 desktop application will differ depending upon how you purchased your copy of Microsoft Office.
>
> Perpetual license holders (pay once use forever) do not receive the Excel 2019 feature updates that are enjoyed by Excel 365 subscribers (who pay monthly).

The *Excel 2019 for Windows* desktop application is a conventional locally-installed application. This means:

- You need a license to use the *Excel 2019 for Windows* desktop application.

- You need to install the *Excel 2019 for Windows* desktop application software onto your computer before you can use it.

- The *Excel 2019 for Windows* desktop application will only run on a computer running the Windows 7, 8.0, 8.1, 10 (or later) operating systems.

- The *Excel 2019 for Windows* desktop application is the only Excel version that includes every Excel feature.

- Workbooks may be saved to (and opened from) either the local hard drive or a OneDrive.

Excel 2019 for Mac desktop application

The *Excel 2019 for Mac* desktop application runs on the *macOS (OS X)* operating system found on Apple desktop and laptop computers.

Excel 2019 for Mac has a reduced feature set and a radically different user interface to the Excel *2019 for Windows* version.

You can see more about this in: *Appendix A: Differences between the Windows and Mac versions of Excel 2019.*

Excel Online

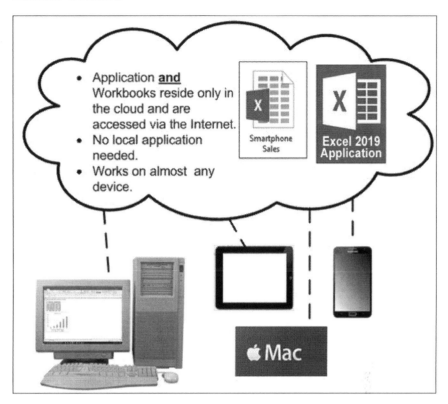

Excel Online is a cloud application that runs inside a web browser. This means:

- You don't need a license to use Excel Online.

- You don't need to install any software to use Excel Online.

- Because a cloud app doesn't directly communicate with the operating system, Excel Online will run on any device that has a supported web browser. This includes the Windows PC, Apple Mac, iPad and almost all recent tablet and smartphone devices.

- Excel Online provides only a cut-down limited-feature version of Excel 2019.

Excel Online makes it possible to share a workbook with just about anybody

If you e-mail a copy of a workbook to another user (as an attachment), you have to assume that the recipient has a Windows computer with a compatible version of Excel installed.

When you send a user a link to a workbook stored on your OneDrive it will open using Excel Online. You can then be confident that the user will almost certainly be able to open the workbook. You'll learn how to share links that open using Excel Online later, in: *Lesson 8-8: Share a link to a workbook*.

The recipient of a link can have any type of device (such as a Windows PC, Windows Surface tablet, Apple Mac, iPad tablet, Android tablet or even a smartphone) and does not have to have a copy of Excel 2019 installed.

Smartphone Sales

Lesson 8-7: Open a workbook using Excel Online

Now that you have saved a workbook to your OneDrive, you can use Excel Online to open it from any device that has a supported web browser (see facing page sidebar). This includes most recent smartphones, tablet devices and personal computers. Even if the device does not have Excel 2019 installed, you will be able to view and edit the workbook using the free Excel Online cloud application.

If you have a tablet computer (such as an iPad), or recent smartphone, you might find it interesting to use this device (rather than your Mac) for this lesson.

1 Open *Smartphone Sales* from a web browser using Excel Online.

1. Open the Safari web browser on your Mac or (ideally) using another device.

2. Enter the url: **https://OneDrive.com**

3. If necessary, enter your user name and password to log in.

4. Click the *Documents* folder. (If you are using a smartphone or tablet computer, see sidebar for the touchscreen gesture that simulates a left-click).

5. Click the *Excel* folder. You created this folder in: *Lesson 8-2: Save a workbook to a OneDrive.*

6. Click the *Practice* folder.

   You can now see the *Smartphone Sales* workbook that you saved in: *Lesson 8-2: Save a workbook to a OneDrive.*

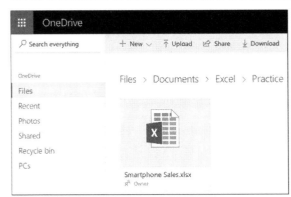

7. Right-click on *Smartphone Sales*.

8. Click *Open in Excel Online* from the shortcut menu (or simply *Open* if you are using a device that does not have Excel installed on it).

In a real-world situation you'd usually select *Open in Excel* (if it is available) because Excel has more features and is faster than Excel Online. For the sake of this lesson, you'll open the file using Excel Online so that you can share the experience of users who do not have Excel installed on their device.

The *Smartphone Sales* workbook opens in Excel Online:

note

Supported web browsers

Excel Online is only supported on recent versions of the five most commonly used browsers: Microsoft Edge, Internet Explorer, Chrome, Safari and Firefox.

Almost all recent devices (such as the Windows PC, Apple Mac, iPad, Android tablet, Microsoft Surface and most smartphones) can run at least one of the supported browsers.

Microsoft Edge is always the best browser to use if it is available. If not, use the latest version of Internet Explorer, Chrome, Firefox or Safari.

If you find that Excel Online does not work correctly with one of the supported browsers, try again using a different supported browser

Excel Online looks very much like the desktop Excel application. Many (but not all) of Excel's features are now available from the Ribbon.

2 **Expand and collapse the Excel Online Ribbon.**

If you are using a smartphone or tablet device with a very small screen, Excel Online may open with the Ribbon minimized.

Just like the desktop Excel version, you can double-click (or double-tap) on any of the Ribbon tabs to minimize or maximize the Ribbon.

Try minimizing and maximizing the Ribbon to see this working.

3 **Close your web browser.**

Smartphone Sales

Lesson 8-8: Share a link to a workbook

When your workbooks are stored on a OneDrive, it is possible to share them without sending a physical copy of the file to the recipients. This is done by distributing a simple hyperlink via an e-mail, or by pasting the link into a Facebook page, Twitter tweet, blog or other web page.

As discussed in: *Lesson 8-6: Understand Excel Online*, this method ensures that the recipient will be able to open the workbook on almost any device, even if Excel 2019 is not installed. The workbook will automatically open using the free *Excel Online* application.

You can also use the technique taught in this lesson to share Word documents and PowerPoint presentations, as there are also *Word Online* and *PowerPoint Online* cloud applications that will open them.

1   Open Excel.

The start-up screen is displayed.

2   Open the *Smartphone Sales* sample file from your OneDrive.

This is the file that you saved in: *Lesson 8-2: Save a workbook to a OneDrive*.

3   Send an e-mail link to yourself to enable the recipient to open (but not change) the workbook.

1.   Click the Share icon at the top right of the screen.

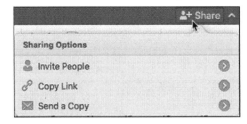

The *Sharing Options* menu appears.

2.   Click *Invite People*.

3.   Type your own e-mail address into the *Type Names or Email Addresses* text box.

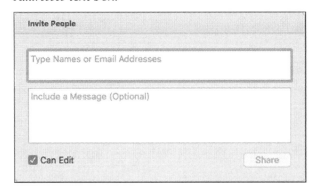

4.   Prohibit editing.

Notice that there is a check box that controls whether the recipient will be able to edit the workbook.

Make sure the checkbox is not checked. This will allow recipients to view but not edit the *Smartphone Sales* workbook.

Checking this box would enable the recipient to make changes to the workbook on your OneDrive. You'll do this later, in: *Lesson 8-9: Edit a workbook simultaneously with other users using Excel Online.*

5. Add a short message.

6. Click the *Share* button.

   An e-mail with a view link is sent to the recipient(s) you specified (in this case yourself).

4 Examine the e-mail that Excel has sent you.

After a few moments you should find that the e-mail has appeared in your inbox.

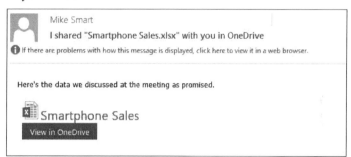

5 Log out of your OneDrive.

While you are logged in to your OneDrive you will always have full access to your own files.

This means that, even though the link is read-only (a View link), you will still be able to edit the file as if it were an Edit link.

To simulate a recipient that is not yourself, you will have to log out of your OneDrive.

1. Open a web browser and go to: **http://OneDrive.com**

2. Click the icon of a person (or your photograph) in the top right corner.

3. Click *Sign out* from the shortcut menu.

6 Test the link.

1. Open the e-mail previously sent to yourself.

2. Click the link in the e-mail.

   The workbook opens in Excel Online.

3. Notice that there is no *Edit Workbook* link on the Ribbon. This is because you sent a View link that does not allow the recipient to edit the workbook.

   Note that the user is still able to save (and then edit) a local copy of your workbook (see sidebar).

7 Close Excel Online.

note

You may find yourself unable to log out of your OneDrive

Sometimes macOS can insist upon automatically logging you into your OneDrive when you open one of your own workbooks using a View link.

If this is the case, you will not be able to test the read-only nature of a View link unless you log in to a different OneDrive account first.

note

Users can save (and then edit) a local copy of read-only workbooks

When you send a *View* link, you can be sure that recipients cannot change the workbook stored on your OneDrive.

This does not prevent the user from making a local copy of your workbook. It is then possible for the user to make changes to the local copy.

To make a local copy the user can click:

… from inside Excel Online.

It is then possible for the user to open and edit the local copy of the workbook.

Lesson 8-9: Edit a workbook simultaneously with other users using Excel Online

When working with Excel Online you never have to save

Excel Online has no save button.

While this seems strange at first, it is actually quite logical.

When you open a workbook using the normal Excel desktop application, the workbook is copied from your hard drive into the computer's memory. When you make changes, they are applied to the copy of the workbook (in the computer's memory) rather than the workbook on the hard drive. If you don't save the workbook, you might lose any changes that you make. The desktop Excel application always works like this, whether the workbook resides on your local hard disk or your OneDrive.

When you open a workbook using *Excel Online*, the workbook is not copied into the computer's memory. You work with the actual workbook on the OneDrive and not a copy of it. This means that any changes are instantly applied to the workbook, making a save button unnecessary (as any changes that you make are being instantly made to the actual workbook file).

This new way of working provides an unexpected benefit.

If several users are all working with the same workbook (and all are using Excel Online), any change made (by any user) will magically, and almost instantly, appear on every other user's screen!

This provides a completely new way of collaborating with other users.

note

If you only have one device

If you only have one device, you can still work through this lesson.

To do this, you will need to open two web browser tabs.

You'll have to imagine that each browser tab is a different user with a different device.

Smartphone Sales

To get the most out of this lesson you will need two devices to simulate two different users. See sidebar if you only have one device.

1   Open Excel 2019 on your Mac.

   The start-up screen is displayed.

2   Open the *Smartphone Sales* sample file from your OneDrive.

   This is the file that you saved in: *Lesson 8-2: Save a workbook to a OneDrive.*

3   Send an *Edit Link* to yourself via e-mail.

   This will enable the recipient to both view and edit the workbook via Excel Online.

   You learned how to do this in: *Lesson 8-8: Share a link to a workbook.*

4   Close Excel.

   It is important that you close Excel. If the workbook remained open in Excel, you'd lock the workbook and prevent other users

© 2018 The Smart Method® Ltd

important

All browsers are not equal

Excel Online officially supports Microsoft's own Edge and Internet Explorer browsers along with the Chrome, Safari and Firefox browsers.

You can always expect Excel Online to work perfectly with the *Microsoft Edge* browser. That's because Microsoft have full control over updates to their own browser and will test Excel Online with each update before release.

Users often report glitches with other browsers after they are updated (and browsers are usually updated very frequently).

For this reason, always use Excel Online with the Microsoft Edge browser if it is available.

If you use a different supported browser and it does not work, try using one of the others (they are all free to download).

For example, if you run into a problem with Firefox, try again using Chrome or Safari.

from editing it using Excel Online. File locking was discussed in more depth in: *Lesson 8-3: Open a workbook from a OneDrive.*

5   Use the *Edit Link* to open *Smartphone* Sales on your Mac using Excel Online.

1.   Open the e-mail previously sent to yourself.

2.   Click the link in the e-mail.

The workbook opens using *Excel Online.*

Notice that there is an *Edit Workbook* link on the Ribbon (this may say *Edit in Browser* on some devices).

This is because you sent an *Edit* link that allows the recipient to both view and edit the workbook.

6   Use the same *Edit Link* to open *Smartphone Sales* on your other device using Excel Online.

Your other device may be a different Mac, an iPad, a Windows PC, an Android device, or any other device that has a supported web browser.

You now are now viewing the same workbook on both devices. This means that any changes made to the workbook on one device will (almost) instantly appear on the screen of the other device.

7   Put both devices into *Edit* mode.

Click the: *Edit Workbook* link on the Ribbon (this may say *Edit in Browser* on some devices).

It is important that you edit the workbook in your web browser.

If a user opens the file using a local copy of Excel, the workbook will be locked and it won't be possible for any other user to edit the workbook using *Excel Online.*

8   Make a change to the workbook on one of your devices.

Notice that the change appears (almost instantly) on the other device.

Note that you won't see the change on the other device unless the device is in *Edit* mode.

9   Close Excel Online on both devices.

There is no need to save the workbook (there isn't even a save button in Excel Online). Your changes were automatically saved to the OneDrive as you made them.

Session 8: Exercise

1   Open *Broadband Speeds* from your sample files folder.

2   Create a new sub-folder in your OneDrive documents folder called: Exercise 8

3   Save the *Broadband Speeds* workbook into the */Documents/Exercise 8* folder of your OneDrive.

4   Send a *View Link* and an *Edit Link* for the *Broadband Speeds* workbook to yourself via e-mail.

    (If you have a slow Internet connection you may have to wait until synchronization completes before you are able to do this).

5   Close Excel 2019.

6   Use the *Edit Link* to open the *Broadband Speeds* workbook using Excel Online.

7   Enable editing within Excel Online.

8   Change the *Average Speed (Mbs)* for *Luxembourg* (cell B4) to: 75.00

9   Close Excel Online.

10   Open the desktop Excel 2019 application.

11   Open *Broadband Speeds* from your OneDrive.

    Note that the average speed for Luxembourg is now 75.00 Mbs.

12   Change the *Average Speed (Mbs)* for *Luxembourg* to: 100.88

13   Save the workbook.

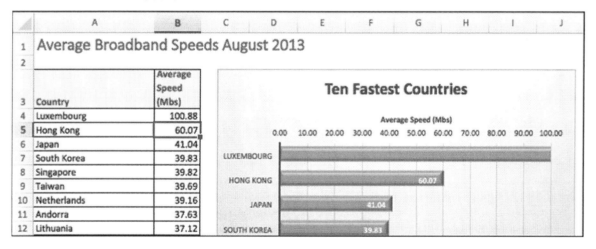

Broadband Speeds

If you need help slide the page to the left

Session 8: Exercise answers

These are the questions that students find the most difficult to answer:

Q 7	Q 4	Q 2
Click: *Edit Workbook* on the *Excel Online* Ribbon (*Edit in Browser* on some devices). This was covered in: *Lesson 8-9: Edit a workbook simultaneously with other users using Excel Online.*	1. Click the Share button at the top right of the screen. The *Sharing Options* menu appears. 2. Click *Invite People.* 3. Type your own email address into the *Type Names or Email Addresses* text box. 4. Make sure that *Can Edit* is not checked. 5. Click the *Share* button. 6. Repeat the same operation for the *Edit Link* (this time checking *Can Edit*). This was covered in: *Lesson 8-8: Share a link to a workbook.*	1. Click: File→Save As. 2. Click: *OneDrive* in the *Save As* menu. 3. Click the *Documents* folder. 4. Click *New Folder.* 5. Type: **Exercise 8** as the name of the new folder. 6. Click *Create.* This was covered in: *Lesson 8-2: Save a workbook to a OneDrive.*

If you have difficulty with the other questions, here are the lessons that cover the relevant skills:

1,10   Lesson 1-7: Download the sample files and open/navigate a workbook.

3   Lesson 8-2: Save a workbook to a OneDrive.

5   Lesson 1-2: Start Excel and open a new blank workbook.

6   Lesson 8-8: Share a link to a workbook.

8,9   Lesson 8-9: Edit a workbook simultaneously with other users using Excel Online.

11   Lesson 8-3: Open a workbook from a OneDrive.

12   Lesson 2-1: Enter text and numbers into a worksheet.

13   Lesson 1-8: Save a workbook to a local file.

Appendix A: Differences between the Windows and Mac versions of Excel 2019

Excel 2019 for Mac and *Excel 2019 for Windows* are not identical products, and there are many differences between the two.

The skills taught in this course will still be useful if you apply them to the Windows version of Excel 2019, but you may find that some features behave differently.

This appendix does not list every difference between the Windows and Mac versions. Instead, it only lists the differences that apply to this *Essential Skills* course.

If any of the features listed in this appendix are of vital importance to you, you can see how to use them in the Windows version of this course.

Important:

Microsoft release regular updates that may implement missing features or change the way that Excel 2019 behaves.

This information was true as of September 2018, but the product may have changed since this book was published.

Additional features available in Excel 2019 for Windows

■ Default file location setting

The Windows version of Excel 2019 enables you to set a default location for saving your files. This setting is not available in the Mac version.

■ Automatic Flash Fill

The Windows version of Excel 2019 tries to automatically detect when you are entering values that could be filled down and automatically uses Flash Fill where appropriate. The Mac version never automatically uses Flash Fill, but you can invoke it manually when you want it.

■ Autosaved Versions of a workbook

The Windows version of Excel 2019 automatically saves 'draft' copies of your workbooks as you work, enabling you to retrieve an older version of a workbook even if you didn't save your changes. This feature is not available in the Mac version.

■ Quick Analysis

The Windows version of Excel 2019 shows a 'smart tag' below selected cells that enables you to quickly create totals, charts, tables and sparklines. The Mac version does not include this feature.

■ The Mini Toolbar

The Windows version of Excel 2019 shows a small toolbar when text is selected, allowing you to easily change font styles, sizes and colors. The Mac version does not include this feature.

■ Multi-item Clipboard

The Windows version of Office 2019 includes a multi-item clipboard that allows you to copy and paste several different things at the same time. This feature is not included in the Mac version, but there are macOS add-ins available that provide this functionality.

■ Redo drop-down menu

The Windows version of Excel 2019 offers a drop-down menu for both the Undo and Redo options, enabling multiple actions to be quickly 'undone' or 'redone'. The Mac version only offers the drop-down menu for the Undo option, meaning you must 'redo' actions on at a time.

■ Pictures in comments

The Windows version of Excel 2019 enables pictures to be placed within cell comments. This is not possible with the Mac version of Excel.

■ Default template location setting

The Windows version of Excel 2019 enables you to set a default location for saving templates. This setting is not available in the Mac version.

■ Effects Sets

The Windows version of Excel 2019 enables you to customize your workbook's visual style using a Color Set, Font Set and Effects Set, but the Mac version only allows the Color Set and Font Set to be changed.

■ Custom Color and Font sets

The Windows version of Excel 2019 allows you to fully customize themes by creating custom Color Sets and Font Sets. The Mac version does not allow new Color Sets and Font Sets to be created, so themes can only be created from the preset options.

■ Live Preview

The Windows version of Excel 2019 contains the Live Preview feature. This is used in many different places throughout the Excel application to show a preview of the effect an option will have when you hover the mouse cursor over it. For example, hovering the mouse cursor over a Theme will preview how the Theme would look if it was applied. The Mac version does not contain this feature.

■ Fill Effects in cells

The Windows version of Excel 2019 allows you to apply a gradient fill to cells. This is not possible in the Mac version.

■ View Side by Side

The Windows version of Excel 2019 contains a View Side by Side option that allows you to easily compare two workbooks, even when many workbooks are open. This feature is not available in the Mac version, although workbooks can still be compared by using the Arrange feature.

■ Synchronous Scrolling

The View Side by Side feature from Excel 2019 for Windows contains a Synchronous Scrolling option that allows you to scroll through two workbooks at the same time. This feature is not available in the Mac version of Excel 2019.

■ Forecast Sheets

The Windows version of Excel 2019 contains a new Forecast Sheets feature that is able to automatically detect seasonal changes and forecast future values based upon a confidence factor. This feature is not available in the Mac version of Excel 2019.

■ Find & Replace Formats

In the Windows version of Excel 2019, the Find & Replace dialog offers the ability to find cells based on their format (for example, the background color) and to replace the format of cells that are found. This option is not available in the Mac version.

■ Full-sized print preview

The Windows version of Office 2019 allows you to see a large print preview of the workbook, including the ability to zoom in and out. The Mac version displays a small print preview that cannot be zoomed.

■ Ribbon Display Options

The Windows version of Office 2019 contains a *Ribbon Display Options* menu that allows the Ribbon to be completely hidden, freeing up more screen space than is possible by simply minimizing the Ribbon. This feature is not available in the Mac version.

■ Chart Data Labels from a Range

The Windows version of Excel 2019 allows you to select a range of cells to be used as data labels within a chart. This is not possible in the Mac version.

■ Chart filters

In the Windows version of Excel 2019, it is possible to apply a chart filter to quickly select the data that should be displayed in a chart. Chart filters do not exist in the Mac version, but you can still change the data that is displayed within a chart by using the Select Data Source dialog.

■ Error printing

The Windows version of Excel 2019 allows you to choose how errors should be displayed when printing a workbook. This setting does not exist in the Mac version, so errors will always be printed exactly as they are shown.

■ **Key tips**

In Excel 2019 for Windows, holding down the **\<Alt\>** key displays 'key tips' for every item on the Ribbon, enabling every command to be accessed using keyboard shortcuts. Key tips are not available in the Mac version.

■ **XPS document format**

Excel 2019 for Windows is able to save workbooks in the XPS document format. XPS is a Microsoft alternative to the PDF format. The Mac version cannot save to XPS format.

■ **Protected view**

Excel 2019 for Windows automatically opens files that were downloaded from the internet in *protected view*. Protected view disables editing and other features to protect you from viruses. The Mac version does not include protected view.

Features that behave differently in Excel 2019 for Windows

■ **Cmd shortcut keys**

Many features of Excel 2019 for Mac can be accessed by holding down the **<Cmd>** key and pressing another key (for example **<Cmd>+<b>** makes the selected cell bold-faced).

Windows computers do not have a Cmd key, so the Ctrl key is used instead.

■ **Fn shortcut keys**

If you are using macOS with its default settings, you need to hold down the **<Fn>** key to use the *F* keys at the top of the keyboard within Excel (for example **<Fn>+<F4>** to make a cell reference absolute).

Windows computers do not usually have a Fn key, so you do not usually need to hold it down to use the *F* key functions. Some Windows laptops with compact keyboards are an exception to this rule and may still require you to hold down a Fn key.

■ **Ribbon and Menu Bar**

Excel 2019 for Windows does not use the Menu Bar that is used for many commands in Excel 2019 for Mac. Instead, all commands are accessed via the Ribbon.

This means that Excel 2019 for Windows has additional Ribbon options to enable access to commands that are in the Menu Bar in Excel 2019 for Mac.

■ **Chart templates**

Chart templates are accessed via a dialog launcher on the Ribbon in the Windows version of Excel 2019. In the Mac version, chart templates are accessed via the Menu Bar at the top of the screen.

■ **File tab and 'Backstage View'**

In Excel 2019 for Windows, the Ribbon contains an additional tab called *File*. This tab takes you to *Backstage View* which contains options for saving, printing and sharing, as well as more advanced Excel options.

These options are accessed via the Menu Bar in Excel 2019 for Mac.

■ **Minimize Ribbon double-click**

In the Mac version of Excel 2019, clicking the selected Ribbon tab minimizes the Ribbon. In the Windows version, the Ribbon is minimized by double-clicking any Ribbon tab.

If the Ribbon is minimized in the Mac version of Excel 2019, it can be restored by clicking any tab. The Windows version requires you to double-click a tab in order to permanently restore the Ribbon.

Hiding and showing the Ribbon is covered in: *Lesson 1-16: Hide and Show the Formula Bar and Ribbon.*

■ **Task pane docking**

The Mac version of Excel 2019 allows task panes to either be 'floating' or docked to the right side of the screen. The Windows version allows task panes to be docked to either the left or right side of the screen (as well as being floating).

Task pane docking is covered in: *Lesson 5-7: Manually format a chart element.*

■ **Copying worksheets by dragging and dropping**

In Excel 2019 for Mac, you can create a copy of a worksheet by holding down the **<Alt>** key and dragging it to the location where you wish to create a copy. Excel 2019 for Windows behaves the same way, except you must hold down the **<Ctrl>** key.

Copying worksheets is covered in: *Lesson 6-2: Duplicate worksheets within a workbook.*

▨ Help system

In Excel 2019 for Mac, the help search system is accessed via the Help menu on the Menu Bar. Excel 2019 for Windows replaces this with a *Tell me what you want to do* option on the Ribbon.

▨ Find & Replace 'look in'

The Find & Replace dialog contains a 'look in' menu that allows you to search in values or formulas. The 'look in' feature is available in Excel 2019 for Mac, but only in the *Find* dialog; it is not present in the *Replace* dialog. Despite this, the *Replace* dialog <u>will</u> behave according to the selected 'look in' option if you set it in the *Find* dialog before switching to *Replace*.

Index

Q

R

selecting non contiguous, 72

unhiding, 238

rulers, showing and hiding in page layout view, 291

rules manager

controlling conditional formatting with, 190

editing rules with, 192

S

sample files

downloading, 15, **34**

organizing folder, 34

sans serif and serif fonts explained, 176

save, 36, 38

select all button, 270

selecting cells, 68

series

dialog, 96

exponential, 96

growth, 96

linear, 96

start value, 96

step value, 96

stop value, 96

serif and sans serif fonts explained, 176

share button, 332

shortcut keys. *See* keyboard shortcuts

smart tag

explained, 68

options, 92

using to paste values, 123

SmartPhone

explained, 324

sparklines, 196

column type, inserting, 197

date axis, specifying for, 200

deleting, 198

empty cells, setting options for, 243

formatting

line thickness (weight), changing, 199

marker (data point) color, 199

markers (data points), 199

single sparkline rather than group, 201

group and ungroup, 201

hidden cells, show/hide on sparkline, 243

inserting group of into a range of cells, 196

line type, inserting, 197

size of containing cell, changing, 199

style, changing with style gallery, 199

type, changing, 199

ungroup and group, 201

uses of, 196

vertical axis, applying common scaling to sparkline group, 198

win/loss type, inserting, 197

spell checking

dictionary language, setting, 152

using, 152

split button, 46

split, window into multiple panes, 150

start Excel, 24

styles

accounting number format, 164

applying cell styles, 178

built-in, for numbers, 164

comma, 164

comma[0], 164

currency[0], 164

custom, 184

importance of using theme colors and fonts, 187

master style book, using, 186

merging, 186

percentage, 165

removing from cells, 178

SUM function

creating manually using formula AutoComplete, 86

creating using AutoSum, 66

surface. *See* microsoft surface (tablet computer)

switch windows, 64

T

tablet computer

explained, 324

tabs. *See* worksheets

telephone numbers, formatting with flash fill, 98

templates

creating, 140

custom, about, 138

potential problems when using samples, 138

using, 24, 142

the smart method

learning by participation, 3

two facing pages rule, 2

themes. *See also* office theme

changing, 178

changing the default, 176

color sets, 176

custom, creating, 182

explained, 176

font sets, 176

Moving to the next level

The next book in the series (Expert skills) covers only the most advanced Excel features.

This book will give you advanced Excel skills that are rarely mastered by the average user. By the end of the book you'll be a true Excel expert, able to use all of the power available from the world's most powerful business tool.

Your Excel skills will be greater and broader than almost all other Excel users in the workplace.

The paper printed book is always in stock at Amazon.

The e-book is published in unlocked, printable PDF format (all of our e-books are published in this way) and is only available from https://thesmartmethod.com (this is the publisher's own web site).

Learn how to apply your new Excel skills with a Smart Method construction kit

For over 900 years craftsmen have traditionally taught their skills to an apprentice. In this model the apprentice learned his trade by observing how the master craftsman used his skills. This construction kit will teach you advanced Excel skills in the same way. Even if you only have basic Excel skills, the construction kit is designed in such a way that you'll be able to construct a complex, polished professional Excel application that would be well beyond the powers of most advanced Excel users. Available as both a printed paper book and e-book. This book was written using the Windows version of Excel but will also have relevance for the Apple version. Full details at: **https://thesmartmethod.com**

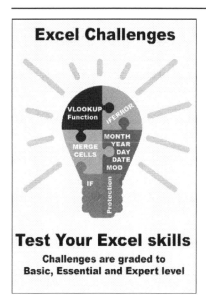

Excel Challenges

Our Excel online challenges are a little like the exercises at the end of each session in this book. Unlike the exercises, the online challenges will test the application of many skills (covered in different sessions in the book).

We began trialling challenges in July 2018 and (at time of writing in September 2018) we'd published three challenges but by the time you read this book we may have produced more.

Access the challenges online at:

https://thesmartmethod.com/excel-challenges/

Use your new Excel skills to teach your own classroom courses

If you've worked through this book carefully you will now have excellent Excel skills and if you progress to the *Expert Skills* book in the series, you'll be a true Excel expert. There is a huge demand, everywhere in the world, for Excel training at all levels. The skills you have learned in this book will enable you to teach an introductory Excel course (providing all of the skills needed by most office workers).

This book is available for all Excel versions in common use (Excel 2007, 2010, 2013, 2016, 2019 and 365 for Windows along with Excel 2016 & 2019 for Apple Mac). You can use the books as courseware during your classes and then give each student a copy of the book to take home as reference material when the course is over.

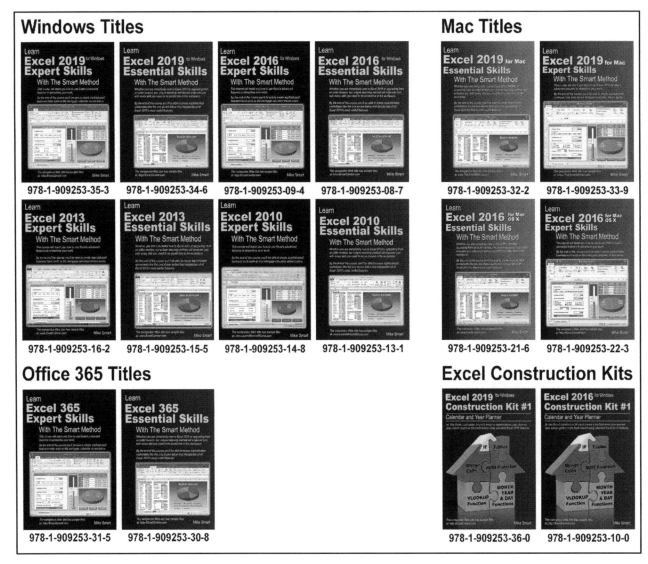

You can quote the ISBN numbers shown above to any book retailer or wholesaler. All major distributors (in every country of the world) have our books in stock for immediate delivery.

Place a direct order for 5+ books for wholesale prices and free delivery worldwide

To place a publisher-direct order you only need to order five books or more (of the same title). To view wholesale prices, go to this web page: https://thesmartmethod.com/wholesale-printed-books

35014057R00199

Made in the USA
Middletown, DE
31 January 2019